T0168923

Cooking by the Book

Cooking by the Book:

Food in Literature and Culture

Edited by
Mary Anne Schofield

Bowling Green State University Popular Press
Bowling Green, Ohio 43403

Copyright© 1989 by Bowling Green State University Popular Press

Library of Congress Catalogue Card No.: 88-64055

ISBN: 0-87972-443-9 cb
     0-87972-444-7 pb

Cover design by Laura Darnell Dumm

for

Barb, Diana, Doreen, Gloria, Janice, Jill, Liz, Mary, Molly,
Sue and Sr. Molly—
nourishers of my body and my soul

Contents

Preface

In *Heartburn*, Nora Ephron/Rachel Sanstatt succinctly observes:

What I love about cooking is that after a hard day, there is something comforting about the fact that if you melt butter and add flour and then hot stock, *it will get thick!* It's a sure thing...in a world where nothing is sure; it has a mathematical certainty in a world where those of us who long for some sort of certainty are forced to settle for crossword puzzles. (117)

Ephron/Sanstatt writes about food because it counts, because it articulates in concrete terms what is oftentimes vague, internal, abstract. Food objectifies and then allows repetition of both the pleasure of the senses and the verifying of these senses. Food cooked, eaten, and thought about provides a metaphoric matrix, a language that allows us a way to get at the uncertainty, the ineffable qualities of life. Thus, to write about food is to deal with the most important and the most basic of human needs and desires. As M.F.K. Fisher remarks in *The Gastronomical Me*, a sentiment that I wholeheartedly second:

People ask me: why do you write about food and eating and drinking? Why don't you write about the struggle for power and about love the way others do? The easiest answer is to say that our three basic needs, for food, security, and love are so mixed and mingled and entwined that we cannot straightly think of one without the others. So it happens that when I write of hunger for it and the love and warmth and richness and fine reality of hunger satisfied, it is all one. ("Forward")

And so it is that *Cooking by the Book*, though ostensibly dealing with food as language in both literature and culture, is really a study and critical examination of the entire spectrum of human life.

The book itself grew out of just such caring for human life. I would like to thank a colleague and friend, Margaret Hundleby, for her great interest, assistance, and knowledge; without her help, *Cooking by the Book* would not have begun, nor would it have ever reached fruition. I would also like to thank Sandy Goodliff and Dorothy Mikolajczk for their editorial assistance. Finally, words of thanks must be offered to my many friends who have so richly nourished me. With their kind words and good foods, they have, indeed, helped me articulate what is vague and abstract about life, love, and literature.

1

Introduction

Cooking by the Book

In *The Spice of Life and Other Essays*, G.K. Chesterton remarks that "Every healthy person at some period must feed on fiction as well as fact" ("Fiction as Food"). Earlier, Thackerary, when questioned about food, had answered: "Next to eating good dinners, a healthy man with a benevolent turn of mind must like, I think, to read about them." Both aphoristic statements underscore the truism that is the *raison d'etre* of *Cooking by the Book*: there is a symbiotic relationship between food and the written word, be it fiction or non-fiction, which whets the appetite (literally and metaphorically) of even the most seasoned of eaters and readers. Clifton Fadiman writes that books about food belong "to the literature of power, those that, linking brain to stomach, etherealize the euphoria of feeding with the finer essence of reflection" (M.F.K. Fisher, *The Art of Eating* xi).

It is the purpose of *Cooking by the Book* to nourish these reflective appetites. The essays collected here (Part One) examine the use writers have made of food as a rhetorical structure that allows them to articulate abstract, internal, and difficult to express concepts; the food rhetoric objectifies the ineffable qualities of life, thus providing the artist with a necessary "imagining power." In the second part, the contributors turn to the larger world and examine the rhetoric of food in the proverbial "market place:" what do food catalogues and McDonalds, for example, really have to say about our twentieth-century culture. *Cooking by the Book* attempts to find answers by presenting a varying menu of critical approaches and topics to this most basic of human needs.

As an appetizer to the main investigations, Anne LeCroy explores the tantilizing conundrum: "Cookery Literature—or Literary Cookery." In her essay she offers us "a sort of appetizer of various writing" that composes the beginning of a bibliography about food and literary cookery: (1) general histories of human cuisine; (2) personal memoirs and essays with recipes; (3) recipes with short essays or anecdotes and (4) fiction with recipes in the text; she provides the reader with sufficient primary sources to promote further exploration and culinary feasting.

Tobe Levin introduces the central concerns of this examination of food as literary language as she explores the eastern European, Jewish immigrant portrayed in the fiction of Anzia Yezierska. The immigrant questions the possibility of assimilation: is one able to retain one's identity and yet still become a part, and a necessary one at that, of the new culture? The answer, Levin argues, is found in the use made of food, both actually and in the food literature of this particular ethnic group. In Yezierska's fiction, mealtimes and table manners measure integration, while hunger becomes the prism through which America is judged— and found lacking.

It is, perhaps, this lack which caused Edith Wharton's characters to travel abroad, in the hopes of finding (?), renewing (?) their cultural roots. Yet, as Cecilia Macheski notes: "Wharton wishes to reveal the Philistine perspective of her characters, whose goals in traveling are little more than to find un-foreign food and hob-nob with royalty." Moving beyond such a parochial view by examining two later and frequently maligned Wharton novels, Macheski traces the menu-to-metaphor, food-to-symbol transformation that Wharton's fiction undergoes as she explores the "American experience" as reflected in food imagery.

"The 'New American Melting' Pot[ter]" described by Lynn Veach Sadler in her essay on the mysteries of Virginia Rich continues this investigation of the "American Experience." Rich's mysteries prove, she argues, that "Contemporary Americans can maintain their old and new world identities and simultaneously meld and enjoy one another and their individual habits and foods."

Hunger also functions as a symbolic matrix in the contemporary novels of Anita Brookner. Food is used as another gauge of self, and Schofield finds that Brookner's heroines, like the immigrants, use food-procurement, preparation, and consumption, as a symbol of self-development and identity. Through the careful and meticulous preparation and serving of a meal to a male, Brookner's middle-aged, single spinsters attempt to find a self-identity and an understanding of their position in society. Basing their own self explorations on the age-old adage about the way to a man's heart is through his stomach, they discover that the way to their own self is through food; it is impossible to know anyone else.

Sharon Wilson also concludes that in an effort to know themselves, women must reject the poisoned apples offered to them by men in their mythic constructs. Examining the male fairy-tale used by Margaret Atwood, Wilson resolves that the women of these tales prove that they are not food to be consumed and destroyed by the male.

Sue Hart takes much the same tack in her essay, "At Home on the Range. Food as Love in Literature of the Frontier," remarking that in "a time when provisions were frequently scarce and anything other than the simplest meal demanded foresight and extra effort on the part of the cook, what better way to illustrate a woman's love—or lack there of—than through her culinary creations?" Sharing food during this westward movement meant sharing life.

The final two essays of the first section continue the examination of regional cookery and literature and return us, full circle, to yet another sort of immigrant experience. Here with Michael Dean's essay we investigate the Florida regionalism of Marjorie Kinnan Rawlings in her *Cross Creek Cookery*. Rawlings uses food, Dean argues, "as a tool to explore the life and customs of her particular region." Delmer Davis provides another taste of "Regionalism" as he investigates the popularity of the 1940s fiction of Betty MacDonald.

In general, the nine essays of Part One emphasize the validity of Thackeray's observation: a man (woman) likes to read about good dinners second only to eating them.

Part Two examines the cultural rhetoric of food and suggests, as Chesterton did, that food feeds more than fiction. Here food has become a narrative strategy and the recipe, or the giving of it, a type of embedded discourse.

It is just this method of *giving* the recipe that Leonardi explores in "Recipes for Reading." A recipe is not a mere listing of ingredients, she argues; it needs a context, a recommendation. It is this reason-to-be that provides the embedded dialogue that takes place in cookbooks between the reader and the recipe-giver, and creates the intertextuality of all good cookbooks.

Kate Kane finds a similar discourse in the seductively democratic language offered by MacDonald's fast food rhetoric. "In many ways fast food is the fulfillment of the domestic science ladies' project. It is efficient, economical, sanitary, and above all-standard." And, Kane argues, supremely alienating.

Since food and eating are about the articulation of emotions, one must be aware that the rhetoric of food is both the positive side examined by Kane and the negative rhetoric reflected in today's society by the plethora of eating disorders and the alienation fostered by fast food. Stubbs addresses this contradictory rhetoric in his essay, "Mourning among Plenty: Eating Disorders in the Shadow of the Persephone Myth."

While Stubbs ranges in literature of all periods, Lynne Gelber reduces his panoramic vision to one more single-minded as she analyzes the use of the food rhetoric in contemporary French society and literature. Finding examples in the culinary mass market, the nouvelle cuisine, short stories, and films, Gelber concludes "that the traditional use of food as a sign for sustenance and membership is often an expression of death or alienation unless one can accept the contradictions of society and the creative process."

It is just this sense of alienation that marks Thoreau's culinary experiments. He notes the contradictions of society's struggle between material possessions and personal commitments and reflects this in his choice of vegetarianism Bruce Henderson argues.

Part of his vegetarian interest mirrors the keen American interest in non-meat meals which Kolodzey explores in "Looking at Early American Cookbooks from an Inter-Disciplinary Perspective." Kolodzey combines this national vegetarian interest with the fascination of old cookbooks and concludes that old "cookbooks can be approached as curiosities, or they can be appreciated as an historical revelation to reconstruct not just past lifestyles, but the tacit philosophies underlying those lifestyles."

Lee Upton's investigations of M.F.K. Fisher's *Consider the Oyster* heighten this tacit philosophy of cookery books, and Upton concludes that the oyster is a "means of exploring our responses to danger, transformation, and trespass as these lead to wisdom."

Karen Madeira's bibliography increases our food wisdom. Why we eat what we eat and the traditions behind much of our popular food are just a few of the issues raised in the articles, books and reviews she cites.

In sum, *Cooking by the Book* offers a tantalizing examination of the new rhetoric, the new language of food. It is a feast to please the most discerning of palates.

Appetizers

Cookery Literature—Or Literary Cookery

Anne LeCroy

The Greeks, who had a muse for every literary genre, failed to provide us with one for gourmandise embedded in poem, essay, novel, and murder mystery. For want, then, of a traditional muse to summon to my aid, I offer Oikonomia as patron for such writers (a multitude) as embellish their works with recipes and detailed descriptions of meal preparation— or those persons who present recipe books that are also literary works for the pleasure of the casual reader as well as the kitchen maven. In a revised edition of *Literary Gourmet*: "Menus from Masterpieces," first published in 1962 (Harmony Books; N.Y.), Linda Wolfe presents menus and recipes she culled from a spectrum of writings, the Bible and the *Iliad*, for example, up through Henry James' *The Ambassadors*. Her collection lays greatest emphasis on fiction, aside from three poets. Her introductions notes:

I had long been noticing that the writers I most admired and from whom I was forever trying to learn literary lessons, invariably used scenes of dining in their works...I could recall hundreds of scenes that had been built by the world's foremost writers around food. (xv)

Wolfe's gathering is by no means exhaustive. I would add in playwrights who made dining the climax of a drama, or at least a major element (Aristophanes, Shakespeare, T.S. Eliot, for example) and a body of mystery writers, a plentitude of essayists, and such humorists as P.G. Wodehouse and Alan King. Lucking upon this book reinforced my long interest in literary-culinary offspring stirred in early college days by reading the essay-cum-recipe *How to Cook a Wolf* of M.F.K. Fisher. A much later venture into the liturgical aspects of eating as motif in the plays of both Aristophanes and Eliot (not such strange literary bedfellows as one might think) encouraged me to feel that investigation into the literature-culinary field might be quite respectable as a scholarly pursuit.

7

The more I worked over this project, the more books slipped into my collection—and they keep surfacing. As a result, I can offer the reader only a sort of appetizer of various writings, most of them fairly recent, that compose a small part of what can become an extensive bibliography. My main criteria for this study have been: 1) that the work include specific material about the cooking procedure so that the reader may try out an interesting dish; 2) that the literary quality of the work be satisfactory to the casual reader whose interest in cookery is such that he cannot boil water without burning the stove. To avoid a chaotic hash of presentation, I have endeavored to sort the various works into a taxonomy of the following four categories:

a. General history of human cuisine with a modest assortment of recipes or suggested uses for foods;

b. Essays, often personal memoirs, with recipes related to the essay topics;

c. Recipes with short introductory essays or anecdotes or comments ranging from historical to philosophical;

d. Fiction, with recipes in the text and use of food woven well into the fictive material, whether to show character, develop plot, or establish setting and atmosphere.

In the first class is a very recent publication, with new recipes as occasional examples. *Perfection Salad* by Laura Shapiro (Farrar, Straus, Giroux; NY: 1986) gives a detailed and fascinating account of women's changing role in cookery and the resulting changes in matters related to cookery, including education and cookbooks. Although the subtitle is *Women and Cooking at the Turn of the Century,* Shapiro takes the reader back to mid 19th-century America when there developed a concern for means to educate the future or present housewife in the skills of homemaking. The growing interest in industry, which had moved from the home to the male-centered factory, and business, a totally male world, took away many of woman's traditional responsibilities as artisan and manager. "The sentimental value of home expanded proportionately," (Shapiro 13) and such persons as Catherine Sedgwick and Catherine Beecher wrote books to professionalize homemaking, especially the "three lessons a day" (Sedgwick) to be learned by children at meals: lessons in cleaning one's plate, eating plain, sensible food rather than rich edibles, being temperate, neat, orderly, and silent unless bidden to speak (all we want from you, my child, is silence, and very little of that). An example is Lydia M. Child. *The Frugal Housewife* provides recipes of the "butter the size of a walnut, a good handful of sugar, bake until done" variety along with handy household hints on how to preserve eggs for three years, whiten teeth, and free a bed of bedbugs. Catherine Beecher added a high moral tone to cookery so that a woman might enjoy virtue even as she prepared the carefully planned, plain menus for the harmonious family.

Shapiro leads us then toward the world of domestic science in the schools (now called Home Ec) and upward to Fannie Farmer's Cooking School with precise measurements, timing, lessons in balanced nutrition, diagrams of various animals for cutting purposes, and full directions for taming of the cast iron stove. Fannie was also, unlike most of her imitators, aware of the importance of taste as enhancement to nutrition, though, like cookbook experts until very recently, she did not encourage experiment and personal creation.

Fannie aside, "by ennobling the recipes over the results [the cooking schools and scientific cooks of the 1890s through the late 1920s], disdaining the proof of the palate, made it possible for American cooking to accept a flood of damaging innovations for years to come...to enjoy food, to develop a sense of flavors, or to acknowledge that eating could be a pleasure in itself had virtually no part in any lecture, course, or written text" (Shapiro 72). According to the major schools of thought, digestibility came first, based on dietary computation; then came garnishing—for looks, not flavor—and last of all taste. A dish sprigged with parsley or a gussied-up raw vegetable encouraged appetites and promoted good digestion. Hence the urge to cut carrots into roses, permanent wave the celery hearts, hide green peas in the croquettes, and present mono-colored meals as examples of the cook's sense of art and symbolism. For a ladies' gathering on St. Valentine's Day one might offer a pink luncheon; a crimson meal honored the Harvard graduate; a bridal shower breakfast should be totally white with a touch of gold provided by the champagne. One example of a menu, for a St. Patrick's Day revelry, has been provided from the archives of my University Home Economics Department:

Grapefruit, broiled, and sprinkled with mintleaves and pistachio nuts
Cream of pea soup
Boiled chicken with parslied sauce
Creamed spinach
Potato balls rolled in parsley
Green ices and tiny petit fours with green filling and frosting[1]

Though the color effect might have charmed the diners, the taste, to judge by the recipes, was bland, the only seasonings being salt, white pepper, and the ever-present parsley.

Shapiro's thesis generally is that the advent of scientific cookery and domestic science training set America's taste experiments and adventurous cookery, at least for the majority of middle-class citizens, in abeyance for over 60 years. Shapiro's work is a literary delight, overall, though rarely offering recipes, other than a few from dismal recollections of her own early days in required Domestic Science. The following example may be sufficient:

I have only made carrot and raisin salad once, the day it was taught to us in seventh grade, but the memory of those bright orange shreds speckled with black morsels and clotted with mayonaise...has been hard to shake. (217)

Other histories of food and cookery offer, on most occasions, numerous recipes with the historical narrative.*

Essay, memoir, history, anecdote, and numerous manageable recipes are ready for the reader in the works of M.F.K. Fisher. Five of her early works are collected in the one-volume *The Art of Eating* (Vintage: N.Y., 1976). The earliest, *Serve it Forth,* offers a history of cooking from Homeric oat porridge and Roman garum (an ancestor of A-1) to a Shakesparean recipe for pigs' feet and a nineteenth century account of the social status of vegetables. *Consider the Oyster* covers every aspect of that popular bivalve: its nature, the philosophy of oyster eating, values of the oyster, and a clutch of recipes. For oyster stew she presents several possibilities, including

a strange stew, made without cream, but even better the sisters murmured with politeness (remembering New Hampshire childhood as they sat in the hot California afternoon under the eucalyptus tree)...it had a stronger, finer smell, they said...it tasted more completely oyster.

Their mother melted a good nubbin of fresh butter in the pan. In another pan she put oysters, a dozen or so for everyone, with all their juices and a cupful more of water for each dozen. She brought the water with the oysters just to the boil, so that the oysters began to think of curling without really getting at it, and then quickly skimmed them off and into a hot tureen. She brought the water to the boil again, and threw in pepper and salt, 1/2 teaspoon of each. She poured hot butter over the oysters and the hot broth over all and the sisters and their other sisters and brothers and grandparents ate it steaming with buttercrackers. (131)

How to Cook a Wolf appeared in 1942, when rationing was in effect, food supplies were limited, and Fisher had befriended several students and resident artists in Paris, all on very tight budgets. Her recipes, comments, and anecdotes focus on how to eat well when both food and money are in short supply, and the wolf is definitely at the door. In part, much of this book looks ahead to the days of "natural" food cookery and the whole earth movement. She presents a recipe for Gazpacho (at that time a soup known primarily to ethnic cooks and not included in standard recipe collections).

*I have not included, because of their tendency to exclusivism and the assumption that Ms. Kitchen artist or her masculine equivalent have endless hours to prepare foods, ready access to gourmet shops of the world, and kitchen equipment worthy of Vincent Price, the Time-Life volumes of world cookery and Julia Child's "from scratch" cookbooks. They do make interesting reading, however, and their literary style is impeccable.

This recipe, which I like very much, is not writ in stone. Like its nature it can vary with the person who makes it... This Gazpacho can be altered to fit what comes from the garden, but it should always have garlic and oil and lemon juice. There should be onion and some other vegetable floating around in it, and it should be very cold. Then it is a perfect summer soup, tantalizing, fresh, and faintly perverse as are all primitive dishes eaten by too-worldly people....It is especially good if you have a barbeque and want some legitimate, not too alcoholic way to keep your guests busy while you cook the entree...(216)

How not to "boil an egg" considers the private quality of the egg until it is broken.

Until then its secrets are its own, hidden behind the impassive beautiful curvature of its shell....It emerges full-formed, almost painlessly...I can make amazingly bad fried eggs...tough with the edges like some kind of dirty, starched lace, and taste part sulfur and part singed newspaper (229). One egg dish I remember we used to make (maybe to show the wolf he didn't scare us!) never earlier than two a.m. or later than 4 on the wine terraces between Lausanne and Montreaux, in a strangely modern kitchen. We put cream and Worcestershire in little casseroles, heated them to bubbling, broke one or two eggs into each, let them sit until they looked done, while we stood around drinking champagne with circles under our eyes and Viennese music in our heads. Then we ate the eggs with spoons and went to bed. (229, 237).

She speaks lovingly of the experience with one's first successful loaf of bread.

You stand and look at [it], even the first time, with an almost mystical pride and feeling of self-pleasure. You will know, as you smell [it] and remember the strange cool solidity of the dough puffing up around your wrist when you hit it, what people have known for centuries about the sanctity of bread. You will understand why certain simple people, in old countries, used to apologize to the family loaf if by accident they dropped it from the table. (249)

Her culinary autobiography is the substance of *The Gastronomical Me* (1949) which she opens with

People ask me: Why do you write about food and eating and drinking? Why don't you write about the struggle for power and about love the way others do?

The easiest answer is to say that I am hungry...but there is more. It seems to me that our three basic needs, for food, security, and love, are so mixed and mingled and entwined that we cannot straightly think of one without the others. So it happens that when I write of hunger for it and the love and warmth and richness and fine reality of hunger satisfied...it is all one. (353)

A fellow cook and literary critic, Leo Lerman, said of Fisher: "[she has] raised writing about cooking to a fine prose art, while giving relentlessly honest, often witty often deservedly scathing, always positive...richly informed views of gastronomy and the world as reflected in the cooking pot. Mrs. Fisher brilliantly vanguarded the culinary revolution in America" ("The Cookbook Shelf," *Gourmet*, 46, January 1986: 96).

History should include some mention of a few venerable reprints. The earliest, *A New Booke of Cookerie* (1615; reprinted Theatrum Orbis Terrarum: Amsterdam, 1972) is a seventy-eight page booklet by John Morrell who offers:

...the newest, most commendable fashion for dressing or soweing eyther Fleshe, Fish, or fowle...[and] the most exquisite London Cookerie. (title page)

Morrell, professing that his travels have given him access to the most timely information about such things as soweing (stewing) Mutton French fashion, roasting Neats tongue, smooring (simmering) and old Coney, boiling larks and Making an Umble Pye, has brief anecdotes and about 150 recipes. Dining with Msgr. X, who describes each dish as it is placed, he comments on Mutton, from the Norman high pastures, sallets from Msgr's. own garden, planted in full moon under the sign of Aries. He also acquired from Msgr. a Lenten Pye with neither Fleshe or Fish:

Wash your green beets clean, pick out middle string, and chop them small with 2 or 3 well relished ripe apples. Season with pepper, salt, and Ginger. Then take your good handful of Raisins and put all in a coffin of fine paste with a piece of sweet butter and bake it; but before you serve it forth, cut it up and wring in the juice of an orange and sugar. (16-17)

Those who like to "cook by feel" could have a fine time with this— as well as with a recipe for Swan pudding which includes "some" blood, oatmeal, milk, nutmeg, salt, pepper, sweet herbs, rosewater, lemon peel, and coriander. No more is said of the preparation, bake time—you're on your own in the King's kitchen, provided you can get the swan.

The 37-book collection, *Cookery Americana* (ed. Louis Szathmary, Arno Press; N.Y., 1973) ranges over 150 years in anecdote and recipe from colonial times to the closing of the American frontier. Not just cookbooks, these include manuals for etiquette, home remedies, household cleaning potions, and general instruction on household management. Among these, I have chosen two: *The Improved Housewife* and *Six Little Cooks*.

Szathmary tells us that *The Improved Housewife* (Mrs. A.L. Webster, 1845) was widely popular and went into six printings in three years, perhaps because Mrs. Webster went further in her book than her contemporaries and included recipes not only from New England but from many other regions. He notes:

Just looking through this book we can...spot a trend that continued...in American cookbooks. Soups, gravies, meats, vegetables, poultry take up only 44 pages, while sweets from Europe as well as America, occupy almost 100. (ii)

Quoting the Proverb, "the good housewife riseth while it is yet dark...and eateth not the bread of idleness," Mrs. Webster says she has been 34 years a housekeeper; her recipes are "to replace those now in use, the results of chance or the whim of a depraved appetite...this book is especially intended as a guide to those who would cook well and *please the palate* at *small expenses*" [italics Mrs. Webster's]. (Preface, 1) She provides diagrams of various animals with cuts numbered and identified, recommended uses for each, and prices (!) supplied. We learn that Sirloin is 10-12 cents; a Rib loin section cost 8-10 cents per pound.*

"A Word for the Dinner Table" gives, in 1 1/4 pages, a quick summary of table etiquette for host and guest:

to host: "do not attempt to eulogize your dishes nor apologize"
"never offer fish or soup a second time"
to guest: "when soup is offered, take it; but if you prefer fish, pass it on to your neighbor"
"enjoy your dinner and make yourself agreeable to the company" (26-27)

She offers one recipe that must have been a boon to 49ers and other folks traveling to the western lands—Portable Soup.

Portable Soup
Let veal or beef soup get quite cold, skim off every particle of fat; boil broth till thick and glutinous. Season highly with pepper, salt, cloves, and mace; add a little brandy or wine and pour over an earthen platter not over 1/4 inch in thickness. Let it be till cold, then cut it in 3" square pieces, set in the sun to dry, often turning them. When very dry, place them between layers of white paper in a tin or earthen vessel. These, if my directions are faithfull attended, will keep good for a long time. Whenever you wish to make soup of them, you have only to put a quart of water to one of the cakes, and to make the water piping. (56-57)

Anyone interested in the construction of those Ginger nuts that the clerk was so addicted to in "Bartleby" can find two recipes for them, both quite simple.

Mrs. Webster's recipes are of the chatty variety with use of "you" and "your" and "some cooks say...but others say." Most vegetables are boiled—corn 30 minutes, artichokes 2 hours, cucumbers stewed 1 1/2 hours—(raw cucumbers were long considered vulgar if not downright

*Among American authors of cookbooks, Mrs. Webster may have been the first to seek to educate the housewife about the cuts and anatomy. This continues with Fannie Farmer and Betty Crocker, but, advisedly, "Ms. Crocker" provides no prices.

fatal to the eater.) There is one rather startling recipe she calls more suitable for children than regular butter:

Black Butter

Allow any kind of berries, stoned cherries, currants & half their weight of sugar, and boil till reduced 1/4. This is a healthful and nice substitute for butter for children. (165)

She commends souffles in a vague sort of way, browned with the aid of a hot shovel held over them:

Take eggs to the liking, mix beaten yolks with milk as for custards. Sweeten and flavor to taste; fill your dish half full and bake. Turn on beaten whites and brown top lightly, by holding hot shovel over it—or otherwise. (213)

Her last recipe is for Punctuality: Fifteen minutes before the time (214).

Six Little Cooks (Elizabeth Kirkland, 1879) presents us with perhaps the first cookbook intended for children. In fictional chapters we meet Aunt Jane, teacher, and six girls ranging from 7 to 13 years, to whom she introduces the mysteries of the kitchen. The chapters of dialogue amongst these characters lead from preparation of simple custards, biscuits, and popovers to a full lunch for adult guests: sweetbreads, salads, potato croquettes, open-faced pie in puff paste.

Often the recipes are developed through dialogue as with that for Mixed Croquettes. The ingredients and procedure are given in a paragraph, with the ensuing conversation:

"We're not going to make these today, are we, Aunt Jane!" inquired Grace.
"By no means," said her aunt, "but I thought I might give you several croquette recipes at once. We can select from among them when we find what materials Aunt Carroll has on hand."
"How can we find whether a tablespoonful is heaping or not...if it isn't water or some such thing?" asked Amy.
    "Salt is always to be measured even; also soda, cream of tartar, and any kind of spice. Of such things as sugar and flour, it is understood that they are to be a little heaped— about as much as the depth of the spoon bowl, unless it is expressly stated even." (65)

Saratoga Potatoes, very new in the American world of edibles, also are part of a discussion.

"Are these the potatoes that puff out like little balloons?" asked Jessie.
"Yes, the very same, and you shall fry them too, so that it will be all your own dish." (73)

Evident is the confusion about this new dish created by an exasperated chef at Saratoga for a finicky diner; Auntie's recipe may profess to be for potato chips, but Jessie will end up with Pommes/souffles, if she's lucky.

Let us take a leap into the present with *Fading Feast* (Raymond Sokolov) which combines regional cookery—and numerous recipes—with account of the recent loss of regional foods in the American diet. Like Ms. Fisher, Sokolov crusades verbally against tasteless store bread, plastic tomatoes, cardboard processed cheese, and prefab gravy. He offers essays and anecdotes on old, honored uses of American edibles—meats, fish, vegetables, greens, fruits. From Iowa comes a prize apple pie; from Indiana, persimmon ice cream; Florida offers raw conch salad and an egg lime soup that must be made with Key limes.

The American passion for beef and, to a slightly lesser extent, pork, has banished lamb almost entirely from the average table:

...the basic picture is dim. The Greek shepherd and his family may eat ground lamb often, or lamb stew in winter, or whole lamb at Easter, but McDonald's doesn't serve McLamb and Arby's has yet to place roast lamb slices on a croissant...(197) Americans who do eat lamb limit their purchases to the most expensive cuts, giving it a high price image, except in ethnic centers of the urban east offering parts no Westerner or Southerner would know how to use, and to costly restaurants on the gourmet circuit. (Sokolov 191 passim).

Barbara Norman-Malanowitzky offers a history of western cookery accompanied by a section of recipes from every era in *Tales of the Table: A History of Western Cuisine* (Prentice-Hall, N.J., 1972). In the historical sections we learn, inter alia, that early humans, after the nomadic hunting period, lived largely on legumes, nuts, and wild fruits, rarely on meat. Acorns, barley, and wheat (made into a sort of mush) were important staples to the majority at the beginning of Middle-Eastern cultures. We learn what to expect at an Egyptian feast (if we are of noble class; the lesser folk ate from a common dish of leftovers):

...on low round tables, one for each one or two guests, set with spoons of wood, ivory, or metal, goblets of glass, porcelain, bronze, silver, or gold, servants placed wild game cuts of force-fed cattle, grilled poultry, and fresh, dried, or salted fish. Breads and honey cakes, fruit piled in pyramids, and jars of wine completed the meal. Food was seasoned with spices and herbs fetched by ship from the Orient. (15)

Athens was famed for pastry, but it was reserved for the rich (who enjoyed cakes of honey, flour, eggs and milk flavored with dried figs, walnuts, poppy seed, almonds, filberts, cheese, or sesame seed.) The poor ate barley cake "bristling with chaff and perhaps one iris bulb or a dainty dish of sow-thistle, perhaps a few figs or a braised mushroom" (Norman-Malanowitzky 25).

Much later, in connection with a common table utensil, we find:

the fork was adapted only very slowly and over great opposition. Were the hands the Good Lord gave us no longer enough to touch His creatures? The fork inspired general ridicule as unmanly and affected.... Cooks felt it spoiled the flavor of food.... Louis XIV would have none of it and forbade the fork at his table....His sister-in-law declared "I have never in my life used anything to eat with but my fingers." (Norman-Malanowitzky 117-118)

Speaking of France, we could have had real problems working through a French dinner at Versailles: 112 dishes, not counting desserts; or later at an English summer meal served by a 17th century Gentleman of lesser quality: 7 dishes in each of 2 courses, including Pike, Veal, Calf's Head pie, a Pig, fat chickens, a couple of lobsters and a dish of tarts. No vegetable is included (Norman-Malanowitzky 119-120).

The poor, lacking such comestibles (or forbidden them) lived largely on bread, rancid butter, and questionable cheese. In earlier centuries they had enjoyed roast pork on occasion but a 17th century ordinance forbade anyone to keep pigs in town or city. Even prison food catered to class levels:

in a fortress prison near Lyons, the people of high rank...all dined with the governor(warden) each day and could spend the revenue of their estate on fine wines, fish and game.... One meal intended for a writer imprisoned in the Bastille consisted of exquisite soup, filet, a quarter of roast chicken, marinated artichokes, spinach, a pear, grapes, a bottle of fine Burgundy and coffee....When Louis XIV and his family were imprisoned, a staff of 13 cooked and served dinners of three soups, four entrees, three roasts, cakes, compites, fruit, bread, champagne, wines and coffee. (Norman-Malanowitzky 128-129)

In the shadow of the guillotine, the night before his death, Louis begged "for but a bit of bread" and was piled with six chops, a half a large capon, eggs, and three glasses of wine (Norman-Malanowitzky 129). He ate with gusto apparently.

The author offers a chapter for trivia specialists on Common and Uncommon Foods, ranging from acorn to whale and wort. Of beef, she notes that a British poet praised mightly roast beef as ennobling the heart and enriching the blood of the Englishman. But, many centuries before, Vergil had deplored eating of beef as godless, leading to readiness for war.

Whale was a popular and princely dish for Lent and fast days, the tongue, split and roasted a delicacy for the bourgeois.

Her recipes, given in the concluding section, are adapted for the modern cook, at least for one with the skills and resources (in grocery stores) of Julia Child or James Beard.

Many of the present generation grew up with Rawling's *The Yearling* as part of their reading list. Perhaps less familiar is her *Cross Creek Cookery*, a food memoir both personal and regional:

Food imaginatively and lovingly prepared, and eaten in good company, warms the being somehow more than mere intake of calories. I cannot conceive of cooking for friends, family [or self] being a chore. Food eaten in unpleasant circumstances is unblessed to our bodies' good.... (2-3)

Each chapter, following a few pages of personal comment and reflections on Florida friends, lore, habits, and personal experiences, offers favorite recipes for Zelma's ice box rolls, Mother's egg croquettes, and swamp cabbage (now called heart of palm; at Kroger's would you pay $2.39 a can for swamp cabbage)? "Better a dinner of herbs where love is," she concludes. Some of the recipes she offers are rich and for "company" but among them are simple ones such as Hoppin' John, cooter, greens, corn bread—all suited for company.

Two elements enter into successful and happy gatherings at the table. The food must be carefully prepared; willingly prepared; imaginatively prepared. And the guests—friends, relatives, the passing stranger—must be conscious of their welcome. Formal dinners of ill-assorted folk invited for the sole purpose of repaying an obligation are an abomination. (217)

Much the same feeling shows in the work of the Most Rev. Robert F. Capon, *The Supper of the Lamb*, "a book that concentrates more on the cracks and interstices of the culinary keyboard than on the conventional notes" (ix). This is, by his own statement, a leisurely book whose opening "outlandish" recipe runs by fits and starts through the entire work, providing "a fixed star under which the length and breadth of cooking is explained."

Capon includes within a text of mixed meditation, Biblical quote, personal memoir and feeling, the recipes that fit into the frame of the book—which allows him a wide range—with others in an appendix. The opening, "ingredients" is stark—Lamb for eight four times.

He "will eat anything...there are almost no foods that cannot be found delectable, given the right cook....I like drink and I have Pellaprat on my shelf, but Fannie Farmer in my heart. I describe myself as a moderately High Church Anglican cook" (6-7).

Capon does detest most electric gadgets, teflon-covered anything; has a mania for sharp knives and iron cookware. Finally, he despises recipes that promise quick results with little work or technique:

Technique must be acquired, and with technique, the love of very processes of cooking. No artist can work simply for results; he must also like to work of getting them...delight in the art of cooking is one of the oldest and dearest things in the world. (7-8)

He avoids mild hams, New York Sate wines, vodka, thin bacon and all diets. "I am against margarine," "prepared foods," broiled grapefruit, and whipped cream in cans...but I am wild about peanut butter, canned fruit salad, process cheese, and I have been known to put mayonnaise on cooked pears....I steal Franco-American spaghetti from little children's plates and am the foremost canned ravioli maven on the East Coast. (8)

Thus advised, you continue at your own risk. The rest of the book drifts about from memories of his wife's and his early experiments in cooking, to the philosophy of bread-making to a Psalm-like paean to water, a discourse on and recipe for puff pastry (that sounds far less complicated than most I have seen), 7 commandments of the guests-for-dinner menu (similar to Rawling's on guests). An experienced Anglican cleric, he is seriously concerned with liturgical acts: vesting the table, serving the meal.

1. Don't crowd the table. Provide your guests with elbow room, even if it means faking out a larger board by putting two tables together.

2. Don't clutter it either. It should be spread as handsomely as possible, but knickknacks, geegaws, and other oddments in the wedding present category should be left in the china closet. Keep things fairly open and business-like. A floral piece in the center, if you like flowers, is always pleasant, but keep it low. Your guests should not have to talk around it. The full array of silverware and glassware required for several courses is usually quite enough decoration for any table. Remember, though, to keep the colors under control. (10)

He concludes with the lamb:

The bread and the pastry, the cheeses, the wine and songs go into the Supper of the Lamb because we do: It is our love that brings the City home.

Raise her not for what she is not;
But lift her up herself
To grace the Supper of the Lamb,
The unimaginable session
In which the Lion lifts Himself Lamb slain
And, Priest and Victim
Brings
The City
Home. (191)

A Feast Made for Laughter (Doubleday: N.Y., 1982) is Craig Claiborne's collection of essays from *The New Yorker* and *The New York Times* from his years as food editor and food commentator. The style is cheerful, chatty, smooth, refreshing—though Claiborne might also be accused at times of a strong streak of egotism and addiction to name-dropping.

The first section, basically autobiographical, includes scattered reflections on food and a few recipes, none very unusual. An example might suffice. Claiborne's mother ran a boarding house and supplied the table with chicken and turkey on a regular basis. Bored with poultry, the family requested something else for Thanksgiving:

almost in unision we asked for Mother's baked spaghetti. So, when the vegetables were heated, a little ground beef was added and a tomato sauce containing cream, Worcestershire sauce and Tabasco sauce. These two sauces were the primary ingredients of my mother's kitchen...Once the meat and tomato sauce were done, the time came to assemble the dish. A layer of sauce was topped with a layer of cooked spaghetti, a layer of shredded chicken, and a layer of grated Cheddar. Layers were repeated to the brim of an enormous roasting pan, ending with a layer of cheese. The pan was placed in the oven and baked until bubbling throughout and golden brown on top. It was served in soup bowls with grated cheese and two curious, but oddly complementary sidedishes—sliced garlic pickles and potato chips. (86)

Claiborne made later acquaintance with master chefs and includes descriptions of dinners elaborate and simple—among them a traditional clambake for 60. After the labor of gathering rocks and seaweed and wood, digging a six-foot pit, and tying into cheesecloth packs 2 bushels of clams, 60 lobsters, 10 pounds of onions, 120 ears of corn, and 200 halves of chicken, burying the whole in sand, weed and burlap, there were 4 1/2 hours to loaf, sleep, read, swim, fish, drink beer or beachcomb. A vital respite!

Claiborne's second section lists the ideal cookbook library with critical comments. The final section contains 100 favorite recipes from homely—grits and cheese, cornbread made with creamstyle corn—to complex—stuffed cabbage that calls for 27 ingredients and a Cuisinart or two. None are in any way so elaborate as his recipe (in Time-Life *Classical French Cooking*) for pheasant pate that requires four days for preparation and 1 1/4 pages of ingredients, including about $150 worth of truffles.

Time forbids any details on books that offer collections of local lore and recipe, usually well presented by the Ladies' Aid, the Local Baptist or other Church circles, the D.A.R., or other local groups, to raise money for a new Sunday School building, the school library, or other worthy cause. I would like to offer two titles, though—*Spoonbread and Strawberry Wine* (Norma J. and Carole Darden, Fawcett: N.Y., 1978) a combination of Black family history and recipes of family cooks and the *Korner's Folly Cookbook* (Beth Tartan, TarBar Ltd.: Kornersville, N.C., 1977), an archival study of Korner's Folly mansion and recipes from the Kornersville collection of cookbooks, mainly personal handwritten copies. Included is a recipe for Confederate Army Soup (ham bone, beef bone, 1 small red pepper, 1 pt. black-eyed peas, boil in 2 gallons of water) (35).

M.F.K. Fisher writes the foreword to *Square Meals* (Jane and Michael Stern, Knopf: N.Y., 1984), a "funny, affectionate American food diary, not regional but topical." "A square meal means plenty of good hot or cold familiar, odorous decent food" (ix). . . .it will consist of decent bread and butter, plenty of meat/fish/fowl, one or two vegetables, cake, pudding or fruit.) The food the Sterns list is decent, familiar, plain pioneer food that boosted us out to the frontier and on into the 20th century. One excerpt should offer a good example:

In the hierarchy of food values, diner grub is far below home cooking; but at least diner food is hot, and a hot lunch always tops a cold one. Compared to the hoi polloi who eat sandwiches, those who feast on hot lunch at noon are living the life of Riley.

Roadside diners are home to a particular genre of hot lunch: meat loaf, liver and onions, and mountains of mashed potatoes. Here is a hashhouse menu:

De Gustibus Gearjammer
Cream of Tomato Soup
Diner Meat Loaf
Mashed Potatoes with Crater Gravy
Highway Patrol Succotash
Crumb Top Apple Pie
Black Coffee (16)

Richard Gehman would probably chuck out 90% of the recipes contained in *Square Meals*. Styled *The Haphazard Gourmet* (Scribner's: N.Y., 1966), Gehman presents a book (I really don't know how to classify such a mix) of anecdote, criticism, memoir, authoritarian cooking advice, formal recipe, vague recipe and chit-chat. Its full title is:

The Haphazard Gourmet, being a carelessly compiled, aimless, alternately infuriating and ingratiating COMPENDIUM of RECIPES, personal REMINISCENCES, and occasional JOKES recalled with AFFECTION, more or less, by RICHARD GEHMAN from good and bad TIMES in his LIFE, inspired by Le Grand Dictionnaire de Cuisine by ALEXANDRE DUMAS and published by CHARLES SCRIBNER'S SONS—NEW YORK

Novelist, biographer, journalist and columnist, Gehman said the cookbook had "been stewing inside him for 25 years" (9) The book is designed for the hungry man on his own, the woman looking for variety, the diligent and the lazy. He detests blenders, pressure cookers, electric stoves, aspics, Bloody Marys, airline food, anyone's gravy but his own, any Hines recommended restaurant. He loves all Pennsylvania Dutch food except scrapple and pickled beets, every sort of fish, cassoulet, his own bean soup, Tabasco, pizza and all forms of sausage. Herewith an example:

Electric Stoves. The man or woman does not live who can cook satisfactorily on an electric stove. No one, not even the president of Consolidated Edison Company of New York, or the trademark man called Ready Kilowatt, can cook satisfactorily on an electric stove. Another example of Progress defeating purpose. Burn things, yes. That, electric stoves can do. Undercook things, oh my yes indeed. That they also can do. Cook things satisfactorily? That, they never can do. If you are househunting and come upon one that has an electric stove in it, look elsewhere. If you move into an apartment where there is an electric stove, shoot the landlord. Start a campaign to eliminate electric stoves from American life! Embroider banners: DOWN WITH ELECTRIC STOVES! Tell your friends, relatives, and dear ones! Join the Anti-Electric Stove league of America! Need I mention that I am president? (78)

He offers multi-page essays on the cause, symptoms and cures for a hangover, history of good steak in Chicago, and Sloppy Leo Morino's philosophy on fish. Recipes wander from a short one for oyster pie, pot roast, and Senegalese soup to a 6-page item on stuffing for roast turkey.

On a personal note. I find him fun to read, he's a superb stylist with wry humor and charming anecdotes (some of which one suspects of being mild fictions). I've tried some of the recipes and had mixed results. But I enjoy reading and rereading his pages while the bread rises or the pot roast slumbers in the crock pot. He died about 1975— I wonder how he would have reacted to the microwave.

Lastly, the literature of fiction with cookery as an integral part. Linda Wolfe pointed out in her book about food in literature: "behavior toward food has been used by writers to demonstrate the innermost workings of their character's personalities" (xviii). Here are the practitioners of the two most ancient arts—narrative and cookery. They speak of their own century, their culture, and their class and I have interrupted them only in parentheses (xx).

We are offered Isaac's red pottage—his means to win the birthright from Esau, because he knew that was the sort of rough basic dish the rough, rural brother would long for (Wolfe 13).

A menu from Boccaccio provides 10 different dishes, each based on chicken, whereby the Marquise shows the king, subtly, that women may be disguised in many ways but they are at base all the same. A simple peasant stew served to Pancho, who fancies for a time that he would be a lordly governor and eat roast partridge, convinces the man that he is at heart a peasant, happiest with peasant food and peasant life (Wolfe 48).

For some of the elite public, mystery stories with a few exceptions are fare for the vulgar; we know better, having read mystery tales, old and modern, that rank in every way with the best of the best. My last two writers are from this category: Charles M. Smith, writer of five mysteries featuring the Rev. Randollph as detective and gourmet; Virginia Rich, with Mrs. Potter, cook, gourmet, and amateur sleuth.

Reverend Randollph and the Unholy Bible (Avon: N.Y., 1984) presents a former football star who has become rector of a large Chicago church (which is also part of a hotel business complex). With his TV talk show wife, Sammy, he lives in luxury (inherited) atop the church-hotel in a two-story penthouse, his life made no less pleasant by the presence of his cook-houseman, Clarence, a gourmet cook who describes his methods and menu choices as, for example:

"Clarence said you would ask about the soup, sir. It is chestnut soup. It contains chopped carrots, leeks, celery, and onions browned in olive oil. Then chestnuts, chicken stock, parsley and cloves are added. After simmering until the vegetables are soft, the soup is pureed, cream and brandy are added, and everything is brought to a boil." (25)

The comment in answer to Randollph's "isn't this a spiritually unhealthy preoccupation with food?" puts into Clarence's words a note reminiscent of several of the writers I have discussed.

"Let me put it this way. Until you came into my household, I had what you would call no palate and didn't even think much about what I ate. Now I think about it. I anticipate my meals. I speculate about what you will be serving. I like to hear you describe a dish. Isn't this a spiritually unhealthy preoccupation with food?"

"Oh, not at all, sir. I should think just the opposite."

"You'll have to explain that to me, Clarence."

"Quite easily, sir. A person who voluntarily eats ill-prepared food is showing disrespect for God's creation. If I may say so, sir, what the average American restaurant serves constitutes blasphemy."

"Oh?" Randollph was surprised at the contempt in Clarence's voice.

"If I understand the story of creation in the book of Genesis—or the two creation stories in genesis—the point is that what we have, all that we have, is a gift from God to us. And that we are to enjoy it. That means we are to treat the gift with reverence. You and madam work hard at your vocations. You try to do the best work possible. Am I not correct?" (45)

Smith, and our last author, Rich, set out—in the midst of murders and mayhem—recipes and menus and talk of food that is never distracting, but a part of the whole context of their mysteries. Mrs. Eugenia Potter, hero of three tales thus far and another about to be published, is a lively 60ish widow, well off, and with an addiction to cookery plain and fancy. In *The Cooking School Murders*, Mrs. Potter appears in a midwest farming community on a lake, the population of a mix of all-year round prosperous farmers and summer vactionists with comfortable homes on the lake. The plot focuses on an advanced cooking class sponsored by fourteen of the mixed citizenry—conducted by a gourmet cook and author recuperating from illness. Amongst such murders as stabbing, drowning, shooting, and strangulation, Mrs. Potter sleuths and cooks. Early, we are given an example of her own basic skills. In the cooking class, encouraged by Mrs. Potter "simply so that she could learn to make French bread" a lesson about knives is accompanied by one on breast of chicken Veronique. Soon after, a member of the class is murdered with a boning knife. Later, the picking of green tomatoes and their storage in a root cellar, sets the scene for murder in the root cellar, and a recipe for green tomato pie. On the end papers of this book— and of her two others— are set recipes for some of the foods involved in the story. After completing the novel with its "suspense-to-the-end" solution, the reader can repair to the kitchen and whip up Five star soup, Eddie's mousse, Ralph and Dottie's pommes de terre.

Her other two books, *The Baked Bean Supper Murders* and *The Nantucket Diet Murders,* with titles that speak clearly of setting and food ambience, offer similar but not boringly repetitious combinations of crime and cuisine—murder by explosion, auto wreck, falling from a high place, starvation, and crushed skull—recipes for Baked Beans, Mussel Soup, Plogues, cranberry cup pudding, hazelnut cheese, and rum pie.

There were two baking dishes of beans. One, Mrs. Potter's preference, the small pea beans, was considered here to be a foreign Massachusetts dish, but it was provided at bean supper to allow for outsiders. These were deep brown with molasses and slow cooking, rich with salt pork, and centered in the pot with a well-browned and tender whole onion, to which Mrs. Potter resolved to serve herself, without apology, along with the beans.

The second bean dish was the favorite of the locality. These were the large yellow-eye beans, also baked long and tender and also rich with salt pork, but sweeter, more golden, and juicer than their Boston cousins.

The steamed brown bread had been made by one of the three local experts—Amanda, the postmaster; Edna, grand-daughter-in-law of the original expert; or Tillie Northcutt, widow of Harvard's brother. By whichever hand, it was a credit to Birdson grandmother— of legendary bad temper but with a sure knowledge of brown bread—who had been their teacher. Each steaming, fragrant slice was almost too meltingly tender to eat with the fingers, and yet uncompromising in the honesty of its stern ingredients—rye meal and cornmeal, whole-meat flour, buttermilk, and molasses—an an invitation to add a too liberal slathering of butter from the dish that followed it. (9)

The gap between the chatty cookbooks—of good literary quality— and the interest in history, philosophy, sociology and literary contexts of cookery lasted about 75 years in America. When cookery turned from art to "science" of nutrition, exact measurement, home ec principles and second-rate imitators of Fannie Farmer, the broader study of the relation between food and humanity disappeared from view. Efficiency, speed, cost, precooked foods, replaced (for many) loving preparation of food, concern for taste, understanding that a plain, simple menu was appropriate for guests as well as family.

Only since about the 1960s, perhaps spurred by Fisher and Claiborne (and the whole-earth combined with true gourmet movement), has interest such as Capon's, Gehman's, and Wolfe's turned many of the populace to read about food and cooking as well as collect recipes from McCall's—takes 45 minutes, feeds 6—or retreat to the local fast-food hangout for an assembly-line burger and the Colonel's extra crispy.

The books I have chosen—from an increasingly vast number fresh off the press—are of high literary *and* culinary quality, fiction, essay, history, memoir, or spiritual meditation. I feel it appropriate to close with Clarence's comment:

Eating is something we do everyday to sustain a life.If the food I serve not only sustains the life of the body but at the same time lifts your spirits, then I have succeeded in my vocation. (Smith 46)

Note

[1]No source for the menu or recipes was provided. I acquired the duplicated sheets for this about 1968. For comparable discussion, however, see Shapiro, p. 84.

Works Cited

Capon, Robert Farrar. The Supper of the Lamb. New York: Doubleday and Co., 1969.

Claiborne, Craig. *A Feast Made for Laughter*. New York: Doubleday and Co., 1982.

Fisher, Mary Frances Kennedy. The Art of Eating. New York: Vintage Press, 1976.

Gehman, Richard. *The Haphazard Gourmet*. New York: Scribner's, 1966.

Kirkland, Elizabeth. Six Little Cooks. Chicago: Janson, McClurg, 1877.

Morrell, John. *New Booke of Cookerie*, 1615. rpt.: Amsterdam: Theatrum Orbis Terrarum, 1972.

Norman-Malanowitzky, Barbara. *Tales of the Table: A History of Western Cuisine*. Englewood-Cliffs, N.J.: Prentice-Hall, 1972.

Rawlings, Marjorie Kinnan. *Cross Creek Cookery*. New York: Scribners, 1942.

Rich, Virginia. The Bake Bean Supper Murder. New York: E.P. Dutton, 1983.

———. *The Cooking School Murders*. New York: Delacorte, 1984.

Shapiro. Laura. *Perfection Salad*. New York: Farrar, Straus, Giroux, 1986.

Smith, Charles. *Reverend Randollph and the Unholy Bible*. Avon, N.Y.: 1984.

Sokolov, Raymond. *Fading Feast*. New York: Vintage Press, 1976.

Stern, Jane and Michael Stern. *Square Meals*. New York: Knopf, 1984.

Szathmary, Louis (ed.). *Cookery Americana*. New York: Arno Press, 1973.

Tartan, Beth. *Korner's Folly Cookbook*. Kornersville, N.C.: Tar Bar, Ltd., 1977.

Webster, Mrs. A.L. *The Improved Housewife*, 1845. rpt. Hartford, CT.: Richard Hobbs, n.d.

Wolfe, Linda. *The Literary Gourmet*. New York: Harmony Books, 1962.

Main Course
Part One

How to Eat without Eating:
Anzia Yezierska's Hunger

Tobe Levin

Writing in a tenement on the Lower East Side during the teens of this century, Anzia Yezierska persevered in spite of want. One anecdote relates how all too soon the $200 income she had received from her first book, *Hungry Hearts* (1920) was gone, driving her to "satisfy her [empty] stomach with stewed-over tea leaves" (Liptzin 128). Sensitive to the politics of hunger in this country, one of her characters, the sharp-tongued Hannah Breineh in "For My People," scoffs:

[the charity lady comes] to see that we don't over-eat ourselves!... She learns us how to cook cornmeal. By pictures and lectures she shows us how the poor people should live without meat, without milk, without butter, and without eggs. Always it's on the tip of my tongue to ask her, 'You learned us to do without so much, why can't you yet learn us how to eat without eating?'

Miraculously Yezierska herself almost achieved this sleight-of-hand, her books a seeming substitute for bread. Ironically, though, when asked in the autobiographical "My Last Hollywood Script," " 'What helped you most to become a writer?' " Yezierska replied: "My greatest stimulus...was the teacher who said, 'There are too many writers and too few cooks,' and advised me to stick to the job that assured me a living. I told him if I had to spend my life cooking for a living, that would be existing, not living" (186). This dementi is both instructive and misleading: accurate in hinting at an alliance in her work between creativity and food; deceptive in that the immigrant never really gave up cooking for writing but rather, perhaps unconsciously, made viscera and palate into the narrative organs of her work, producing a body of texts obsessed with "meat and mink," "ryebread and rubies" ("Hester Street " 169).

The origins of this obsession are not hard to find, announcing themselves in titles like *Bread-Givers* (1925) or *Hungry Hearts* (1920). Especially revealing is an anecdote narrated in "My Last Hollywood script," a tale whose frame, as in many Yezierska stories, is a banquet, dinner or kitchen table. Here the autobiographical persona, having achieved distinction, is guest of honor at the dais of a women's college where she is to answer questions about her career. "An elaborate dinner was served," "Yezierska writes, "but I could not eat" (184). Not the anorexic symbol of the present age nor the stage-fright of a novice speaker, this appetite loss suggests acute awareness of the abyss in terms of class and privilege separating her audience, "born into the good things of life" (184) from herself, the 'successful' alien still nursing the hungry inner waif. She is inclined to eat, however, after tearing up her script, preferring to the text of rags and riches the following tale:

...in the throes of my second story, I was starving. I went to my sister [who] had nine children. They never had enough to eat, but occasionally they let me have a bite from the little they had. [Letting myself in, I found] a pot of oatmeal...boiling on the stove, I seized the pot, rushed with it to the sink, added a little cold water to cool it and began wolfing it. That whole pot of oatmeal only whetted my hunger. There was a loaf of bread in the breadbox. Just as I started to break off a piece the children stormed in, and seeing me at their bread, tore it out of my hands. At this point my sister returned, saw the empty pot. Her shriek raised the roof of the flat. (187)

The author defends herself uneasily by claiming literary parenthood: after all, she lives not for herself but for her writing, and just as "a mother has a right to steal to feed a hungry child [so has she] a right...to finish [her] story—"(188). This excuse, however, fails to impress her sister who pushes the fledgeling author to concede, " 'All right, then....Call a policeman!...say I've robbed. If it's a crime to want to give your thoughts to the world, then I'm a criminal. Send me to prison. I'll have something to eat till I finish my story' " (188). Yezierska claims that "every step in [her] writing career was a brutal fight, like the stealing of...oatmeal from hungry children" (188). Thus, one who might have choked to death on Tillie Olsen's 'silences' survives on metaphor: writing is fighting, is eating. Yezierska's transplanation to foreign soil resonates with textual incursions onto the fenced-in literary lands she has come to forage.

And because she was hungry as she wrote, her stories are the echoes of her craving. Hardly a one neglects the thesaurus of food images; several equate assimilation with the adoption of American foodways, thus making the table carry the burden of plot and theme. Daughters curse mothers and young women reject suitors should their preferences for food betray their origins, sexual attractiveness symbolized by what we eat, the Yezierska heroine angling for an Anglo-American mate. The author arrives at the position of Ellison's invisible man who declares "I yam what I am!" yet her tales are tense from the strain of accepting ethnicity in a hypocritical 'melting pot' culture that relishes the meat but scorns the spice.

*   *   *

I've often heard Jews of my mother's generation (describe to gentiles) how the prototypic Ashkenazi dishes of chopped liver, potted herrings, sweet and sour evolved through our foremothers devising ways to create nourishing and interesting meals out of the cheapest and least appetising foods—and lament to each other how they are now delicacies...(Burman 66)

Between the long years of creative penury and the present moment of ethnic chic lies a third movement: rejection of the immigrant mothers' efforts by their second generation children avid to assimilate, who shrink from the embarrassing cooking smells and table manners of old world elders in subserviance to an alien cultural ideal. Yet if youth thereby prides itself on adopting the right chauvinistic stance, it might do well to consider Chinese philosopher Lin Yutang's words. "What is patriotism," he asks, "but love of the good things we ate in our childhood?" Turned around, this means that what we eat in our childhood is good and to reject our native dishes is to sap our psychic strength. Erica Berman amplifies this, pointing out that "the contradictions [Jewish women in particular] experience in relation to food express the complexity of negotiating the meaning of...identit[y] within cultures dominated by Christianity,...by men" (64) and, for the immigrant, by New World cultural chauvinism pitting ethnic specificity against acceptance, ethnic pride against inferiority.

In several short stories by Anzia Yezierska, mealtimes and table manners measure integration. Chronicler of the Yiddish-speaking East European immigrant experience, Yezierska dramatizes intergenerational conflict through issues of food, balancing a critique of 'archaic' preferences with empathy for older people to whom nourishment is both sustenance and symbol of a former life. This is particularly true in her prize-winning tale, "The Fat of the Land" (1919), the idiomatic title offering an ironic commentary on the metaphor of satiety without satisfaction for the heroine's rise from penury to riches means adopting alien foodways that threaten her identity and Weltanschauung.

Illuminating the conflict in this piece is an essay by Erica Duncan which explores the effects of deprivation on the mothers:

Too well we know the Jewish mother our male writers have given us, the all-engulfing nurturer who devours the very soul with every spoonful of hot chicken soup she gives....Too well we know the feeder whose hard-wrung offerings are imbibed as poisons. Yet we do not know enough of the other hungry one who feeds others because it is the only access she knows to a little bit of love. In Jewish literature by women, mothers...the 'bread givers'...are themselves starved in every way, sucked dry and withered from being asked almost from birth to give a nurturance they never receive. They are starved not only for the actual food they are forced to turn over to others, but for the stuff of self and soul, for love and song. (Duncan 28)

The tenement dweller Hannah Breineh is such a woman whose hunger is revealed from the moment we meet her absorbed in contemplating the fifty pounds of chicken ordered for the Melker daughter's wedding. " '...and such grand chickens!' " the neighbor, Mrs. Pelz, exclaims. " 'Shining like gold! My heart melt[s] in me just looking at the[ir] flowing fatness...' " Smacking her "thin, dry lips" at this intelligence, "a hungry gleam in her sunken eyes," Hannah "gasp[s], 'It ain't possible'," for in Savel, Mrs. Melker had had far less prestige, existing on a diet of "potato-peelings and crusts of dry bread picked out from the barrels." Now, however, her children in New York factories provide " 'meat for dinner every day [and] eggs and buttered rolls...like [for] millionaire[s]'." So naturally Mrs. Melker will be able to "chop up the chicken livers with onions and eggs for an appetizer,...buy twenty-five pounds of fish,...cook it sweet and sour with raisins, and...bake all her shtrudels on pure chicken fat' " ("Fat " 181). " 'Some people work themselves up in the world'," Hannah sighs. The menu is the measure of success.

With five small children, Hannah is not yet successful, since she depends on Mrs. Pelz' hospitality for her first taste of food that day. But the gefülte fish on bread with gravy hosting a bit of onion and carrot performs miracles, for the beleaguered housewife "relax[es]...and expand[s]...and even grow[s] jovial" (189) at this succulent intermission from life's recurrent struggle. For most times, her household is embattled:

...the children...seeing nothing on the table...rush...to the stove. Abe pull[s] a steaming potato out of the boiling pot, and so scald[s] his fingers that the potato [falls] to the floor; where upon the others pounce...on it.

'It['s] my potato,' crie[s] Abe, blowing his burned fingers, while with the other hand and foot he cuff[s] and kick[s] the three...struggling on the floor. A wild fight ensue[s], and the potato [is] smashed under Abe's foot amid shouts and screams. (190)

Hannah, returning from the market, tops "their cries with curses and invectives," but the ravenous children ignore her words. " 'Mama, I'm hungry!' " they shriek, " 'What more do you got to eat?' " Ripping the bread and herring out of Hannah's basket, they "devour[] it in starved savagery, clamoring for more" (191). " 'Savages'...'Murderers!' "she shouts at the cannibals. " 'What are you tearing from me my flesh? From where should I steal to give you more" (191). She has already done her best, "trudg[ing] from shop to shop in search of the usual bargain, and [has] spent nearly an hour to save two cents" (190). It is not surprising then that 'everlasting cursing and yelling' " (217) about gluttony should permanently ruin relationships to food. Thus prosperity does not bring peace:

From the squalor the scene shifts to the opulence into which Mrs. Breineh's grown-up children have placed her. The trouble is, of course, that the "successful" children are ashamed of their mother and want to Americanize her. She finds her plight unbearable, flings groceries all over her Persian rug and rushes off to live with Mrs. Pelz. But she is too old and pampered to live in poverty and must return to the hateful elegance of Riverside Drive. (Guttmann 35)

Back home she continues to skirmish with her offspring, defying all their efforts "to make [her] over for a lady" ("Fat " 261).

'Making oneself over for a[n American] lady' means precisely altering one's diet to conform to the female stereotype of Victorian ineffectuality, stifling the energetic Russian *baleboste* whose life is her bargaining, cooking, and relishing herring and onions. She differs radically from the American norm when it comes to attitudes toward food as described by Jillian Strang in her review essay of *Perfection Salad: Women and Cooking at the Turn of the Century* (1986):

[For women influenced by the home economics movement] food appears as an adversary, something that conflicts with the delicacy and gentility of the preparers who, in Laura Shapiro's words, were "proud of their lifeless palates."...In their hands salad became...fashionable and ladylike. (Strang 8)

Hannah Breineh, whose *shtell* heritage has prepared her to bear the economic burden of a family, earning the living if need be, is deaf to the call of Ladyhood. Loud where the American is silent, assertive where she is decorative, forthright where she is simpering, with a lusty appetite where she is prepared to live on lettuce leaves, the Jewish immigrant finds the lady an impossible, self-annihilating model. Hannah's inability to conform to this stereotype is codified in her rejection of American cuisine.

Having been installed by her prosperous children in a kitchenette apartment, Hannah, deprived of her function as nurturer feels "robbed of the last reason for her existence" (210). Nor can she endure "the public dining-room [for] no matter how hard she trie[s] to learn polite table manners, she always [finds] people staring at her, and her daughter rebuking her for eating with the wrong fork or guzzling the soup or staining the cloth." Nor is the menu appealing.

'I am starved out for a piece of real eating,'[Hannah tells Mrs. Pelz]. 'In that swell restaurant is nothing but napkins and forks and lettuce leaves. There are a dozen plates to every bite of food. [And what] looks so fancy on the plate, [is] nothing but straw in the mouth. I'm starving, but I can't swallow down their American eating.' (218)

As Claude Levi-Strauss suggests, "The origin of table manners, and more generally that of correct behaviour, is...deference towards the world— good manners consisting precisely in respecting its obligations" (quoted in Nicholson 41). Hannah therefore is a rebel, her preference for traditional cuisine signaling refusal of assimilation's strictures. What she desires in prosperity is the same dish relished in adversity: herring and onions.

Generational conflict over menu and manners is central to another tale, "Children of Loneliness," which opens as an angry Rachel challenges Mrs. Ravinsky: " 'Oh, Mother, can't you use a fork?' " The immigrant daughter, afraid of being rejected by the American man she loves, cannot bear to see the woman eating with her fingers and complains, " 'It drives me wild to hear you crunching bones like savages. If you people won't change, I shall have to move and live by myself....I'd die of shame if one of my college friends should open the door while you people are eating.' " Her mother is willing to adapt, but her father refuses. " 'Yankev'," Mrs. Ravinsky pleads, " 'stick your bone on a fork. Our teacherin sa[ys] you dassn't touch no eatings with the hands.' "

'All my teachers died already in the old country,' retort[s] the old man. 'I ain't going to learn nothing new no more from my American daughter.' He continue[s] to suck the marrow out of the bone with that noisy relish...so exasperating to Rachel. (145)

Although living in New York, the orthodox Mr. Ravinsky will not become acclimatized if assimilation means giving up the foods he loves and his exuberant manner of enjoying them. If to be become American means to exercise repression, he will have none of it, telling his daughter that her "insistence upon the use of a knife and fork spell[s] apostasy, anti-Semitism, and the aping of the Gentiles" (146), a weaving together of elements which gains in meaning if we consider that in fact, the daughter's goal is to marry a Protestant goy, bringing sexuality and slurping into symbolic proximity.

"Children of Loneliness" concerns Jewish identity codified in foodways that "stand between [Rachel] and the new America...[she's] to conquer." As Kim Chernin aptly notes, "an obsession with food is always, at heart, an expression of some attempt to bring about either profound personal transformation or entry into collective life and its spiritual meanings" (168). For Rachel, the focus on food is both: precisely because "[she] can't strangle [her] aching ambitions to rise in the world," she is tempted to reject her parents, to "break them and crush them" because she "can't stomach their table manners" (157). Although expressed somewhat facetiously, Rachel's bitterness is realistic, for table manners are political. As anthropologists have noted, food is "as basic to socialization and social relations as it is to bodily existence.... Food demarcates power relationships" (Nicholson 38).

To distance herself from powerlessness, escaping the "dirt" and "squalor...of her Ghetto home," Rachel moves out, but one evening, feeling very lonely, she returns to stand outside her parents' window and is momentarily seduced by the scene she views. Freed from bodily associations with gastronomy, the tzadik praying sweetens his daughter's bile:

The father of the daylight who ate with a knife, spat on the floor, and who was forever denouncing America and Americans was different from this mystic spirit stranger who could thrill with such impassioned rapture. Thousands of years of exile, thousands of years of hunger, loneliness, and want swept over her as she listened to her father's voice. (154)

Cleansed of his appetite, he finds acceptance as Rachel also sees her mother free from stain. Although she lays the table and urges her husband to eat while "it is hot yet," Mrs. Ravinsky "only pretend[s] to [swallow] her slender portion and Rachel realizes "it ha[s] always been like [this], her mother [taking] the smallest [amount] for herself." "I don't want to abandon them!" she thinks (156). Still, "broken in upon by the loud sound of her father's eating," the daughter's good intentions crumble. As ascetics, they can be reclaimed; indulging, they are themselves engulfed in the economy of devoured and devouring. Her father's noisy gulps, "audible swallow[s] and smacking of the lips" are an embarrassment in the Anglo world, so the second generation daughter turns away, certain that, "if [she hasn]t the strength to tear free from the old, [she] can never conquer the new" ("Loneliness " 157).

The tale concludes in a restaurant but with an unexpected twist. During a date she had so looked forward to, Rachel learns that her suitor, a sociology M.A., romanticizes the Ghetto Jew in a misguided effort to avoid chauvinism. Rachel, however, seeing that she can be only an exoticum for him, never an individual, gives him up, feeling doubly the pain of having broken with her family to enter alone, another child of loneliness, the born-American's well-fed world.

If the sociologist's egotism and complacency offend the heroine, male individualism inspires her, as in the story "Hunger," the female protagonist wishing to model herself after the American man. Courted with promises of "dove's milk to drink," factory worker Shenah Pessah declines the role of leisured lady offered by her Jewish immigrant suitor because " '[he] can't make [her] for a person' "; rather, she must " 'push [her]self up by [her]self, by [her] own strength' " (61). Identifying with the Anglo-Saxon Brahmin, the greenhorn woman cannot accept one of her own, limited as she is. And less interested in marriage than in androgyny, she finds the WASP appealing not for himself, but for the life he symbolizes (Laufer 154). " 'He ain't just a man,' " Shenah Pessah tells Sam Arkin. " 'He is all that I want to be and am not yet. He is the hunger of me for the life that ain't just eating and sleeping and slaving for bread' " (62).

Bread, a metonymy for both material comfort and spiritual ease, is also literal in Yezierska. Especially in the story "Hunger," each major turning point in plot is marked by a culinary image, betraying an underlying preoccupation with food. First, janitress Shennah Pessah, broom in hand, daydreams of her American man until rudely awakened by a woman trailing "the smell of herring and onions...through the dim passage" (36). Then her dallying earns her the following reproof— " 'Worms should eat you!' " scolds her uncle, an appropriate threat, as Nicholson notes, "...if you are weak, you are edible; if you are edible, you are weak" (39). And Shenah's other misdemeanors? Gustatory negligence: " 'Yesterday, the eating was burned...today [she] forget[s] the salt.' " Is this merely being picky? Not according to the highest authority: " 'In the Talmud it stands a man has a right to divorce his wife for only forgetting him the salt in his soup' " (37). As Nicholson again reminds us, "Food is to the individual what sex is to the species" (37), the Talmud too conflating appetite and love. Thus, with a sigh of understanding, Shenah resumes her sweeping. But the old man's order of herring and onions—the "ugly things and ugly smells [that]...sicken her" (38)—drives her away from his house for good.

In the factory, Shenah meets Sam Arkin who falls in love with the "mother's milk...still fresh on her lips" (42), an image repeated after she rejects him, the street appearing lined with "young mothers [and] their nursing infants" (62). Fresh from the motherland, Shenah embodies that home Sam preserves in his vitals, ingesting it daily in his preferences for food. Shenah, however, having refused to be devoured by her uncle, is equally wary of Sam who, proposing in a restaurant, duplicates the other's error: "chopped herring and onions for two" (56) will not win the girl. When Shenah Pessah asks, "Ain't there some American eating on the card?" he "laugh[s] indulgently," compounding his faux pas: "If I lived in America for a hundred years, I couldn't get used to the American eating. What can make the mouth so water like the taste and the smell from herring and onions?" (56). She replies:

There's something in me—I can't help—that so quickly takes on to the American taste. It's as if my outside skin only was Russian; the heart in me is for everything of the new world—even the eating. (57)

In his discussion of "assimilation and the crisis of identity," Allen Guttmann asks how another popular dish, chicken soup, has come to be understood as almost synonymous with Jewishness. "How did it happen that Americans often assume that the folkways of *Mitteleuropa* or of the Russian *shtetl* are really the essentials of Jewishness?" Ironically a minority that adopted many of the traits of its European neighbors is now distinguished in the eyes of its American neighbors by these adopted characteristics rather than by the fundamental differences that originally accounted for minority status. (10)

In Yezierska we encounter one solution to the conundrum: Jewish authors themselves make secular foodways the emblem of identity.

A more general bonding of identity and food shapes the autobiographical "Bread and Wine in the Wilderness," whose title equates integration with 'communion.' Events are launched when the heroine, inheriting $800 from a fish peddlar, moves to a New Hampshire village hoping to "write again with the honesty [she] knew on Hester Street" (192). Prosperity allows the exploration of foreignness and the reaffirmation of Jewishness.

But underlying these overt themes is an unmistakable preoccupation with food to match that of Yezierska's ghetto tales. For example, no sooner does the heroine arrive than she is ushered directly into the "sunny kitchen"; her first gesture is to open the ice box stocked magically with her neighbors' donations of milk, eggs, butter and homemade bread; the following day she visits her contact for tea where the conversation concerns her "first lunch," opens with the heroine's assertion: " 'Only a city person could appreciate the flavor of fresh, creamy milk and fresh homemade bread—' " (196). The loaf leads to its baker, a fellow poet, who however cannot dispel the malaise swelling in the 'stranger in the village', for she finds a small town is unlike the city where the lonely go to cafeterias whose fellow patrons enter "for a nickel cup of coffee, or a ten-cent sandwich," smile and "start...talking to you at the counter [or] across the table"; Fair Oaks, in contrast, makes the heroine feel like "an outsider, a stranger" (198). Though the talk is almost exclusively of edibles and growing things—"You know what makes my jelly so good? I put a crab apple into my grapes..." (199)—the narrator's sense of exclusion is heightened. With "the smell of a New England boiled dinner, pork, cabbage, turnips and onions" in her nose and, in her ears, complaints about the weasel munching on the best of the chickens thus eliminating "any boughten things for the table," the heroine continues "plagued with doubts" about her right to independence in a rooted world so self-sufficient, torn between what "[she] was," an undernourished greenhorn, and "what [she] wanted to be," (200) well-fed and American.

The author, now mature and affluent, nevertheless continues hungry for acceptance as her narrative moves from one feeding to the next until, at dinner in a colleague's home, she realizes the "futility of all...attempts to become a Fair Oaks villager" (205), the symbol of Anglo-America. Goaded by an Anti-semitic remark, she reembraces her religion, acknowledging that "the battle [she] thought [she had been] waging against the world had been against [herself], against the Jew in [her]"

(206). Denying her ethnicity, she finds, had been "like cutting off part of [her]self" and had translated into metaphors of loss and craving. Thus, when, on her last morning at Fair Oaks, archetypal mainstream town, she is awakened by the milk truck on its way to meet the freight train, the lactic image seems well-placed: if New Englanders replenish the continent's bodies, immigrants can offer sustenance for minds.

In the tale "My Own People," a writer's attempts at self-expression are equated with a mother's drive to feed her young. Between them they move, like the author herself, "from bitterest agony to dancing joy," and their optimism in the face of misery suggests the flavor of Yezierska's work: " 'Who'll say no in this black life to cake and wine' " (239).[1]

Note

[1]I would like to thank Jo Myers-Dickinson for her careful reading of an earlier version of this essay.

References

Berman, Erika. "Love and Knishes: Jewish Women and Food," *Shifra* No. 3 and 4, Chanukkah 5747/Dec. 1986, 64-66.

Chernin, Kim. *The Hungry Self, Women, Eating and Identity*. N.Y.: Random House, 1985.

Duncan, Erika. "The Hungry Jewish Mother," in *On Being a Jewish Feminist*. ed. Susannah Heschel. N.Y.: Schocken, 1983, 27-39.

Guttmann, Allen. *The Jewish Writer in America. Assimilation and the Crisis of Identity*. N.Y.: Oxford U.P., 1971.

Laufer, Pearl David. "Between Two Worlds: The Fiction of Anzia Yezierska," *Dissertation Abstracts International* 42. No. 11 (May 1982): 4827A.

Liptzin, Sol. *The Jew in American Literature*. N.Y.: Bloch, 1966.

Nicholson, Mervyn. "Food and Power: Homer, Carroll, Atwood and Others," *Mosaic. A Journal for the Interdisciplinary Study of Literature*. Vol. 20, No. 3 Summer 1987, 37-55.

Strang, Jillian. "Too Many Cooks," *The Women's Review of Books* Vol. 3, No. 12, September 1986, 8-9.

Yezierska, Anzia. "Bread and Wine in the Wilderness," in *The Open Cage. An Anzia Yezierska Collection*. ed. Alice Kessler Harris. N.Y.: persea, 1979.

—— "Children of Loneliness," in *The Open Cage. An Anzia Yezierska Collection*. ed. Alice Kessler Harris. N.Y.: Persea, 1979.

—— "The Fat of the Land," in *Hungry Hearts and Other Stories*. N.Y.: Persea, 1985. [Originally published 1920].

—— "Hester Street," in *The Open Cage. An Anzia Yezierska Collection*. ed. Alice Kessler Harris. N.Y.: Persea, 1979.

—— "Hunger," in *Hungry Hearts and Other Stories*. N.Y.: Persea, 1985. [Originally published 1920].

—— "My Last Hollywood Script," in *The Open Cage. An Anzia Yezierska Collection*. ed. Alice Kessler Harris. N.Y.: Persea, 1979.

—— "My Own People," in *Hungry Hearts and Other Stories*. N.Y.: Persea, 1985. [Originally published 1920].

In the Lands of Garlic and Queer Bearded Sea-Things: Appetites and Allusions in the Fiction of Edith Wharton

Cecilia Macheski

"The creative mind thrives best on a reduced diet," Wharton claimed in her autobiography, *A Backward Glance* (Wolff 15). The implications of this observation fuel Cynthia Griffin Wolff's psychological study, *A Feast of Words: The Triumph of Edith Wharton*. Wolff argues that Wharton's early years were marked by emotional deprivation, and that the novelist uses food imagery frequently to suggest that words became her nourishment, a replacement for parental and marital love.

The frequency with which such images occur throughout Wharton's work suggests, however, that there is conscious as well as subconscious choice at work. While there is no question that Wolff's analysis makes sense, it is clear we must go further and see Wharton's choice of literary menu and metaphor as a deliberate act of creation and an important clue to Wharton's development as a novelist from the early days of *House of Mirth* to her more complex and frequently misunderstood later works, particularly *Hudson River Bracketed*. If Wharton lived on a "reduced diet," a limited menu in which the love she needed often proved as illusive as Prospero's banquet, there is no stinting of verbal calories as she creates style and amasses allusions in her fiction. Yet readers have failed to digest her later books, perhaps because their palates are unaccustomed to the rich and ethereal flavors heaped upon the fictional trenchers.

Consider, first, the American aristocrats abroad whom we meet in *The House of Mirth*.

On the Promenade des Anglais,... [Selden] received a deeper impression of the general insecurity.... How anyone could come to such a damned hole as the Riviera—any one with a grain of imagination—with the whole Mediterranean to choose from; but then, if one's estimate of a place depended on the way they boiled a chicken! Gad! What a study might be made of the tyranny of the stomach—the way a sluggish liver or insufficient gastric juices might affect the whole course of the universe, overshadow everything in reach—chronic dyspepsia ought to be among the 'statutory causes'; a woman's life might be ruined by a man's inability to digest fresh bread. Grotesque? Yes—and tragic—like most absurdities.... (MIRTH 200)

Selden's tirade is a combination of jealousy and concern for Lily Bart, whose connection with the Dorsets he finds distasteful. Selden is also contemplating an earlier encounter with the band of Americans who accosted him with the pitiful plea, "We're starving to death because we can't decide where to lunch." The absurdity of the situation is revealed as they continue: "Of course one gets the best things at the Terrasse, but that looks as if one hadn't any other reason for being there; the Americans who don't know anyone always rush for the best food. And the Duchess of Beltshire has taken up Becassin's lately..." (191). As the argument develops, Wharton's irony builds. We recognize as her target the rich New York society people whose lives are without an awareness of genuine taste—in all senses—and who have discarded nourishment in favor of snobbishness, and who, despite the appetizing offerings that surround them, prefer the humdrum platters familiar from childhood to more adventurous fare, or choose for their visual display alone the magical but inedible banquet such as Prospero commands Ariel to conjure in *The Tempest*.

For if we turn to Shakespeare's feast, we find at least one clue to Wharton's themes. In *Act 3, Scene 3* we find a stage direction, "Enter several shapes, bringing a banquet...." Sebastian, Gonzalo, and Alonso are astonished. Shipwrecked and in desperate straits, the travellers can only express astonishment at the vision: Sebastian calls it "a living drollery," and begins to place himself in the long tradition of travellers and the literature of travel as he exclaims, "...now will I believe/ That there are unicorns...." His companion, Antonio, continues, "...travellers ne'er did lie,/ Though fools at home condemn 'em."

Seemingly more lucky than Selden and his compatriots, who lack such willing tour guides to provide for their needs, the shipwrecked men attack the fairy banquet, only to find that their hunger cannot be sated by these spoils. Enter Ariel like a Harpy; claps his wings upon the table, and, with a quaint device, the banquet vanishes.

Wharton, like Prospero, causes her characters in *The House of Mirth* to get "shipwrecked" on a foreign shore though her comedy is more wicked, for she has them choose, from motives of the most blind snobbery, their own ports. If we consider again Alonso, we find him courageous to some degree, willing to make the best of his situation, as he declaims to his fellows: "I will stand to, and feed,/Although my last—no matter, since I feel/The best is past...." Wharton's rich Americans, cast from their yacht on foreign shores in quest of food and society, *would* rather starve than eat in the "wrong" place, as they explain to Selden. If they are naive or narrow-minded in their culinary tastes, they are not innocent in their choice of companions. They are their own Prosperos, creating their own false storms and monsters. Removed from the stage and placed in the novel, the Calibans and Ariels survive in the psychological traits of the characters who will devour Lily Bart when she is no longer able to satisfy them with her beauty. When Lily must in turn ask for nourishment, Selden becomes a kind of winged harpy, snatching away the banquet of love and leaving her to starve.

The food imagery in *The House of Mirth*, in short, leads us to the conclusion that in the dining rooms of the Gilded Age, the deceptive dishes and treacherous tables of epic and Elizabethan lore are still very much standard fare. The chief difference is that while Ariel's labors gain him freedom, and Prospero puts aside his book in favor of his daughter's happiness, the rich Americans in Wharton's fiction seldom acquire the self-knowledge to know when to break their staffs, and thus continue to cause starvation and death.

In *The House of Mirth*, then, food is literal, and the references reveal the texture of the social fabric, as the characters judge their environment on the availability of well-cooked peas and terrapin. In "False Dawn," a short novel collected in *Old New York*, Lewis Raycie hungers for home while on his Grand Tour. He finds that "though not a large or fastidious eater when at home, he was afterward, in lands of chestnut-flour and garlic and queer bearded sea-things, to suffer many pangs of hunger at the thought of [the] opulent board [of his parents' New York home]." Lewis conjures up an extravagant, near fantastical feast, much like the one over which Ariel hovers:

Oh, that supper-table. The vision of it used to rise before Lewis Raycie's eyes in outlandish foreign places; for though not a large or fastidious eater when he was at home, he was afterward, in the lands of chestnut-flour and garlic and queer bearded sea-things, to suffer many pangs of hunger at the thought of the opulent board. In the centre stood the Raycie *epergne* of pierced silver, holding aloft a bunch of June roses surrounded by dangling baskets of sugared almonds and striped peppermints; and grouped about this decorative 'motif' were Lowestoft platters heavy with piles of raspberries, strawberries and the first Delaware peaches. An outer flanking of heaped-up cookies, crullers, strawberry short-cake, piping hot corn-bread and deep golden butter in moist blocks still bedewed from the muslin swathings of the dairy, led the eye to the Virginia ham in front of Mr. Raycie, and the twin dishes of scrambled eggs on toast and broiled blue-fish over which his wife presided. Lewis could never afterward fit into his intricate pattern the 'side-dishes' and tomatoes, the heavy silver jugs of butter-coloured cream, the floating island, 'slips' and lemon jellies that were somehow interwoven with the solider elements of the design; but they were all there, either together or successively, and so were the towering piles of maple syrup perpetually escorting them about the table as black Dinah replenished the supply.

They ate—oh, how they all ate!—though the ladies were supposed only to nibble; but the good things on Lewis's plate remained untouched until, ever and again, an admonishing glance from Mr. Raycie, or an entreating one from Mary Adeline, made him insert a languid fork into the heap. (*False Dawn* 21-22)

This is a fairy banquet for Raycie, but the Ariel who claps his wings may in fact take the form of Mr. Raycie, Lewis's father. There is no real nourishment for the son not because the food is imaginary, but because the food is no adequate substitute for love. That "lanquid fork" bursts the reveries like the snap of the harpy's wing.

As Wharton reminds us in *The Decoration of Houses*, there was once a time when even the homes of the wealthy contained no formal dining room.[1] Such rooms emerge, at least in part, because of a new consumer-oriented conspicuous consumption society, where display of wealth and food became a by-law of the leisured class. Lewis's food fantasy, like the vision of Sebastian and his companions, vanishes, just as his role in society vanishes when he returns from his Grand Tour having purchased not the great painting by Raphael that his father requested (and for which he advanced funds) but the then unheard of work by such Italian "primitive" painters as Fra Angelico and Giotto. For Raycie, when the fairy banquet—the dream of a loving family—vanishes, he turns to art for nourishment. It is no coincidence that he and his wife literally starve to death, having spent their money on the paintings they admire rather than following their family taste and dining safely at the silver-laden family table.

While Shakespeare's characters, looking at Ariel's feast decide:

> I will stand to, and feed
> Although my last—no matter, since I feel
> The best is past

such resignation is not quite Lewis Raycie's position, but he makes the same decision in his transference of food to art: to "eat" the art his eye treasures is indeed to eat his last. That this courage is justified after his death as the family fights to take possession of the glorious paintings that have proven, too late, immensely valuable, is the final irony so typical of Wharton.

Food, then, in Wharton's fiction after the early *House of Mirth*, becomes increasingly metaphoric, and more significant to the themes of the fiction. If the choice of imagery does emerge, as *The Feast of Words* suggests, from Wharton's own life, we must not overlook the evidence that the novelist consciously and cleverly wove the images into the texture of her stories, conscious of the craft she employed. Wolff implies that the food imagery is unconscious; I suggest that it is, on the contrary, quite deliberate. Understanding the choice and recognizing the craftsmanship that informed Wharton's language is crucial if we are to appreciate her most misunderstood work, *Hudson River Bracketed*. While the stories in *Old New York* have received warm praise from virtually all of Wharton's critics, who see them as fairly spineless nostalgia pieces on the whole, the later novel, and its sequel, *The Gods Arrive*, have suffered severe condemnation. If we turn to these in light of Prospero's feast, however, a new reading emerges.

Cynthia Griffin Wolff is among the strongest critics of these later novels, calling them "deplorable" (*Feast* 391), and indicting the author as "a bore" who preaches rather than creates fiction in this two-volume long tale of young Vance Weston's journey from the Midwest to life as a successful writer in New York. Curiously, Wharton's own feelings about *Hudson River Bracketed* are radically different: "I am sure it is my best book, but I have little hope that the public will think so" (Lewis, 490). While W.R.B. Lewis labels the novel "laborious and unsure," Wharton again offers the other side: "I never minded [the critics] before, but as my work reaches its close, I feel so sure that it is either nothing or far more than they know. And I wonder a little desolately which" (Auchincloss 173).

While authors are not necessarily reliable as critics of their own work, the intensity of Wharton's defense suggests that the two novels deserve a second look.

Hudson River Bracketed and *The Gods Arrive*, though published as two separate novels, are, in fact, two parts of one longer tale. While there is space here only to discuss *Hudson River Bracketed*, the reader must consider the first novel in light of what happens in the sequel in order to grasp the whole story.

Vance Weston, the long-suffering hero of Wharton's tale, reaches the end of his modern odyssey when he receives a copy of St. Augustine's *Confessions* and is deeply moved by the fire of the saint's language. No experience works its magic so much for Vance as reading: "And thou didst beat back my weak sight, dazzling me with Thy splendour, and I perceived that I was far from Thee, in the land of unlikeness, and I heard Thy voice crying to me: 'I am the food of the full-grown. Become a man and thou shalt feed on Me'" (*Gods* 418). Vance finds Augustine's prose "concentrated spiritual food to nourish him in his lonely rambles," just as Raycie found in the menus of his childhood sustenance for *his* solitary wanderings. If, then, we turn back to *Hudson River Bracketed* with the hindsight of Vance's revelation, we are in a better position to recognize the significance of these two novels to Wharton's *oeuvre*: for only Vance, in all the tales I have cited, learns the secret of eating the fairy banquet.

The first novel opens with Vance Weston leaving the Midwest after a prolonged illness in order to rest and recover at the home of his relatives in Paul's Landing, a small upstate New York town, at the time of the depression. Once on the east coast, the young man begins to pursue his career as a writer. For Wharton, this means Vance learns something about history and architecture, tools by which his powers of perception are enhanced, a theme familiar in all of her novels. In this case, the hero discovers the Willows, once the home of an elderly spinster who has died and left the house, with its well-stocked library, uninhabited and in the care of relatives, the Spears, who hire Mrs. Tracy and her daughter, Vance's relatives, as housekeepers. Vance marries Laura Lou, his young, fragile cousin. The marriage proves a mistake, and the hapless young woman will die of tuberculosis, freeing Vance to begin an affair with Halo. His career as a writer, like his romantic life, advances slowly, and only after much adventure will he finally return to the Willows, and find in Halo the peace and stability he has been seeking. He comes to terms not only with love, but with his role as an artist during his long journey from a struggling writer of short fiction to a successful and popular novelist.

The Willows, in Paul's Landing, is a place where Vance lands, emotionally and physically wrecked, much akin to Sebastian, Alonso, and Gonzago, and, as the name implies, to the freshly converted St. Paul. But Vance's fairy banquet manifests itself in a metaphoric form: the food for which he hungers, at least in part, is knowledge. The most revealing question Vance asks comes early in the first novel: "Why wasn't I ever told about the Past before?" (*HRB 59*). But our hero, like the Italians on Prospero's island, wants what a modern analyst might call instant gratification. Vance demands the right to consume the contents of the library at the Willows, without for a moment asking if he has a right to do so. Like St. Augustine and St. Paul, he must learn that spiritual and intellectual epiphanies cannot be ordered up like fast food in a restaurant. Instead of simply appropriating unto himself the contents of the library, or for that matter the love of a woman, he must, like Ferdinand, pass trials and tests before he can accept the gifts of love and learning. Like so many young artists, Vance attempts to be both Prospero and Ariel, unwilling to relinquish his self-centered view of the world and acknowledge the power of a muse. He is not yet ready to accept the paradox of conversion, that, as Donne puts it, "I/Except you enthrall me, never shall be free,/ Nor ever chaste, except you ravish me."[2] In the interests of length, a few short examples must suffice to illustrate Wharton's technique for portraying Vance by means of his human appetites and spiritual and literary allusions.

Vance and Laura Lou arrange a honeymoon, despite the fact that it is December, in a rustic beach house on Long Island. No sooner do they arrive at the little bungalow, than Vance must rush toward the Atlantic shore and explain to the innocent Laura Lou: "Didn't you know Venus was our goddess, and that she was born out of the waves, and came up all over foam? And that you look so like her that I feel as if you'd just been blown in on one of those silver streamers..." (*HRB 231*). Caught up in his own myth-making, Vance fails to hear the true note in Laura's response: "Vance, I never did hear such things as you make up about people." If this were not evidence enough of their opposite natures, the meal scene which immediately follows confirms the reader's impressions that this is an ill-fated marriage. When Vance asks his wife, as they sit on the Atlantic beach in December, if she is cold, she "shook her head, nestling down against him. No—but I'm hungry, I believe." He is delighted by her reminder: "Hungry? Ye gods! So am I" (231).

They embark on the first of their many eccentric meals together as Vance spreads a picnic on the frozen sand:

He was unwrapping, and spreading out on the sand, beef sandwiches, slices of sausage and sticky cake, cheese, a bunch of grapes and a custard pie, all more or less mixed up with each other; and he and Laura Lou fell on them with hungry fingers. (231)

Unlike the Raycie cornucopia, this banquet conjures up memories of nursery teas or "playing house." And, indeed, we soon recognize that the young couple are, in fact, little more than children performing their own fairy banquet as they stuff themselves despite the increasing wind and cold, until Vance extracts "a half bottle of champagne and a corkscrew—and looked around him desperately for glasses. 'Oh, hell, what'll I do? Oh, child, there's nothing for us to drink it out of!'"

As they laugh at "the pantomime of his despair," Vance "running along the beach came back with a big empty shell. 'Here—our goddess sends you this! She sailed ashore in a shell, you know.'" Unable to uncork the bottle, Vance must break the neck, "and the golden foam came spiring and splashing into the shell and over their hands" (232).

This peculiar meal is one of many that have no doubt left readers puzzled about the author's attitude toward her hero, and her intention in the lengthy fiction. Veiled in ambiguity and mock heroic, the picnic presents Vance as a dreamer and a narcissist and leaves the reader unwilling to trust him as a traditional hero. The fact that Vance is a writer, and, we want to assume, some version of Wharton's own self, leaves us even more puzzled. If we continue to look at the food scenes, we begin to clarify our vision and recognize that Wharton is no teller of simple autobiographical tales, but a richly complex artist accomplished in the portrayal and control of multiple perspectives and voices. Vance, to put it another way, sometimes speaks in tongues.

The critics' failure to appreciate the novel arises from their mistake of reading Vance as a mere one-to-one correspondent of Wharton herself. The seaside wedding banquet, and the following scene, as the young couple approach the rented bungalow, reveal again that Wharton is far more allusive than autobiographical as she creates her hero:

Once in most lives things turn out as the dreamer dreamed them. This was Vance's day, and when he pushed open the door there was the stove, with a pile of wood and some scraps of coal ready for lighting, and a jug of milk and loaf of bread on the table. The

bare boarded room...was as clean as if it had been recently scoured, and the drift of
sand and crinkled seaweed on the floor merely suggested that a mermaid might have done
the cleaning. (*HRB* 233)

The seashore marriage feast is a far cry from Lewis Raycie's reverie,
yet Wharton's tone, set by "once in most lives" urges us to take the
words at face value, to privilege the experience despite its eccentric nature.
Like the Willows, the banquet is a way for Vance to find out about
the Past, but like too many young writers, he fails to see the natural
beauty of the edenic scene because he is too busy embroidering it in
passages of overwritten prose. Vance, at this moment, is as much a parody
of a writer as he is the writer-as-hero.

Too soon, his marriage will degenerate as the beautiful but frail
Laura Lou proves unable to meet his needs; she is neither a good housewife
nor an intellectual equal able to share his ideas as a writer. The beach
house becomes, indeed, a prelapsarian world. As their lives slip into
poverty, near starvation and squalor, mermaids no longer scrub floors;
fairies no longer deliver fresh milk, and when they do not, Vance is
unaware of how to provide it for himself. Within months, we find the
young couple leaving "a decent rooming house" that was "clean,
hygienic, not too dear," in fact, would have suited them exactly if, as
cold weather came on, Laura Lou's colds had not so often prevented
her going out for her meals. She tried preparing their food on an electric
cooker, but the dishes she produced were "unpalatable and
indigestible..." (382). So, they move into a "leprous brownstone survival
of an earlier world. When Vance entered the greasy hall a smell of canned
soup and stale coffee told him that dinner had begun" (382). Vance's
vanity about his art and his status as an artist has chased him from
Eden, though as we will soon see he continues to grope toward the
apple he craves.

Vance comes to see his life as a failure, despite the success of his
first novel, *Instead*. Food and meals become not a shared romantic
adventure but the subject of quarrels with his wife in the world beyond
their beach:

'See here—there'll be nothing left to eat if we don't go down,' he reminded his wife.
   'I don't want anything. I'm not hungry. Besides, it's too late...you're always too
late....' (387)

Laura Lou is, in fact, upset because Halo Spear (now Halo Tarrant)
has just visited, arousing suspicions and jealousy that the young wife
tries to hide. Vance, as usual, misunderstands her anger and leaves her
behind as he goes out to sulk and dine alone: "In the first chophouse
that he passed he found a table, ordered sausage and potatoes, with a
cup of coffee, and devoured them ravenously...." (*HRB* 387)

As their fortunes continue to decline, due largely to the merciless contract by which Vance is tied to Lewis Tarrant's magazine, *The Hour*, Vance and Laura Lou move to "a bit of bedraggled farmland" on "the fringes of the Bronx" containing "a shaky bungalo...some rattan chairs, a divan and a kitchen range" (487). Laura Lou's health worsens, though Vance, again caught up in ideas for a new book, ignores her symptoms, unable as he seems to be to empathize with other people—a curious obstacle for a novelist, and one which suggests why readers have found the character so difficult and the book so puzzling. In this moment of poverty and crisis, Vance again turns away from reality and mythologizes the situation. Just as he fed the shivering Laura champagne from a clamshell, so now Wharton alludes to Christian myths as Vance finds "inspiration" for a new work of fiction. The ambiguity we feel toward him in the scenes that follow arises, once again, from the response readers have had that the hero, because he is a novelist, is some version of Wharton herself, and we hesitate to be too severe in our condemnation. Yet we cannot overlook the situation in which Vance finds his muse: his wife is dying from tuberculosis, and they are living in a sordid cottage in the hinterlands of the Bronx, yet as readers aware that we are reading a text about writing by a writer, we cannot but feel we are peering almost illicitly into the private spaces where creativity happens, and we do not want to disturb the author, the magician, lest the story end. To understand the complexity of the scene and the rich allusive strategy Wharton employs here and throughout *Hudson River Bracketed*, we need to look closely at a sample of her language.

A significant paragraph describes Vance's moment of heightened experience or "inspiration":

Just outside the cottage window an apple branch crossed the pane. For a long time Vance had sat there, seeing neither it nor anything else, in the kind of bodily and spiritual blindness lately frequent with him; and now suddenly, in the teeming autumn sunlight, there the branch was, the centre of his vision.

It was a warped unsightly branch on a neglected tree, but so charged with life, so glittering with fruit, that it looked like a dead stick set with rubies. The sky behind was of the densest autumnal blue, a solid fact of a sky. Against it the shrunken rusty leaves lay like a gilt bronze, each fruit carved in some hard rare substance. It might have been the very Golden Bough he had been reading about in one of the books he had carried off when he and Laura Lou left New York. (483)

The language is rich, poetic—and yet disturbing; too rich. The very density of images is atypical of all the rest of the book's style. The key, I think, is to see the moment not in reference to Wharton's autobiographical impulse, but rather as an allusion to the life of another American writer she admired, Edgar Allen Poe. The cottage in the Bronx, the fragile wife sick with tuberculosis—and, the language of an opiate dream—all lead us to read this scene as an allusion to the pathetic life of the addicted poet. Still, as when Vance is in the Willows, "book knowledge" is something external; his allusions emerge self-consciously from "one of the books," rather than from a private spring of feeling or vision.

Before discussing the meaning of this allusion to Poe in the text, I want to look at a second passage that occurs only a few pages later, after Vance has gone for a walk to escape his squalor and meditate on his vision. He returns to a silent house and finds "The table was laid with a box of sardines, potatoes, and pickles. All was orderly, and inviting; but Laura Lou was not there" (493).

This passage describing the simple everyday fare that awaits Vance contrasts sharply with the apple bough vision, and provides us with another reading of the hero's character. Those glistening, gem-like apples prove inedible as Vance cannot write the novel he envisioned without first consuming pickles and potatoes. Unless nourished with the ordinary and the practical, his visionary tree bears no fruit. It is a lesson about art Vance is still not ready to accept, but he will begin to weigh its importance when his wife's condition pushes him, finally, to contend with the unavoidable demands of hunger. He takes a job, offered out of kindness by his wife's former fiance, writing advertising copy. As one might expect, Vance finds the task difficult as his artistic yearnings conflict with practical demands:

> He clenched his fists and sat brooding over the model 'ads' till it was time to carry in the iced milk to Laura Lou. But he had not measured the strength of the force that propelled him. In his nights of unnatural vigil his imagination had acquired a fierce impetus that would not let him rest. Words sang to him like the sirens of Ulysses; sometimes the remembering of a single phrase was like entering into a mighty temple....(517)

No longer feeding Laura Lou champagne from a clam shell, he now brings her "milk out of the icebox." This diet—milk, sardines, pickles, bread, potatoes—may not be fruit plucked from the Golden Bough, or the tree of good and evil, but it is nevertheless a vast improvement upon the sticky cake and custard pie all mixed up together with champagne from a broken bottle that the couple consumed only a few months before. The cottage food is at least "orderly and inviting." The problem is that the improvement has come too late, at least for Laura Lou.

When the poor girl is close to death, Bunty Hayes, her former lover and now employer of Vance, comes to visit, sensing the desperate straits in which the couple are living. He proves immensely strong and practical, cooking the first hot meal the cottage has seen, repairing the broken stove. But he is too late, arriving only to help Vance close his wife's eyes and help with arrangements for the funeral.

Laura Lou's death marks the end of one major episode in Vance Weston's career, although his story continues for a few chapters in this volume, and then in sequel, *The Gods Arrive*. Such a vast and sprawling tale, particularly one with so scanty a critical history, is too much to digest here, but the point must be made that the two volumes comprise, in fact, a single tale. Vance, as the tale continues, will transfer his affections to Halo Tarrant, who will leave her husband to travel and live with Vance. The illicit nature of their relationship, as well as Vance's perceived needs as a writer, send the pair off to Europe. After a long journey which results in the separation of the two lovers, Vance suffers the loss of his grandmother, whose bequest to him includes a copy of St. Augustine's *Confessions*. The epiphany which this crucial text precipitates sends Vance back to the Willows, where he finds Halo, unsure of her future, as she is carrying a child. This work, the longest of Wharton's fictions, leaves the reader with the least permanent sense of closure. Whether Vance will prove a responsible mate is suggested but not confirmed. If we continue the parallel to Poe, of course, Vance will never marry Halo and will die shortly after the tale ends. Later evidence in the texture of the allusions, however, leads us to a happier conclusion.

To return to Poe is to return to the central problem of the text: our ambivalence about Vance Weston. There is no question that Wharton admired Poe's literary achievement, ranking him with Whitman and Emerson as "the best we have—in fact, the all we have" (Lewis 236). And the parallels between Weston's and Poe's lives are too striking to rank as coincidence: both began life estranged from their families, secretly married child-brides who were cousins (while boarding in their aunt's homes), won fifty dollars for their first short story, watched their young wives die of tuberculosis in the Bronx, and promised to marry another woman whom they had admired before their respective marriages (*Norton Anth* 778-79). If we continue the parallels, as I suggested above, we do not have much hope for Vance. But further questions are raised by the connections between the real and the fictional writers, and require that we glance back to an earlier scene in the Willows Library. Miss Lorburn, the former owner, required in her will that the room be arranged in a particular way, with a copy of "Kubla Khan" open on the reading table. It is the first work Vance reads in the house, and the one which triggers his awakening to literature and history. Poe's frequent use of laudanum, and Coleridge's report that his poem was the product of an opium dream thus frame our reading of Vance's life in *Hudson River Bracketed*. Is Vance's fairy banquet merely a drug-induced hallucination?

What disturbs us, then, at this point close to the end of the first volume, is that we are left with the dilemma of wanting to respect the two American writers for their talent, but despising them for their sordid lives. While Laura Lou is never presented in a very sympathetic light, she is nonetheless dead, and largely as a result of Vance's "artistic temperament." Are we being asked by Wharton to weigh *Eureka* or the unwritten *Magic* against the lives of the women? And do we believe that Wharton herself viewed the creative process as one stimulated by selfishness and opiates?

However strong Wharton's avowed admiration for Poe the writer remained, her text in *Hudson River Bracketed* presents an incomplete answer to the questions, unless we read *The Gods Arrive* as the completion of the story. Only there, with the final and significant allusion to St. Augustine, are many of the contradictions resolved.

The passage cited earlier in which Vance quotes the *Confessions* occurs at the turning point in both Augustine's and Vance's lives. The saint, in his imagined conversation with God, says in the section preceding the one Vance cites, "When I first knew you, you took me up, so that I might see that there was something to see, but that I was not yet able to see it" (171). He speaks, of course, with the hindsight of conversion, but his text is as much the narrative of a human as a spiritual quest. Augustine learns to see God, but he also sees himself and the world more clearly. That Vance should find the text spellbinding suggests that Wharton leads her hero not down the road Poe chose, but the one travelled by Augustine and St. Paul. "Night after night," we read, Vance "returned to those inexhaustible pages, again and again after that first passionate encounter he re-read them slowly, brooding, weighing them phrase by phrase...carrying away each day some fragment of concentrated spiritual food to nourish him in his lonely rambles" (*Gods* 418).

This is a turning point in many ways. It is, we recognize, the first time that Vance has read any text with maturity and patience. He has come a long way from the youthful impatience with which he first tried to devour the entire library at the Willows in a single afternoon. He has learned some humility in the face of better writers than himself. " 'And Thou didst beat back my weak sight, dazzling me with Thy splendour, and I perceived that I was far from Thee, in the land of unlikeness, and I heard Thy voice crying to me: I am the Food of the full-grown. Become a man and thou shalt feed on Me' " (*Gods* 418).

We have travelled a long way from the lands of garlic to the land of unlikeness. Perhaps our response to Vance is much like the ambivalence we feel toward the text of the *Confessions*; we revel in Augustine's recollection of his preconversion prayer, "Give me chastity and self-control—*but not just yet*...(418). Perhaps Vance, then, will learn to surpass his mentor Poe if he replaces the opium-like dreams of gem-like but inedible apples with the "food of the full-grown." Perhaps he will also become a major writer.

Whatever his chances, Vance still remains better nourished, in the end, than any of the other characters who have shared the fairy banquets. For most, greed or snobbery snapped the harpy's wings, made the banquet vanish. For Vance Weston, we want to believe that the spiritual epiphany will have enduring results, that the banquet will become edible and nourish him and his art. For by placing him so closely in Poe's shadow—that Poe who ranks as "all we have,"—Wharton has empowered Vance Weston not as just any writer, but as a great American writer.

Whatever the results, readers are certainly fair in concluding that in these neglected volumes by Edith Wharton, "We've run down a little place *at last* where you can still count on the caviar" (*Gods* 221).

Notes

[1]*The Declaration of Houses* is Wharton's first published work, and valuable in understanding the rich architectural descriptions present throughout her work. About dining rooms she notes, "it was only in grand houses, or in the luxurious establishments of the *femme galantes*, that dining rooms were found" (155) in eighteenth-century France. Her discussion covers England and America, and furniture as well as architectural space.

[2]See John Donne's *Holy Sonnets* for more examples of the paradox. This reference is to "Batter My Heart."

Works Cited

Auchincloss, Louis. *Edith Wharton: A Woman in her Time*. New York: Viking, 1971.

Augustine of Hippo. *The Confessions of St. Augustine*. Trans. John K. Ryan. New York: Image Books, 1960.

Bradley, Sculley, *et. al. The Norton Anthology of American Literature*. Vol. I. New York: W.W. Norton, 1967.

Lewis, R.W.B. *Edith Wharton A Biography*. New York: Harper and Row, 1975.

Shakespeare, William. *The Tempest*. Ed. John Dover Wilson. Cambridge: Cambridge University Press, 1980.

Wharton, Edith. *A Backward Glance*. 1933. New York: Scribner's, 1985.

_____ and Ogden Codman, Jr. *The Decoration of Houses*. 1902. New York: W.W. Norton, 1978.

_____ *The House of Mirth*. 1905. New York: New American Library, 1964.

_____ *Hudson River Bracketed*. 1926. New York: Scribner's, 1957.

_____ *The Gods Arrive*. 1932. New York: Scribner's, 1960.

_____ *Old New York*. "False Dawn." 1923. New York: Appleton, 1924.

Wolff, Cynthia Griffin. *A Feast of Words The Triumph of Edith Wharton*. New York: Oxford University Press, 1977.

The New American Melting Pot[ter]:
The Mysteries of Virginia Rich

Lynn Veach Sadler

Virginia Rich's three "theme" mysteries—*The Cooking School Murders* (1982), *The Baked Bean Supper Murders* (1983), and *The Nantucket Diet Murders* (1985)—have established Eugenia "Potter" as the mistress of culinary crime and the sharer of local recipes. Solid and entertaining, the books also seem to have another agenda: proving that contemporary Americans can maintain their old and new world identities and simultaneously meld and enjoy one another and their individual habitats and foods. Food, indeed, is often the mechanism that cuts through class lines and finds common ground as characters from different parts of the country and different Old World countries (an approach especially dominant in *The Nantucket Diet Murders*) interact.

Rich's "detective" is upper-middle and professional class and moves easily among her home place in Iowa (*The Cooking School Murders*) and three retirement locales: a ranch in Arizona, a cottage in Maine (*The Baked Bean Supper Murders*), and the house of a friend in Nantucket (*The Nantucket Diet Murders*), where she and her deceased husband Lew once owned a summer home. Milieux are developed with loving detail; and Rich genially—Eugenia Potter is better known as "Genia"—comments on the passing of old ways, yet welcomes some of the changes. Even the motivations behind the murders are "as American [and as 'human'] as apple pie": "...people don't kill for real estate. Money, power, revenge, sexual conquest—none of these seemed to [Mrs. Potter] more than secondary reasons for killing. One person destroys another only if he is threatening the essential *me* that one's whole life is dedicated to preserving" (*The Baked Bean Supper Murders* 247).

Author Rich, now deceased, relies heavily on her own experience, which, we infer, she has found pleasant and sustaining. One of the appeals of her writing is her ability to convey personal satisfaction with her life and offer others some modeling without being pompous, self-righteous, or condescending. Born in Sibley, Iowa, which is as small as Mrs. Potter's "Harrington," Virginia Rich wrote a food column for the *Chicago Tribune* under the pseudonym "Mary Meade" and was food editor for a magazine (*Sunset*). She and her husband also owned a working

50

cattle ranch in Arizona and spent some months each year at another home in a small town in Maine. Clearly, one of her purposes is to offer a commentary on the American landscape viewed by Genia Potter for some sixty years. A point is that, though times and America have changed, often for the worse, the old values and traditions are intact.

In the three books, Eugenia Potter remains a consistent character and detective. She often loses hairpins from her shining gray-blond hair. Though she occasionally considers a new style, she always decides to keep her simple bun. Similarly, she chooses clothes that are simple and timeless. From at least her college days, she has made lists and taken notes and has come to find clarity and answers in writing out the givens of a situation on her "ubiquitous yellow pads" (*The Baked Bean Supper Murders* 88), which now find a place in her suitcase as she moves from one locale to the next. As her college roommate says, they are her way of "settling all the problems of the world" (*The Nantucket Diet Murders* 33). She frequently falls asleep over them at night and wakes up in the morning with at least some of the mysteries solved and answers found. She also operates from a sixth sense of danger, of something being wrong. This feeling usually, in fact, sends her to those yellow pads for finding and testing hypotheses. She uses social calls to investigate her suspicions and writes out scenarios for murder that involve all of her friends—but not without feeling guilty.

Mrs. Potter is a model of the generally right-thinking individual aware of and even enjoying her own small foibles. Entirely circumspect and trustworthy, she will not read her dead mother's diary because she was never encouraged to do so while Mrs. Anderson was living. She is always ready to learn something new (fly casting in *The Baked Bean Supper Murders*) and is constantly seeking to find the master recipe and tame the culinary challenge (e.g., of French bread in *The Cooking School Murders* and *The Baked Bean Supper Murders*, Portuguese bread in *The Nantucket Diet Murders*, and lobster pie in *The Baked Bean Supper Murders*). If she is disappointed in the too-technical lecture on Portuguese bread that she receives from Hans, the Harvard Business School graduate, she is pleased when his fiancée, Mary, uses her Radcliffe olfactology expertise to lure customers to their shop with "Attar of Yeast." Though an accomplished cook, Mrs. Potter knows her limitations and may even, when uninspired, resort to "a dish of cold canned pears, a glass of milk, and a few limp graham crackers" for supper or produce a "badly poached egg" (*The Baked Bean Supper Murders* 134, 136). She is not above substituting Club Soda for Perrier when a guest puts on airs and does not believe that people are unavailable for last-minute invitations: "Very few of us are really booked up with an impressive social calendar" (*The Baked Bean Supper Murders* 61-62). She can momentarily suspect that her powers are slipping (*The Nantucket Diet Murders*), talks to herself, resents being considered "elderly" (though she has thought about what she will do if she becomes incapacitated and about her will—*The Baked Bean Supper Murders* 98, 160), is shocked to discover that the locals think her to have an accent (*The Baked Bean Supper Murders* 232), and knows how "unprogressive" she is in resisting going to church without a hat. Her mechanisms for coping with unease and grief include creative cooking; preparing company meals; eating good food; walking; observing the wildflowers in Northcutt's harbor, the snow in Nantucket, and the maples in Maine; working with her hands; and finding "catharsis in her yellow pad scribbling of the night" (*The Baked Bean Supper Murders* 249). She appreciates such ladies' men as MacKay Moore (*The Cooking School Murders*) and Carter Ansdale (*The Baked Bean Supper Murders*) but does not take them seriously, though she can still turn her thoughts to men (e.g., Deke MacDonald in *The Baked Bean Supper Murders*) while worrying about her college roommate wanting to marry for the fourth time.

Mrs. Potter has her own prejudices and pet peeves, of course, but, again, knows them for what they are. She is vehemently opposed to new, high-priced kitchen gadgets; will not have a food processor (*The Cooking School Murders* 178); and could never get a facelift. She does not want lawns introduced artificially on the coast of Maine. She hates tasteless restaurant jelly served in paper squares with "infuriating plastic covers" and prefers the approach in Sis's restaurant, where the owner spoons out whatever kind of her own preserves or jelly is available. "If you didn't eat it all, she scooped it back into another jar of mixed fruits and juices she saved as moistening for her mincemeat, as a proper Maine housewife should" (*The Baked Bean Supper Murders* 140). Eugenia is equally adamant about the tasteless tomatoes grown outside of Iowa.

Rich seems to feel, too, that another mixed view of Mrs. Potter—this one on Women's Liberation—deserves a hearing. As with serving alcohol at dinner parties (*The Nantucket Diet Murders* 120), she can see the pros and the cons. Her mother, indeed, was emancipated for her era, since she went downtown once a month with her children in tow to pay the family's bills. Although ignorant of the identity of Lucretia Mott (*The Nantucket Diet Murders* 71), Mrs. Potter has agreed with her husband Lew that her friend Gussie has to be married because she is not so independent as Genia, and Gussie later admits that she wants a man around the house (*The Nantucket Diet Murders* 152). Even Mrs. Potter is more comfortable when a man is available to carve and to open the wine. Nonetheless, she is irked by Lew's response to her query as to why she will have a trust if he dies first but not the reverse: "He muttered something about 'women sometimes get carried away by their emotions, especially as they get older.' That, from Lew! And about *me*! I told him I thought he was just as likely to get wacky in his old age as I was" (*The Nantucket Diet Murders* 47). She admits that she and the rest of Les Girls indulge in manwatching (*The Nantucket Diet Murders* 146) and recognizes that they stereotype: they "know" that men like desserts (*The Nantucket Diet Murders* 30) and prefer more light at the table (*The Baked Bean Supper Murders* 61). While noncommital herself on whether Amanda and the United States Post office are correct to eschew the term "postmistress" (*The Baked Bean Supper Murders* 4), she acknowledges two serious problems caused by faulty man-woman relationships. First, she and her friends in *The Nantucket Diet Murders* are taken in by the elegant, sophisticated "swordsman," Count Tony Ferencz, and ignore square-looking, solid Peter Benson, driving him to murder and suicide. Second, in *The Baked Bean Supper Murders*, Olympia, whose husband has betrayed her with another woman, feels that she can never trust a man again, competes with men on the job, and allows her distrust to sour her relationship with her daughter and with Deke. At the other end of the spectrum is the Down East housewife whose most persistent phrase is "my Louis says" (*The Baked Bean Supper Murders* 180). Nor is Mrs. Potter entirely pleased with Leah's assumption of the role of World's Most Bereft Widow or Mary Lynne's Southern Belle helplessness (*The Nantucket Diet Murders* 17, 10), though Roger Two is just as bad for his Praxitelean poses (*The Cooking School Murders* 10).

Some of the changes in the American landscape Mrs. Potter mourns. Doors are still not locked in Harrington, Iowa (though she comes to wish that they were), but they are on Nantucket, where the church is no longer open at all hours. Her high school is long since gone, and the new one sports a nearly flat roof in snow country. Similarly, she misses the "real bridge" of her youth. Women in Harrington can now be accused of being lovers, and Mrs. Potter is a bit surprised by Eddie Boy's blue eye shadow but refuses to apply the term *gay* to him on the grounds that such usage would be "a meaningless waste of a lovely, lighthearted word" (*The Baked Bean Supper Murders* 84).

The contemporary world Mrs. Potter studies, comments on, and enjoys, though she would correct it, is ours. It is filled with anorexia nervosa (*The Nantucket Diet Murders*); husbands whose sexual disabilities drive their wives to drink (*The Cooking School Murders*); cancer and attempts of the victim and her family to cure it with natural foods (*The Cooking School Murders*); "ovo-lacto" vegetarians (*The Cooking School Murders*); hippie communes (*The Cooking School Murders);* generation gaps (*The Baked Bean Supper Murders* and *The Cooking School Murders*); children cutting across their neighbors' lawns with tricycles but adults shooting them with salt and buckshot (*The Cooking School Murders* 130); widows whose husbands have died in hunting accidents and from heart attacks (*The Nantucket Diet Murders*);

the well-to-do letting a captured mallard starve to death (*The Cooking School Murders*); Meals on Wheels (*The Nantucket Diet Murders*); erosion (*The Nantucket Diet Murders*); a need to rename the church basement the "Undercroft" (*The Nantucket Diet Murders*); society matrons who can refer to their help, after twenty years of service, as "colored" (*The Nantucket Diet Murders*); references to "wap" and "dago" and hints of the Mafia in Down East Maine (*The Baked Bean Supper Murders*); vain people who refuse to wear hearing aids (*The Nantucket Diet Murders*); television exercise shows and a general health and beauty mania (*The Nantucket Diet Murders*); migrant camps (*The Baked Bean Supper Murders*); teenagers on the pill (*The Baked Bean Supper Murders*); people lacking in simple human decency (the Wyncotes forgetting Frances at the funeral of her employers in *The Baked Bean Supper Murders*); fundamentalist preachers (*The Cooking School Murders*); boys and girls whose "permed" hair makes them look alike (*The Baked Bean Supper Murders*); soap operas that set patterns of "passion and revenge" (*The Cooking School Murders* 105); and civilians who try to get the military to buy liquor for them on the base (*The Baked Bean Supper Murders*). *The Cooking School Murders* opens with Leonard Silsby sniffing in the way of a native Iowa farm boy, and the smell of the victim's blood recalls Vietnam. Ultimately, however, Mrs. Potter, "at sixty, [i]s shocked by very few things except cruelty, major or petty" (*The Cooking School Murders* 70). She says of another character what is true of her and what Rich means us to understand about her and to emulate: "You must have grown up knowing so much that we didn't, particularly in *learning tolerance* and in *being at ease with different kinds of people*" (*The Cooking School Murders* 115; my italics).

Rich and Potter make us remember a past that has confronted problems as great as these and has sent us a heritage of resistance and resilience, as in the homesteading experience and work on the "land-grant" college in Ames, Iowa, of Eugenia's grandfather; the oral history of Harvard Northcutt, who dies in his eighties; and the daily living through which "women [Mrs. Potter's] age ha[ve] learned to be both strong and resilient" (*The Nantucket Diet Murders* 269). An artifact like an arrowhead connects Eugenia, her father, and generations of Iowa farmers (*The Cooking School Murders* 153) or the previous American landscape of Indian life with a memory "treasure of serendipity" shared by mother and son (*The Nantucket Diet Murders* 254). Continuity reigns whether we call creamed chipped beef *dried beef gravy* (*The Cooking School Murders* 8) or a little of something a *mite, dite, tad, or s'koshi bit* (*The Cooking School Murders* 281). Mrs. Potter, indeed, often reflects "on the similarities of Iowa country cooking with that of New England"; "actually, there was nothing so mysterious about it...since her Middle

West forebears had mostly come from New England stock" (*The Cooking School Murders* 10).

Mrs. Potter's increasing perception of truth in each book makes her the target of the murderer. Yet the situation is alarming only in retrospect: when the reader stops to think that a sixty-year-old-female-pillar-of-the-community type can be so frequently threatened. We also receive the subliminally calming message that this atypical "detective" can restore order after the most violent aberrations and can, with good, ordinary common sense and fellow feeling, trace aberration to the source: exclusion from the dominant social pattern. At the same time, however, we are forced, along with Mrs. Potter, to accept our guilt and responsibility for what the murderer has become. In *The Cooking School Murders*, Bertha destroys three people and tries to kill "Mrs. B. Lewis Potter" because she has always both hated and wanted to be part of the "big-shot high-muckety-muck" set, as has her mother before her. Yet the rest of her family has understood "that whatever Bertha did in her attempt to change the social pattern that dominated their very small town, it wasn't going to work" (194). Eugenia feels the guiltier because she had known the inequality of the situation but had not permitted herself to think of the possible consequences: "Talk of a classless society in small-town middle America is absolutely phony. There is a right and a wrong side of the tracks, even in Harrington. . . . There are the Haves and the Have Nots, and Mrs. Potter knew very well (and had always known) that Grandpa's money and her father's gentle and generous presence as president of the Harrington bank had ensured that she and Will were permanently enrolled among the former" (57). The blindness has been a legacy. From the point of view of the town family, farm girls like Bertha's mother come not just to help with spring cleaning but to learn to cook from Eugenia's grandmother and to set a table and give a luncheon from her mother. Such unconscious condescension offends even the mentally and spiritually healthy like Harvard Northcutt in *The Baked Bean Supper Murders*: "And then Teddy Pettengill's crowd, here all the time, God help us, all of them with new pickup trucks they don't need any more than two left feet, all in new houses on their five-acre lots, taking over town meetings and starting something called a planning board, and *doing good*. That's the thing I've most got against them. I don't appreciate being done good to, and neither does anybody else in these parts" (17-18).

The problem is not so simple, however, as upper versus lower class. Teenager Rodney Pickett, allowed to believe that his sailor father, shipwrecked in Northcutt's Harbor, was English aristocracy, kills ultimately because his "warped and uncertain *me*," "looking for acceptance and recognition," feared and found ridicule in not only Mrs. Potter but Harvard (*The Baked Bean Supper Murders* 271) and because he was not accepted as an equal. Peter Benson, who has fought his way up from short order cook in a greasy spoon to owner of the Scrimshaw Inn on Nantucket kills when an outsider takes over his world, his island, and Les Girls (the group of seven to whom Mrs. Potter belongs). His "rage to be loved" has been overlooked; she and her friends have simply taken him for granted (*The Nantucket Diet Murders* 267, 269).

Rich, through Potter, then, is intent upon some social correctives— but of humans in general; she does not merely play off Haves and Have Nots or Insiders and Outsiders. In *The Cooking School Murders*, upper-crust Helen is guilty of disparaging her daughter Lolly publicly, but the Veersteegs, of farm stock, have haunted their niece with the fear that she will go bad like her mother (98). Still, Eugenia knows that Miss Bee, the local hairdresser, looks so much older because she "hadn't grown up with the good food, the good care, that most of the rest of them had" (157).

Each locale struggles for the best mix, though every group will continue to be known by its cars, for example (*The Baked Bean Supper Murders* 96). Even Harrington, Iowa is trying to bring into balance such groups as the summer resorters, the native townsmen who are the "decision-makers and opinion-formers" (*The Cooking School Murders* 57), and the prosperous farmers who remain outsiders. A major point is that, contrary to popular belief, "Everything that happens in New York happens here [in a hamlet in Vermont, for example]. . . . The only difference is that here *you know the people*" (*The Cooking School Murders* 171). Even when such social pulls do not end in violence, they take their toll. The DeWitts, of farm stock in *The Cooking School Murders*, have worked so hard to make the Country Club Set that they are lacking in humor and take themselves too seriously, prefacing most of their statements with "It is my firm belief" (59). Worse perhaps are the outsiders who would re-make the adopted area in their own image through buying up the land and building condominiums and boutiques on Nantucket, which has survived intact only because the whale oil crash left too little money for architectural renovation. Or, in the manner of Teedy in *The Baked Bean Supper Murders*, they become professional Yankees, exaggerating their accents and misapplying the language of the sea and generally incorporating stereotypes without plumbing local ways to discover that Down Easters pat rather than shake hands, give finger waves, take their meals at specified times at odds with the rest of the world, and generally adhere to a social pattern that is good manners to them if apparent indifference to outsiders. His wife, similarly, fills their house with beach-pebble bric-a-brac and kit-issue needlepoint and serves instant coffee, non-dairy creamer, and stale doughnuts.

In all of her ports of call, Mrs. Potter makes herself a part of the several groups, never "too rigidly" identifying with any of them (*The Baked Bean Supper Murders* 18), and feels guilty about her lightship basket and its association with old money throughout *The Nantucket Diet Murders*. She does admire a combination wedding and baby shower given by the mother of the husband-to-be: "how solidly practical and how comfortable in its acceptance of facts" (*The Baked Bean Supper Murders* 226). Rich asks for recognition that any of her locales, while lacking "city crime and international violence," can produce equally troubling situations to be remedied only by human caring and community responsibility (*The Baked Bean Supper Murders* 168, 210).

Mrs. Potter shows us what the individual can do to help effect correction. She refuses to cut herself off from change or judge by appearance and thus can easily end up talking to "hairy, gentle" bear hunters: "At times, Mrs. Potter felt that all her life had been conditioned to saying, 'No, do tell me more' " (*The Baked Bean Supper Murders* 220). She wishes that everyone could share the rewards. Charley (Charlene), for example, looks as though she would sing protest songs to the accompaniment of her own guitar but serves her guests Souchong tea, with generations-old linen napkins, and provides homemade raisin bread. Brought up by her father to hunt, she now hates guns but saves Mrs. Potter's life by shooting Bertha. The hippie-looking couple who does odd jobs turns out to be James Russell Markham, III, and Anne-Marie Loeb, who are very much the opposite of what they appear to be and will, with her help, end up revitalizing the local inn in *The Baked Bean Supper Murders* with their excellent cooking. Mrs. Potter is interested in the *Young*, gives a dinner party for them in *The Cooking School Murders*, and tries to understand them, though she maintains her belief in old-fashioned marriage and knows that she will have to return to the ranch if her nephew asks his girlfriend to move in with them. In another smaller dinner party in *The Baked Bean Supper Murders*, Eugenia uses the occasion to take Laurie off in the kitchen and try to sort out her problems with her mother while leaving Olympia and Deke alone to work out their own difficulties, though Mrs. Potter is herself interested in the man.

Finally, however, food is the most important means by which the Rich books link cultures and families and destroy generation gaps. It is the ultimate expression, Rich seems to say, of our community and communality. Our history can be told with such dishes as Beef Wellington. Our knowledge of others is enlarged by food, as in the "great rush for [that] of the Middle East, and the parsley-bulgur salad called *tabbouleh*" or the wild rice that was gathered by the American Indians and fed to Midwesterners for breakfast (*The Cooking School Murders* 88-89). "Fashions in food" are communicated with the quicksilverness of jokes:

"Food fads are like jokes. . . . You don't understand how they get around, but all at once everyone in the country is repeating the same one" (*The Cooking School Murders* 118). Similarly, the history of modern dieting (*The Nantucket Diet Murders* 272-275) teaches us more about ourselves than about food, as "menus, almost as much as houses, are a reflection of personality, or so Mrs. Potter had long felt" (*The Cooking School Murders* 132). In *The Nantucket Diet Murders*, Eugenia finds that she is slender enough by the standards of her girlhood but "fat" in modern terms, as, more seriously, Oscar deBevereaux's "plump and beautiful" Marthé, "as round and sleek as a young seal" (1), becomes obsessed with her obesity and dies. The opposite can also be found. In *The Cooking School Murders*, Mrs. Potter has returned to Iowa to decide what to do with her grandparents' and parents' home. Her brother has asked her to take in his son Gregory, whose bout with hepatitis has interrupted a Stanford research job. He gains on her high-protein meals, and the "good Iowa food" is "restorative" (3) as anticipated, taking the dull from his blue eyes and the drab from his blond hair and beard.

Food serves many other purposes from the point of view of Rich and Potter. It links past and future as we remember our great grandmother's recipe for orange bread (*The Nantucket Diet Murders*) and our grandfather's claims that the Wealthy is the best apple (*The Cooking School Murders*) and as Frances, in her seventies, passes on the art of cooking to the teenager Laurie (*The Baked Bean Supper Murders*). We remember the way cream and ice were once delivered (*The Cooking School Murders*); the days when and the places where even the delivery men expected a cup of coffee (*The Cooking School Murders*); and the best meals of our lives, often the best moments of our lives as well, and often spent "at somebody's coffee table" (*The Nantucket Diet Murders* 155). The books themselves, like us, move easily back and forth from the lowly to the sublime—from rat cheese, head cheese, and end-of-the-garden soup to the *haute* or *nouvelle cuisine* imported into Harrington, Iowa by the food columnist teaching a Continuing Education course. Food, too, can be a social divider as the Cogswells thrive with blueberries and lobsters while the lobstermen themselves cannot afford to let their families eat their catch except on the most special occasions. Mrs. Potter even believes that "newcomers feel more at home when they're immediately pressed into service" at a dinner party (*The Baked Bean Supper Murders* 68). Food is also a personal salvation: "When you don't know what else to do [to allay grief, for example], cook something. . . . Get out your cookbooks and try something new!" (*The Cooking School Murders* 173). Her own ability as a detective may have started in a curiosity about the ingredients of food; Gussie calls her a "very good detective" when her only failure is substituting an apple for a ripe Comice pear in the glass of juice that contains carrots, parsley, watercress, and parsnip

(*The Nantucket Diet Murders* 104). She remembers her ranch for the tequila *puro* and chili beans to be shared "with the brand inspector and the stock-truck drivers before the year's calf crop...was driven off to the feedlots" (*The Cooking School Murders* 200) and for the morning question of its Mexican doves (*"Who Cooks for you?"—The Nantucket Diet Murders* 276). As surely as Shakespeare takes the measure of a character who does not like music, Rich types Helen Latham in *The Nantucket Diet Murders* with the report that, though she has a cook, she sets a poor table and reveals the true state of a friend's finances when Mrs. Potter finds Mittie making lamb stew with cheap bones. Contrastingly, "Anyone who begins a recipe with 'I just happened to notice some nice...' " or who comments "Only in place of the..." I substituted...to make it "a little more lively" "is destined to be one of the world's good cooks" (*The Baked Bean Supper Murders* 282, 285). Mrs. Potter is apt to get a bit out of sorts with those who will not let food continue its magic after the cordiality of a dinner party has passed. They disappoint her when they do not call or write, and she will telephone her hostess at the risk of interrupting a sleep-in the next morning (*The Cooking School Murders* 120). Guest and host not only give and receive compliments but a running (and, to Mrs. Potter at least, necessary) commentary on their world, small though it may be; out of small communities larger are made. Rich and Potter return to its original use the admonition (Peter 4:9) mangled by the DeWitts in *The Cooking School Murders*: "Use hospitality one to another without grudging" (61).

Rich uses food structurally, too, in an almost form-as-meaning effort. *The Baked Bean Supper Murders*, the best example among the three novels, opens with the communal supper that brings in all groups in the town and is for the benefit of the local Grange. By the end, a native who wants to be an aristocratic outsider has murdered two one-time outsiders, now permanent residents; the town patriarch; and his own mother and has made several attempts on Mrs. Potter, in addition to killing her dog. On the way to resolution, the whole town responds to Eugenia's needs, and the book ends, in the classic manner of Elizabethan tragedy, with order restored through ceremony, this time another communal dinner, though on a smaller scale, a lobster pie cook-off in which all of the competitors, all friends, win.

Recipes abound in the books themselves and are printed in the inside covers with the names of or references to the characters, e.g., "Creamy Mussel Soup (as taught to Laurie by Frances)," "Grandmother Andrews' Green Tomato Pie," "Peter's Scrimshaw Inn Rum Pie." The technique pulls the readers unresistingly into the world that has been constructed. We not only accept the recipes but the "receipts" for living that have issued from this "new American Melting Pot[ter]." The amalgam that results is a view of food as not just for sustenance but for life at its most responsive levels: "The sunny patches around the cottage supported only [Mrs. Potter's] much loved banks of *Rosa rugosa* and a low-growing carpet of wild strawberries, blueberry plants, and highland cranberries. Each, in its season (right now it was nearly strawberry time), provided a small feast for the palate, and each, at all seasons, provided a changing feast of color for the eye" (*The Baked Bean Supper Murders* 24).

Works Cited

Rich, Virginia. *The Cooking School Murders*. New York: Ballantine Books, 1983.
_____ *The Baked Bean Supper Murders*. New York: Ballantine Books, 1984.
_____ *The Nantucket Diet Murders*. New York: Dell Publishing Co., Inc., 1986.

Spinster's Fare:
Rites of Passage in Anita Brookner's Fiction

Mary Anne Schofield

Important stages in the life cycle are marked by celebrations, orchestrated with food and drink. Farb and Armelago in *Consuming Passions* note that the

birth of a child becomes the occasion for a feast. Initiation rites and graduation ceremonies are celebrated to mark the launching of a new breadwinner. A marriage frequently entails the exchange of scarce or prestigious foods between the two families. And the dead pass to another world feasted by those who remain in this one. (73)

Food celebrations, indeed, are the mark of initiation.[1] Such food-initiation ceremonies figure most prominently in the life cycle of the female, who as the prime nurturer of mankind, is most intimately involved in the food/life-cycle matrix. Mircea Eliade enumerates the stages that occur during primitive tribes' female initiation:

1. the removal to a sacred ground where initiation can take place
2. the separation from the mother and the conditions of childhood
3. the instruction by older women
4. the entry into distinctive female bonding through the choice of special foods and the practise of special rituals
5. dietary restrictions and taboos
6. physical ordeals of self denial and overcoming
(*Rites and Symbols of Initiation* 4-5; 41ff)

It is just this classic pattern of withdrawal, instruction, restrictions, trials, and success which Anita Brookner utilizes in her fiction. In her six novels (1981-1986), she examines the problems of becoming female by anatomizing the identity problem each woman (no matter of what age) faces as she projects herself away from her mother and toward a definition of her own selfhood. Food becomes "the principal way the problems of female being come to expression in women's lives" (xi) Kim Chernin tells us in *The Hungry Self*. Food takes on a transformative function as women progress to and extend themselves beyond traditional roles and ideas of womanhood. It is a process that, in the final analysis, leads to a new civilization and identity, but it is a process that is oftentimes ambivalent, even contradictory. And, as the plethora of books about eating disorders, female images, cookbooks and the like make clear, it is a progress or rite that is extremely timely in these turbulent decades of self re-evaluation and definition.

It is not odd that such a process of self-study revolves around food (its preparation and consumption). Jean Anthelme Brillet-Savarin in his treatise, *The Physiology of Taste*, said a century and a half ago that one is what one eats. More recently Claude Levi-Strauss (*The Raw and the Cooked* 1969) noted the importance of cooked food in the civilizing and defining of man: man is transformed from savage to cultural agent through the food process; cooking raw foods provides a sophistication that is synonymous with culturizing.[2] Chernin notes the importance of this initiation rite:

The purpose of a rite of passage in a premodern society is to move the individual from an earlier phase in the life cycle, to separate [s/he] from childhood and make possible the movement into the next stages of [s/he] development. The novice emerges from [t]his ordeal endowed with a totally different being from that which she possessed before the initiation;[s] he has become another. But the initiation ceremony must also awaken the individual to a sense of social and collective responsibility. In modern terms, we could say that initiation puts an end to the natural man and introduces the novice to culture. This rite of passage in tribal society accomplishes two fundamental purposes: the transformation of identity and the entry into culture. (166)

Chernin ultimately claims that "an obsession with food is an attempt to provide a ceremonial form by which women can enter culture" (166). This assimulation for the female involves a movement away from the mother as child-nourisher, as model cook and provider, and toward a self definition of the initiate. It is this action which is worked out and through ritualistic food initiation processes.

Brookner's use of food as feminine dialogue is just one example of the encoding language that women have adopted in order to be able to talk to one another. This encoding effect has developed out of their need to tell their story, yet it is a tale that is told within the confines of the patriarchal, censorship structure.[3] Adopting the gender-based language of food (or what Nancy K. Miller would label a "posture of imposture"). i.e.—meats are masculine, vegetables feminine (Moore 80)[4]— women explore the validity of such a language. Is it possible, they question, to establish a new rhetoric, a language of food that applies specifically to the female? Brookner's heroines explore this possibility as they participate in their initiatory passages. For the Brookner female, this rite involves the preparation of a meal for a male. With the preparation and participation in this ceremony, she becomes a "woman," defining herself through the civilizing and culturizing activity of feeding the male. But, I would argue, she does so first by acquiescing to the male-specific language of food, then, when the meal fails, her heroines discover that feminine food is itself sustaining; they find that they have no need of masculine food nor a need for the male. Through their culinary epic of initiation, her heroines learn to define themselves in terms other than those usually applied to the female and her role as nourisher and civilizer; they learn to cook and eat a spinster's fare.

In her novels, Brookner rewrites the language of food making it applicable for today's woman. Considered *en masse*, her novels form a feminine cookery book that could borrow its title from contemporary cook, Michele Evans, and her *Fearless Cooking for One*, who argues that cooking for one is a celebration of privacy (xiii). She goes on to observe that the "solo cook is the producer, creator, performer, director, and audience" (xiii), concluding: "Fearless cooking for one means more than the courage to dine alone; it means enjoying the pleasure of your own company" (xvi). Reading Brookner and participating in the initiatory rites of her heroines allows the reader the same pleasure of discovering the fulfillment of one's own company and the nourishment that can come from spinster's fare.

Brookner's first novel, *The Debut* (1981), is the best example of her presentation of this epic female search for self, a discovery that involves food preparation and consumption. In fact, the two stage "debut" of forty-year old Dr. Ruth Weiss, university professor, involves, first her moving from the parental home to an apartment of her own and the preparation of a dinner for Richard Hirst, a colleague and would-be male companion. Her failure there leads to the second stage, a relocation in Paris and an affair with Professor Duplessis. Again the moment of initiation involves a shared meal, this time not dinner, but sweets and wine. Through both stages, the reader witnesses Ruth Weiss's coming of age and coming to terms with herself; at the conclusion, Brookner gives another variation on the growing up/growing down[5] theme as Weiss, a good cook now, prepares a meal for herself and her father. She has learned that the initial promise held out to her that "Cinderella shall go to the Ball" is one not capable of fulfillment in all female lives. Unable to find Prince Charming, she cannot attend the ball, but she can learn to cook, to live alone and to be happy. Contrary to much of the preceeding feminine literature, her initiation into the adult world is not the ambivalent one of growing down to submission and dependence; instead, she does, indeed, grow up to independence and self-sufficiency.

Ruth's coming of age saga beings with her mother, who, the reader quickly learns, "hated cooking[.] [She] never put on weight, and was delighted to have her husband's domestic arrangements planned and her daughter's timetable supervised" (12). She is a flamboyant character initially who deteriorates slowly throughout the novel due to self-imposed starvation. Clearly, the mother cannot nourish the daughter because Helen Weiss herself never underwent the initiatory process her daughter is about to undertake. Helen never came to terms with her own mother and her own self, and instead remains dependent, coddled, non-assertive, a child; (even her body atrophies back to a baby-like state; her limbs become useless and she becomes bed-ridden). It is the elder Mrs. Weiss who is the life sustainer, the nourisher in this novel; she feeds the child Ruth; and the dining room and its table comes to symbolize the moral rectitude of eating properly and at the regular hours that Mrs. Weiss insists on. Brookner writes:

The dining-room table was permanently half laid, although all members of the household tended to eat separately; Mrs. Weiss longed to preside over a roomful of sons and spouses, but was forced...to sit, first with George at breakfast, then with the child and the nurse at lunch, and with the child and nurse at tea, and at their supper. (12)

The dining room belonged to the grandmother and the child Ruth soon comes to associate heavy meals, a miasma of gravy and tea and a doleful atmosphere as part of the universality of life and eating. "In that dining room while her grandmother buttered a poppy seed roll for her, the child learned an immense sense of responsibility" (13). Ruth also knows that "without her grandmother there might be no more food" (17). Such is, indeed, the case, for with the grandmother's death, all vestiges of normalcy in food preparation and consumption vanish. Mrs. Cutler is hired as the housekeeper-cum-companion. "She produced meals at unpunctual intervals, so that Ruth found herself always too late or too early" (20). Mrs. Cutler is a slut in the kitchen:

She only washed up once a day, was in favor of letting things soak in murky water. Tins of soup and packets of cereal made up the contents of the storage cupboard; the refrigerator yielded a plateful of sardines, some tomatoes, many pints of milk with the cream poured off, and a jar of chicken *en gelee*. The teapot had not been emptied. (942-3)

Ruth, as part of her initiation ritual, will remove herself from such surroundings and will create a setting directly antithetical to this one. Her first step (stages one, two, four and five of Eliade's schemata) is to begin preparing her own meals. She makes excursion to different parts of town in an effort to purchase her supplies.

So Ruth took to getting her own food, instinctively skirting the expensive store-bought pies and pates and tinned vegetables preferred by her father and mother and above all Mrs. Cutler. She made herself eggs and boiled potatoes and salads, but this spinsterish fare did not sit well on the dining-room table...so she took to eating in the kitchen. (21)

Not only has she begun the ritual withdrawal from the mother and the shopping/preparation, but she has relocated the place of consumption as well.

Though the initiation process involves breaking away from the mother (since her mother has been so unmothering), the first steps involve Ruth in a search for a surrogate mother.[6] For a time, school performs this function. "She looked on school as a sort of day nursery which could be relied upon to supply comfort in the form of baked beans and sausages, stewed prunes and custard" (24). But Ruth continues to be "starved for company" (31), and next turns to her colleagues for comfort and nourishment, and the commons room at the university provides yet another place of temporary refuge and possible food preparation, but here, too, nothing substantial and nourishing can come from a small electric kettle and hot plate. Ruth is forced to confront her situation: she must cease looking for mother substitutes and begin to search for her own self.

She finally begins the actual process (stage one) and finds a "flat for herself and for Richard, (or at least his dinner) in Edith Grove, a dusty but not unpleasant thoroughfare near the World's End, reverberant with heavy traffic" (43). She had "removed" herself to the sacred place, thus physically separating herself from the mother and from childhood locations. Instruction comes in the form of cookbooks which Ruth "read...to find the perfect meal for Richard" (44), and Mrs. Cutler instructs Ruth in food preparation giving her a recipe for a chicken casserole; Mrs. Cutler even goes so far as to watch cookery programs in an effort to improve her skills in the kitchen and to teach to her "pupil."

Time passes; the first initiation is about to occur.

And Ruth begins what can only be described as *the* ritual preparation. But it is a ceremony, interestingly enough, to which, she does not go completely happy and willing. As Brookner observes:

she was restless. And even unhappy. The break in her routine, occasioned by her extreme dedication to the idea of the godlike Richard, was, she knew, wrong, not sensible, doomed, in fact. But it was appropriate that she spend the day alone, for the very strength of her feelings had already removed her from normal contact, and certainly from normal conversation. But how very sad it was to be alone with these feelings, when in ideal circumstances, she might be motivated to share them. On an impulse she telephones her mother. (50)

But her mother, unused as she is to mothering, can provide no advice, no solice. So Ruth is left to her own know-how and the cookbooks for the big event. "Half reluctantly she made some sort of a timetable: the preparation of the meal, the bath, the insertion of the dish into the oven, dressing, and then what Mrs. Cutler called the finishing touches" (55). She rigourously prepares for the oncoming confrontation. Chapter Seven is devoted to this painstaking preparation.

Needless to say, the "celebration" goes awry. Richard is dreadfully late, the dinner is spoilt, and Ruth becomes uncaring. When Richard's only topic of conversation is Harriet, a poor unfortunate young mother whom he has befriended, Ruth only wishes to be alone. She concludes: "There was no point in keeping the flat on now" (65), and she returns home until her autumn departure to France. The first stage of Ruth Weiss's initiation has been completed—successfully? Clearly, her talents as a cook have been tested and she has failed: a burned, ruined main course, a failed dessert, cannot pass muster. Yet there is a positive result of this first stage: Ruth has learned that all cannot depend on the male; she has learned self-reliance, the most important lesson for the single female and has taken the first steps toward female aggression and growing up.

The second stage of her initiation involves her return to her parents' home and instruction by Mrs. Cutler. Her parents have left for a last vacation, and Ruth and Mrs. Cutler use their absence as a bonding time: Mrs. Cutler gives Ruth cooking lessons, recipes, and advice (stages two, three, four). Ruth continues her scholarly preparation by trying to "put her notes into some kind of order" (93) as she prepares to leave for Paris. Unfortunately, the withdrawal does not provide the escape, the freedom, the growing up that she expected, and she reasons:

The impossibility of her present life was apparent to her as it had never been before. She was a prisoner in her cell, and, in addition to her physical restraints, she had imprisoned herself in a routine as destructive of liberty and impulse as if it has been imposed on her by a police state. Every morning she caught the same bus to the Bibliotheque Nationale. Every lunchtime she ate a sandwich in the same cafe. Every evening she presented herself for her bath and returned, chilly, to her room where, she was beginning to realize, problems of increased loneliness awaited her. (105)

It is at this juncture that she meets the Dixons, Hugh and Jill. The next step of the growing up saga begins as they shepherd her through the maze of life in a foreign city, and soon they have worked magic and the ugly duckling is transformed:

There was no doubt that her looks improved. She put on weight and brushed her hair and learned the difficult Parisian art of being immaculately turned out....Her heels clipped along the corridor with authority these days, and she was no longer afraid of having time on her hands. (110)

As Ruth gains self confidence, she again approaches the crisis time in this stage of the initiatory process; she meets Professor Duplessis and begins a relationship that will again end in a feeding ritual. But, in order to carry out her plan, she must have a room of her own she reasons. Fortunately, the friendship with the Dixons helps here, and as they prepare to return to England, Ruth sublets their apartment. She reasons rapturously:

A flat of her own. In the rue Marboeuf. She could work at home and cook her own meals and not go out after her bath into the chilly spring nights; there would be a place for her books and a writing table and a telephone, and oh, God, she could see Duplessis there.... She would nurture him until summer took hold, and then, somehow, they would go away together. (148)

This second round of initiation does not involve a complete meal but rather a communion of bread and wine (actually a cake called "le Marquis" 155). There is little preparation for this coming together— she only makes the cake once as a trial run. Perhaps because of their age difference, because he takes a role more of mentor than lover, it is possible for them to share a sweet communion rather than a meal. Even more importantly, Ruth has learned about herself and finds that she does not need to feed Duplessis. Having come to terms with herself, with feminine aggression and selfhood, she can return to England and her dying mother. She is able to return because she has come to terms with the role and function of this non-mothering figure in her life. Ruth has uncovered her own self and has learned the importance of having a room of her own; she has learned not to grow down, like her mother, but to grow up by asserting herself, by becoming independent—in short, by becoming the antithesis of her own mother. After her mother's death, when she keeps house for her father, she still retains the apartment in Edith Grove; there, in her own place, she writes her book, even cooks a meal for herself. In these years, Ruth has become a good cook; she nurtures and nourishes her father and cares for him unlike the mother. She also marries and feeds her husband. Mercifully, he dies soon after the marriage, and Ruth is free to return to her independent self.

Providence (1982), Brookner's second novel, is also a tale of feminine initiation. Kitty Maule, comes of age professionally as she talks on "The Romantic Dilemma" and emotionally as she learns about her position in the complex male/female world. Kitty Maule is a typical Brookner woman. Single, middle-aged, a university lecturer, fatherless, she is a woman who was raised by her mother and her maternal grandparents, whose life focuses on "the centrality of food" (6). Both her mother and grandmother are seamstresses, and, oddly enough, in this household, it is the grandfather who does the cooking. He was "an enthusiastic cook" and "would put plates of food before her at odd times, urging her to taste his latest creation, which was usually both pungent and idiosyncratic" (12). Food is offered with love during Kitty's youth, and when she gets a flat of her own, returning only on weekends to the grandparents' home, she "came to dread the weekends which were symbolized for her by the food thrust lovingly in front of her" (16). Kitty counteracts this overwhelming food-love matrix by not being interested in food when by herself.

When dining alone, Kitty Maule tended to dispatch the meal as quickly as possible and also to distract herself from the actual business of eating. She found it helpful to balance a tray on her knees rather than to sit down forlornly at an empty table, and to read, listen to the radio, or even sometimes to wander about, as if only lending herself to the task of digestion. (17)

Like Ruth Weiss, Kitty is as unsuccessful with sexual relationships as she is with food. As the novel opens, she is continuing a two-year affair with a department colleague, Maurice Bishop. The non-fulfillment of their relationship is mirrored in the atmosphere of the university and its English department. Department meetings are held in the former dining room of the estate, and they are always followed by a ritual tea. "Tea and biscuits at the staff meeting were, for Kitty, the high point of an otherwise socially unadventurous week" (34). "The ceremonial plate of chocolate biscuits handed round by Jennifer's assistant, all this seemed to her stranger and more desirable than the home life of her grandparents with their variants on normal dress and eratic impromptu meals" (35). Because she has not had a youth of well-balanced, three nutrient-group meals, Kitty is unable to apply nutritional balance to other facets of her life. She has only unfulfilling affairs. For example, when Maurice tells Kitty of his unfulfilled love for Lucy, Kitty attempts to succor him, as "she took him in her arms and held him, and as they sat together in the darkening room, she felt her whole heart dissolving in sadness and wander" (57). But she cannot feed Maurice; she cannot nourish him and provide the material food that he needs to survive.

Like Ruth Weiss, part of Kitty's growing-up saga involves a trip to Paris. While there, she plans a meeting with Maurice and attempts yet again to nourish him. Unfortunately, they are only able to get together for one day; they begin, naturally enough, by lunching together. Brookner records the momentous affair:

My love. Darling. Kitty took more nourishment from these words, and from the sight of Maurice's teeth biting into a plateful of radishes, than she did from her own tomato salad, to which she referred abstractedly from time to time. She took an inventory of his lowered eyelashes, his pale brown skin, his careful hands. Then she switched their plates so that he could finish her tomato salad, as she knew he wanted to do, and took more bread and gave it to him. Her earlier disappointments had faded from her mind and she could only concentrate on what she had in front of her: Maurice, captive, his mouth limpid with oil....Are you going to eat your potatoes, Kitty? She handed over her plate. His physical presence so bemused her that her own awakened appetite seemed subsumed into his. He was eating for them both, and that was how she would have it.

To feed him, at that moment, was all she wanted to do; the food was enhanced by his enjoyment of it and she speared a potato from his plate because it looked so much more appetizing than when it had previously featured her own. (115-6)

Though they are "nourished," it raises only false hopes in Kitty, for it is not a meal she prepared herself; it is restaurant fare, and thus she avoids the ritual confrontation. She is not even able to provide a homemade tea for him.

She had some tea sent up, and she watched him striding about, with his cup in his hand.... She had slipped next door to the cake-shop and bought two apple chaussons and two croissants filled with almond paste. They ate ravenously, their mouths perfumed with the sweet mixtures. When they kissed, they exchanged breaths, and she made a vow that she would never forget that particular taste as long as she lived. (121-2)

Because Kitty has finally had some nourishment, it is she who is awakened. Brookner's record of the evening meal is pointed:

They ate at a small obscure restaurant near the hotel, for the rain had now settled in for the night. This time it was she who was hungry and he watched her. She was flushed and animated; she took small pieces of meat on her fork and put them on his plate. He was rather silent, had completely lost his earlier ebullience. (122)

He has lost his energy because Kitty has not fed him. Kitty, on the other hand, gains momentum. She has discovered that her enjoyment of Maurice does not depend on her care and feeding of him. She has begun to find another language.

Her initiation shifts to engulf her professional self, and upon her return to England she plunges into final preparations for her university-wide lecture. Then follows a ritual withdrawal and a coming to terms before the actual ceremony takes place. Notice, in the following passage, that her new direction of life includes a new venture in eating:

As she sat in the garden of her grandparents' house, she was aware that the time had come to say goodbye to those who she had been with on the first half of her journey, and that she must now prepare to live a different sort of life. No more clairvoyants, no more waiting in hotel rooms, no more glum acceptance of Caroline's advice. From now on she would be more definite, more admirable, she thought. She would eat reasonable meals, she would not panic before her lecture, she would deal sensibly with everyone, but would allow no one to dominate her. (143)

Because her final self definition involves her professional person, Kitty has been uninvolved in food preparation itself. The final irony of her growing up process comes in her successful lecture and Maurice's cooking of the celebration dinner. When she finally discovers that John Larter, a former pupil, and not Maurice is to be her dinner partner, further that that Maurice has a date of his own, Kitty can only conclude:

They took their places at the table, Maurice and Miss Fairchild at either end. I lacked the information, thought Kitty, trying to control her trembling hands. Quite simply, I lacked the information. She had the impression of having been sent right back to the beginning of a game she thought she had been playing according to the rules. And there was the rest of the evening to be got through.... And picking up her spoon, she prepared to eat. (182-3)

Her fate is the fate of the typical Brookner heroine: highly successful professionally, but very unlucky in love. Kitty cannot be nourished by another. Like Pauline Bentley, unmarried, university professor, who rarely notices what she eats (81), Kitty Maule can nourish minds, not men's bodies. Her spinster fare will continue; she has been initiated to herself.

Brookner continues her initiatory explorations in her third novel, *Look at Me* (1983), as Frances Hinton, unmarried reference librarian, comes to terms with her mother's death, her place in the world and her single state. Though she catalogues pictures of madness and dreams (6), Frances's real vocation is her writing. Indulged in secretly before bed or in the evening when she has nothing else to do, Frances is a fanatic about her journal. She writes, she tells us several times, because she wants to say "look at me."

Her obsession began innocuously enough:

I used to make my mother laugh when I went home in the evenings and described the characters who came into the Library.... She knew all their habits, and where they lived; it was like a serial story to her. She encouraged me to write it all down, and so I bought the usual large exercise book and kept a sort of diary, and I like to think that one day I will use this material and write a comic novel, one of those droll and piquant chronicles enjoyed by dons at Oxford and Cambridge colleges (16)

Yet after her mother dies, Frances finds that she continues to write. "When I feel swamped in my solitude and hidden by it, physically obscured by it, rendered invisible, in fact, writing is my way of piping up" (19), she confesses. Her writing is her way to reach out to the world, ultimately she tells us to say "I hurt" or "I hate" or "I want" (84). Just as Hinton codes her alienation and longing in the guise of her comic, guileless stories, so Brookner examines the plight of loneliness under the mask of food in this novel as well. Frances's lack of interest in food combines with her lack lustre concern with the house; she is unable to declare herself a person, take charge of the house, and audibly say "look at me." Instead, she lets the ghost of her mother dominate the house; she still consumes sickroom or nursery food—"a cup of soup, a little chicken, some stewed fruits, all in tiny portions" (25)—Frances Hinton has no concept of a separate self; she is merely the extension of the dead mother. Brookner charts her exploitation of her personality using the food matrix.

Frances's heroine-process of self discovery begins as she meets the Frasers, Alix and Nick, and begins to share meals with them (52). Because Alix is a negligible housekeeper and a cook only of steak and spaghetti (32), meals are most often taken in restaurants. Such meals are heady stuff for Frances who was used to a much less rich diet, and soon she finds herself "addicted" (59) to them. The restaurants provide the sacred ground, Alix instructs her, and the new lifestyle gives her many different things to eat. Frances is well on her way in her initiatory rite. However, unlike Kitty and Ruth, initially she does not totally neglect her former being. In the beginning, Frances finds the new diet not too rich, and she continues to write, once again turning the library into fiction, this time for Alix. But such a rarified diet cannot but effect her in the long run, and with the arrival of James Anstey, colleague and friend, she ceases to write (84) as she becomes embroiled in the *menage*. But a diet consisting mainly of restaurant food, late hours, and constant company does not allow Frances the precious time she needs to write. She will write only after the initiation is over.

Unlike previous Brookner heroines, Frances's rite of passage does not involve learning to cook for a man. She never cooks for James, but relies on Nancy, the housekeeper, to supply then with hot milk and biscuits, nursery tea and sweets when they return from their night walk. But the carbohydrates do not nourish him for long and only create a temporary feeling of satiety. When they finally do eat a meal, alone, together, it is the beginning of the end of their relationship. As Frances notes:

I could eat very little at the restaurant, although I believe that the food was excellent at this Italian place: James lunches there most days. He did not seem to notice as I cut up the food and pushed it around my plate; he did not even look at me, although he was in good spirits and very talkative. He seemed to be addressing a point somewhere to the right of my head. (125)

She has not proceeded through the approved stages of initiation and food preparation; she remains uninitiated, a child in an adult world. (For example, she has nursery tea when she visits Miss Morpeth; see 64, 136). Frances's refusal to kow-tow to the sweet, submissive, docile role assigned to her forces her to grow up and find another, more forceful and aggressive role for herself.

Yet Frances does complete her epic rite; she does take over the flat and make it her own (94); she learns to assess herself and by so doing is allowed to begin her long walk "home." Brookner describes this evening amble in epic terms (167-68), complete with an illness of sorts and a long sleep of recovery (176-77) at its end. Her final passing of the initiatory rite is marked by a food event: she has tea with Nancy in the kitchen (172), the indication of her final takeover of the house. This passage has been successful: the house is reclaimed; Frances returns to writing and seems capable of continuing her life. Nancy becomes the food provider, and Frances, unable to sustain a successful career while catering to a man, can now return to her writing, to her new, known self.

Brookner's Edith Hope (*Hotel du Lac* 1984) is another writer-feeder heroine, and in her fourth novel, Brookner investigates once again the failed-male-civilizing yet successful feminine-initiatory process as Edith Hope feeds the wrong man, yet learns through the catering and pampering of the Hotel du Lac how to be her own person.

Edith Hope is one of Brookner's initially more forthright women: "I am a householder, a ratepayer, a good plain cook, and a deliverer of typescripts well before the deadline" (8). Writing as Vanessa Wilde, she seems to lead a romantic life of her own, or does she? She writes that women still want heroes, which is why she continues to write gothic thrillers, and romances. And she tries to get some of the same thrill in her own life. She has an affair with David, a married man, but the love relationship continues in the same pattern that Brookner has presented to us in her earlier novels: the woman becomes the provider of food; in fact, here she gives David " 'Food fit for heroes' and would sigh contentedly" (29).

Anxious in her nightgown, she would watch him, a saucepan of baked beans to hand. Judging the state of his appetite with the eye of an expert, she would take another dish and ladle on to his plate a quivering mound of egg custard. (29)

She keeps the house constantly filled with food because of his voracious appetite. But the woman cannot continue to feed the man and get nothing in return; the affair is one-sided as is the eating relationship; though she cooks meat for him, she is unable to civilize him, to have him love her or take care of her own self. Her caring is one-sided, and Edith Hope learns, like the earlier Brookner heroines, that feeding oneself is the only initiation process that matters.

In fact, it is Edith's failure to find reciprocity with several men that has landed her in the Hotel du Lac, off season, as a recuperator. The hotel will have to feed and nurture her so that she can return, after her cure, to the routine of a normal life. The entire initiation process is reversed here in *Hotel du Lac*. Her attempt at civilizing the male has occurred off stage. (She has already gone through the process that we watch Ruth Weiss and Kitty Maule indulge in.) Edith Hope provides the reader with a portrait of the second stage of the initiation process; her rite of passage is exclusively devoted to herself: she must assert herself. She must not prove her femaleness by caring for another, but instead will find herself by being cared for and fed by others. What the reader watches is the second stage of female development: professional feeding and caring of the wounded self in preparation for a return to the world of the single self: grown up, independent, and healthy.

This act of re-establishing selfhood involves the majority of the patrons of the Hotel du Lac, for the hotel is composed of women with various sorts of eating disorders. Interestingly enough, the gathering place for these women is the salon for afternoon tea or after dinner for coffee or in the main dining room for the evening meal: they always meet over food. And, the eating habits are even more interesting. Monica is the most extreme example: she is anorexic. Brookner records:

Monica has what is politely referred to as an eating problem: at least that is how she refers to it. One is always reading articles about this sort of thing in magazines. What it means in practice is that she messes her food around distastefully in the dining room, already slightly off-colour from acute and raging boredom, and ends up smuggling most of it down to Kiki, who is seated in her lap. In between meals she can be seen in a cafe near the station eating cakes. The story behind this is interesting. Her noble husband, in urgent need of an heir, has dispatched her here with instructions to get herself into working order; should this not come to pass, Monica will be given her cards and told to vacate the premises so that Sir John can make alternative arrangements. Naturally she sulks. She eats cake as others might go slumming.... She is so beautiful, so thin, so over-bred. Her pelvis is like a wishbone. (80)

Unable to fulfill the womanly function, given her by the male, she is considered useless. Monica, too, must learn to feed herself.

Penelope and Iris Pusey provide another example of eating disorders. The mother and daughter team use the dining room more as a platform or stage to exhibit their own eccentricities and personalities (83), rather than as a place for nourishment. When the hotel has a birthday party to celebrate Mrs. Pusey's seventy-ninth birthday, Edith concludes "that this was all for show, that everything was a pretence, that this had been a dinner of masks, that no one was ever going to tell the truth again" (112).

Hotel du Lac is a haven of failed women, women who do not eat properly, who cannot provide for men, and who, therefore, cannot sustain a relationship. They have failed to be submissive and dependent, and so the male society has herded them together and cast them off. They are all binge-eaters like Monica, though she is the only diagnosed one; they all snack and over-indulge at Haffeneggers, the coffee ship, gorging themselves on sweets and caffeine, and they do so because they think they cannot function as women anymore. But they can: they need only a nourishing diet and self-esteem; they must learn to value themselves. Edith Hope, for example, needs a diet of meat and potatoes and real love, not romance. As she writes:

I am not a romantic. I am a domestic animal. I do not sigh and yearn for extravagant displays of passion, for the grand affair, the world well lost for love. I know all that, and know that it leaves you lonely. No, what I crave is the simplicity of routine. An evening walk, arm in arm, in fine weather. A game of cards. Time for idle talk. Preparing a meal together. (98)

Her stay at the Hotel, her rite of passage and self-seeking has proved to be positive; though she does not leave highly nourished, nor has she learned the art of "cordon bleu" cooking, she has learned about herself. She will remain a plain cook, one unable to entice and keep a man with food because she will not be as untrue to herself as that risk requires. She will continue to write in the room of her own and feed herself a spinster's fare.

Brookner eschews her usual pattern in her 1985 novel, *Family and Friends*, and, rather than present another female epic of self discovery, this novel offers a pastiche of male and female explorations. Food matrixes are not obtrusive, and instead of large family gatherings with the requisite meals, the reader finds lots of coffee drinking and not much else. Brookner portrays the female world of the wedding rather than of the kitchen; it is the still photograph of the ceremony that is presented rather than the progressive preparation. Though Sofka supervises all the meals, it is a cook who does the actual preparation. Confrontation scenes do not occur at meal times; there is no civilizing or taming of the male or female that occurs over a meal. Brookner's usual pattern is eschewed in this novel as she concerns herself with family rather than individual, female guests.

Brookner returns in *The Misalliance* (1986) to an examination of the single woman and the self exploration she undergoes in her continual passage toward self understanding, only this time she uses Blanche Vernon, divorceé, as her target. Blanche tenaciously adheres to the civilized forms, most especially those of eating purposefully, consciously, proclaiming herself unchanged by her new marital status.

She addressed herself to the business of shopping, of buying an evening newspaper, of preparing her return. Still conscientious, she shopped scrupuously, testing everything for freshness, regretting that she was too disciplined to buy great quantities, indulging vast imaginary appetites, piling tables with profusion. But she restrained herself, for on whom would this waste be wasted? (9-10)

Her fastidiousness spreads to her own home and food preparation. "She was conscientious about her well-being and thought it poor-spirited to descend to the sort of food that people tend to eat when they are alone; bits of cheese and fruit and the ends of anything that had not already been eaten. She liked to set a table, even now, and did so as if, were she to be surprised, all would be in order, civilized, devoid of self pity" (15). And Brookner continues:

Blanche determined to shop and to cook as if she were a normal woman with normal household concerns. She bought supplies that would see her through the week, in case—always the lurking fear—she was kept at home by illness, and on her return did some more baking. (32)

But all this excellence does not count, for her husband whom she had nurtured and nourished for many years of marriage has abandoned Blanche for the aptly named Mousie, a computer expert. She is the antithesis of Blanche, and cannot even cook.

When Bertie required her to give a dinner party herself, she ordered everything from a caterer and dressed up to the nines to compensate for the fact that the dishes tended to emerge from the oven at the wrong temperature. (33)

What has Bertie done? Clearly, something totally incomprehensible from Blanches's point of view. Blanche is unaware that she must traverse a rite of passage: from wife to divorced woman. She must learn to feed herself and care for herself. She is the most pathetic of Brookner's heroines, for she is unwilling to confront the central issue, which is her own self, and instead, after her husband leaves, she finds surrogates to feed and nurture. At the hospital where she does weekly volunteer work, she meets and befriends Mrs. Beamish and her daughter Elinor, when she sells them tea and cake. Blanche things: "I would not let her have any more cake.... It is synthetic and horrible and will do her no good. I would let her have a banana and some fruit juice; she would find the banana easier to eat and it would be better for her" (38). Suddenly, Blanche has someone to nourish and mother, and one of the first things she does, as child-sitter, is to take Elinor to her flat and give her lunch—a meal of "scrambled egg and brown bread and butter, add...stewed apricots" (57). Elinor does not speak and does not express her thanks.

Blanche aches to nurture the child, to fill up the void that she now experiences in her own life. Brookner notes: "Blanche saw, with what seemed to her to be a true insight, that she was a child who would respond to regular meals, sensible food, traditional games, and a respectable, even self-effacing mother" (47-8). Mrs. Beamish, the reader learns, is not really the natural mother, but has inherited Elinor with her marriage to Paul; but since he is away, she must take care of the child. When Blanche visits their flat, she is not at all surprised with the things she sees, and her remarks about the kitchen are especially timely.

The kitchen was indeed all that she had expected, and possibly more.... The draining board of a stone sink held a washed pile of mugs, plates, and cheap knives and forks. Since there appeared to be no cupboards, most of the kitchen's contents were piled on the table: half a loaf of bread, standing in its own field of crumbs on a breadboard, an open packet of Earl Grey tea, two jars of spaghetti sauce, two green apples, a bottle of milk, a carton of orange juice, a very expensive flowered enamel saucepan, something in a brown paper bag, some kitchen foil, and a brown earthenware teapot with a chipped spout. Removing the lid, Blanche found this to be full of cold tea and could not refrain from tipping it out and rinsing the pot. Having done this, she was led naturally into removing the washing-up from the draining board, but on second thought rinsed it through again and left it, neatly stacked, where she had found it. The bread she covered with the foil, disturbing one of the flies as she did so. The cake went back into its bag. She started guiltily, as if surprised in a luckless form of trespass, as Sally Beamish and the child materialized behind her. (64-5)

Blanche judges correctly when she sees Sally's life as one of "a diet of hedonism, from which the fibrous content of real life had been removed" (77). Sally's eating habits clearly reflect this hedonism: "unlike Blanche she would have thought it poor spirited to eat a proper meal without the appropriate company and service" (78). But Sally does not have to worry about meals; she is not going through a transitional, initiatory stage from one kind of life to another, and so Brookner cannot worry about her food. But Blanche must worry as part of her experience. This rite of passage becomes so momentous, that, for a time Blanche seems incapable of finding herself in her new state.

She herself ate without pleasure or interest these days, and even the memory of the beautiful meals she used to cook now seemed insubstantial, as if divorce had cancelled them or reckoned them to be of swindling significance, like a lost reputation. The things she ate these days—a single chip, an isolated Dover sole—seemed to her rather more suitable subjects for still-life painting than for consumption. (99)

Blanche seems incapable of finding value in the single diet. Brookner intimates that divorce is not a state similar to singleness, and she softens the end of the novel. Recovering from a stress-induced illness, Blanche learns to appreciate the community of women—she is nursed by her neighbor, Mrs. Duff and she begins to see value in her life. Though still a novice in the single lifestyle, the final chapter finds Blanche mobilizing herself for a great single venture: she cuts her hair and plans a trip abroad. The reader is pleased to see that she had moved forward. Ironically enough, Brookner places a boomerang in the final sentences— Bertie returns. The divorced woman is reclaimed—or is she?

Brookner does not answer the question. Instead, she has outlined the journey the single female must make as initiatory rite before she is able to accept her position in society and answer the question for herself. She must clearly define herself, move away from definitions of self that link her with the mother. She must learn to cook for herself and to feed herself healthily and properly. She becomes the nurturer of her own self, not another. She must learn to find value in the spinster's fare.

Notes

[1]Eliade (*Rites and Symbols of Initiation*, x) defines "initiation" thusly: "The term initiation in the most general sense denotes a body of rites and oral teachings whose purpose is to produce a decisive alternation in the religious and social status of the person to be initiated. In philosophical terms, initiation is equivalent to a basic change in existential condition; the novice emerges from his ordeal endowed with a totally different being from that which he possessed before his initiation; he has become *another*".

[2]Eliade confirms such a theory; he observes that one "could say that initiation puts an end to the natural man and introduces the novice to culture" (xv).

[3]See Carol Christ, Sandra Gilbert and Susan Gubar—passim.

[4]"It is testimony to the strength of this symbolism that eggs have never been able to make the grade—though most housewives rationally know that eggs are a good substitute for meat, they are a last resort and don't let a cook feel she has 'done right' " (80).

[5]See Annis Pratt, passim.

[6]Isabel E.P. Menzies in "Psychological Aspects of Eating" notes that "people never eat alone or uninfluenced by others, since they always eat in the context of the internal society" (223).

Works Consulted

Brookner, Anita. *The Debut*, New York: Random House, 1981.

————. *Family and Friends*, New York: Pantheon Books, 1985.

————. *Hotel du Lac*, New York: Pantheon Books, 1984.

————. *Look at Me*, London: Panther Books, 1983.

————. *The Misalliance*. New York: E.P. Dutton, 1982.

Chernin, Kim. *The Hungry Self. Women, Eating and Identify.* New York: Harper and Row, 1985.

Christ, Carol. *Diving Deep and Surfacing. Women Writers on Spiritual Quest.* Boston: Beacon Press, 1980.

Douglas, Mary. "Deciphering a Meal." *Daedalus*, 10 (Winter): 61-81.

Eliade, Mircea. *Rites and Symbols of Initiation. The Mysteries of Birth and Rebirth.* New York: Harper & Row, 1958.

Farb, Peter and George Armelagos. *Consuming Passions. The Anthropology of Eating.* Boston: Houghton, Mifflin, 1980.

Gilbert, Sandra and Susan Gubar. *The Madwoman in the Attic. The Woman Writer and the Nineteenth-century Literary Imagination.* New Haven: Yale University Press 1979.

Knutson, Andie L. *The Individual, Society and Health Behavior.* Russell Sage Foundation, 1965.

Levi-Strauss, Claude. "The Culinary Triangle," *Partisan Review. 33: 586-95.*

————. *The Raw and the Cooked. Introduction to a Science of Mythology.* Chicago: University of Chicago press, 1969.

Menzies, Isabel E.P. "Psychological Aspects of Eating," *Journal of Psychosomatic Research*, 14 (1970): 223-7.

Miller, Nancy K. *The Heroine's Text.* New York: Columbia University Press, 1985.

Moore, Harriet Bruce. "The Meaning of Food." *Diet Therapy*, 5 (1957): 77.

Pratt, Annis. *Archetypal Patterns in Women's Fiction.* Bloomington: Indiana University Press, 1981.

Fairy-Tale Cannibalism in *The Edible Woman*

Sharon Rose Wilson

As Margaret Atwood has admitted on several occasions, fairy tales, particularly those of the Grimm brothers and Hans Christian Andersen, have influenced her work, including *Power Politics* and her recently published watercolors. She read the Grimms when "very young," and some of the tales have the "depth for [her] that certain Biblical and Greek stories also have" (Tape). Even the poems she wrote as a child foreshadow her later interest in the "protean changes in shape" so characteristic of fairy tales. According to Atwood, when she saw "Snow White" for the first time at "some too-early age (5?)... I was [riveted] with fear. The transformation of the evil queen into the witch did me in forever" (Rosenberg 2). Throughout her career, Atwood has used fairy tales as intertexts,[1] causing both inner and frame narratives self-consciously to reflect, and reflect upon, one another. In *The Edible Woman*, Atwood's first published novel, the fairy-tale intertext focuses on food, recalling ancient images of witches, wizards, parents, and spouses, who, deliberately or not, eat the precious "food" of other human beings.

The Edible Woman was written in 1965, the same year Atwood was a graduate student in Cambridge, Massachusetts, a scene to which she returns in her novel *The Handmaid's Tale* (1985, 1986). The two novels are more similar than they seem: in addition to their implicit or explicit parody of graduate school (Atwood has joked that *The Handmaid's Tale* is an expose of the Harvard English Department [Conversation]), both novels are enriched with some of the same fairy tales. Like "Hesitations Outside the Door," *Lady Oracle, Bluebeard's Egg,* and the "Fitcher's Bird" watercolor (Wilson, "Bluebeard " 386), both novels draw on the Grimms' "Fitcher's Bird," a tale about a groom who chops up brides daring to open the forbidden door. In addition, as in *Bodily Harm*[2] and "The Robber Bridegroom" poem and watercolor, [passive] *The Edible Women* embeds the Grimms' "The Robber Bridegroom," a parallel tale in which a groom literally consumes fiancées, is embedded in *The Edible Woman*. Like *The Handmaid's Tale, The Edible Woman* alludes to the Grimms' "Little Red-Cap" (Wilson, "Off the Path") and to a number of other fairy, folk, and nursery tales involving cannibalism, deadly consummation, or metamorphosis through the act of eating.

Eating and food images are evident throughout Atwood's work, particularly in "Speeches for Doctor Frankenstein," *Power Politics, Lady Oracle*, an untitled, undated watercolor, and a magic marker drawing, entitled "Amanita Caesarea, Egg, Cross-Section on Cloud" (about 1980 [Atwood, Tape]). The visual art, housed in the University of Toronto Thomas Fisher Rare Book Library, depicts, respectively, a dinosaurian creature eating a fish, suggestive of the food chain, and a sliced, womb-shaped, amanita mushroom, suggestive of "bodily harm," like the novel's background painting of a cut-open melon (Wilson, "Camera-Images" 45, 48). The photographed flour-and-salt Christmas decorations on the cover of *Two-Headed Poems* illustrate Atwood's own skill in culinary arts. According to Atwood, once a home-economics major who was and still is a good cake decorator, her interest in edible art was "part of the impetus for the cake in *The Edible Woman*, an anthropomorphic *objet* made of foodstuffs, such as candy brides and grooms and Donald Duck cakes in Woolworth's" (Tape).

Even working in a company described as food, *The Edible Woman*'s Marian consumer-product-tests a society in which everyone and everything, including nature, is product and consumer. As several critics have recognized, the central metaphor of this novel is food: "more than food gets eaten in life—our very souls and beliefs live by the conquering and consumption of other people's souls and beliefs" (9). No one has commented on Atwood's use of fairy-tale intertext, however, or on the significance of "The Robber Bridegroom" and "Fitcher's Bird" in this novel.[3] Atwood rarely mentions the tales that have most influenced her: little-known to the general public, they include several ("The Robber Bridegroom," "The Juniper Tree," "The White Snake") (Atwood, Telephone Call) in which eating images are predominant. Since Marian, who gradually renounces eating, also narrates the novel, with Parts One and Three in first-person, Two in third-person, food metaphors not only satirize contemporary culture but also reveal Marian's recognition of societal cannibalism. She has paradoxical, mock-gothic fears of eating, being eaten, suddenly changing into someone else, and being unable to transform at all.

From the first pages of the novel, the remarkable references to food, eating, and cooking are, like these characters' obsession with oral functions, more characteristic of fabulation than realism. As in *Lady Oracle* and several of her watercolors, Atwood develops a marvelous comic-gothic. Marian is on her way to make breakfast as she encounters her roommate, Ainsley, a professional tooth-brush-tester, nursing a hangover from a party focused on "the insides of people's mouths." Feeling as if she is contained in a plastic bag as she rushes to her job with Seymour Surveys, she is immersed in the "soup" when she enters her hot-as-a-furnace-office. Her company, "layered like an ice-cream sandwich" with her department being the "gooey middle layer," is under the watchful eye of Mrs. *Bogue,* who, since Marian is neither man nor machine, represents the only possibility of metamorphosis (*EW* 9, 12, 16, 18, 19, 22). There the dietician, Mrs. *Withers* asks her to pre-test canned rice pudding; and the Accountant, Mrs. *Grot,* a woman "with hair the color of a metal refrigerator-tray," demands that Marian sign up for a pension plan in which people would "feed off (her) salary." Mrs. Bogue even recounts office folklore of interviewers breaking legs in meat-cleaver encounters and being smeared blood-red in tomato-juice taste-tests (19, 23, 16, 168). After handling a complaint about a fly in raisin cereal, Marian arranges respondents to a "Moose Beer" ad that refers to "Manly flavour," "tang of the wilderness," and "hearty taste" associated with cannibal stories of the *Decameron,* Shakespeare, and the Grimms. Duncan, a subject who plays Baby Bear to Marian's Goldilocks, identifies "the pattern:...the husband kills the wife's lover, or vice versa, and cuts out the heart and makes it into a stew or pie and serves it up in a silver dish, and the other one eats it" (24-25, 53).

Preserved, baked in a witch's oven, and eventually served as food, Marian is, by turns, Gingerbread woman, Cinderella, Sleeping Beauty, Rapunzel, Goldilocks, Alice in Wonderland, Little Red-Cap, the Pumpkin-eater's wife, Gretel, Fitcher's bride, and, especially, the Robber Bride.

The Grimms' "The Robber Bridegroom" focuses on a maiden who does not trust or love her prospective husband "the way a bride-to-be should" but feels "a secret horror," "shudder[s] in her heart," when thinking about him. He insists she visit him and his guests Sunday in the dark forest, where he will scatter ashes. Feeling uneasy, she also marks her way with peas and lentils. When she reaches the dark and solitary house, it is "deadly silent" until a voice cries twice: "Turn back, turn back, young maiden dear,/'Tis a murderer's house you enter here." The voice comes from a bird in a cage; otherwise, the house seems entirely empty as the maiden proceeds from room to room, coming at last to the cellar, where an extremely old woman, whose head bobs constantly, again tells her she is in a murderer's den: "You think you are a bride soon to be married, but you will keep your wedding with death." A kettle of water is on the fire; "When they have you in their power, they'll chop you to pieces without mercy. Then they'll cook you and eat you, because they're cannibals. If I don't take pity on you and save you, you'll be lost forever" (Hunt and Stern 200-01; Magoun and Krappe 151-52; Zipes 153-55).

The maiden then hides behind a barrel, where she is told not to budge or move, just before the godless robbers return, dragging another maiden, whose heart bursts in two after she is forced to drink three glasses of wine: one white, one red, and one yellow. The prospective bride realizes the fate planned for her as the victim is chopped into pieces and salted. The hiding maiden is almost discovered when the victim's chopped-off finger springs into the air, falling into her lap (in some versions, bosom); but the old woman calls the robbers to dinner and drugs their wine. They both escape, following the sprouted peas and lentils home, where the maiden tells her father, the miller, everything. (Hunt and Stern 201-02; Magoun and Krappe 152-53; Zipes 155-56).

On the day of the wedding celebration, the bridegroom appears with all the miller's friends, and each person is expected to tell a story. When the bride sits still and does not utter a word, the bridegroom says, "Come, my darling, do you know nothing?" She then relates a "dream," finally presenting the victim's chopped-off finger. Because the bride speaks, the Robber Bridegroom is executed: it is the groom, not the bride, who marries death (Hunt and Stern 202-04; Magoun and Krappe 153-54; Zipes 156-57).

"Robber Bridegroom" motifs figure prominantly in *The Edible Woman*. In addition to explicit fear of being chopped up and eaten, the fairy tale features distrust of the fiancé, path-marking on a forest journey, a visit to the bridegroom's home, unheeded warning, hiding, passivity, consumption of beverages, heart-break, amputation, communal eating of precious food, assistance of an elderly "godmother," return to society, communal telling of the crime, presentation of an emblem representing the victim, and, finally, communal punishment/retribution. Most of these motifs, integrated with several from "Fitcher's Bird" and other closely-related tales, occur comically in *The Edible Woman*.

The Grimms' fairy tale, "Fitcher's Bird," is one of many Bluebeard stories, including the recently translated "Bluebeard" and "The Castle of Murder" (Zipes 660-63, 670-71), the better-known Perrault "Bluebeard," and the anonymous English "Mr. Fox" (Yearsley 127-28). "Fitcher's Bird" is about a disguised wizard (sometimes death, the deadly sun, Sin, a troll, or the devil) (Leach; Jobes, vol. 1) whose touch forces pretty girls to leap into his basket. When he takes them to his castle, he gives each of them an egg which they must carry everywhere and keys to every room but one, that they are forbidden to enter. Most versions of the tale deal with three sisters: the first two are curious and open the door, discovering the chopped-up bodies of former brides. Fitcher/Bluebeard, seeing the egg's indelible blood stains, recognizes their disobedience. The third sister, who cleverly leaves the egg outside, passes the test, thus gaining power over the wizard. Before escaping, disguised as a marvelous bird, she leaves a substitute (a decorated skull) to fool the groom and rejoins the severed pieces of her sisters, recreating rather than destroying life. As in "The Robber Bridegroom," the groom marries death, this time in a communal execution that also destroys his friends and the skull-bride (Hunt and Stern 216-20). The ancient Greek version of this tale features a corpse-devouring death as the murderous husband (Leach); "The Castle of Murder" includes the old woman in the cellar, edible victims, and the tale-telling trap (Zipes 670-71); and "Mr. Fox" features the warning, a severed hand, the bride's tale, and a cut-up groom (Grace f.n. 250).

The *Edible Woman* again features or parodies most of the motifs in "Fitcher's Bird": disguise, enslaving touch, test-orders, a forbidden chamber, amputated brides, stained honor, power reversal, a decorated substitute, the victims' re-membering and rebirth, revenge, and restoration of community. Like "The Robber Bridegroom," "Fitcher's Bird" is a paradigm of the sexual politics underlying Atwood's work: together they are the basis for the menace of the room (or unopened door to the room) from *The Edible Woman, The Circle Game,* and *Power Politics* to *The Handmaid's Tale* (Wilson, "Bluebeard" 390).

Before Marian reaches the bridegroom/Fitcher's foreboding home, however, she has home, forest, or burrow encounters with a number of characters from other popular tales. Marian's roommate, Ainsley, plays the Prince to Len's Sleeping Beauty and Fish's Cinderella in the book's double parody of the "Cinderella"—"Sleeping Beauty" stories. *The Edible Woman* is an anti-comedy in which the wrong person gets married (Atwood in Gibson 20-21); and the subplot mirrors the main plot, reversing the sexes of the Marian—Peter—Duncan triangle. Paradoxically, Ainsley is also a soulless, no longer little, mermaid (85) who, unable to please her first prince, catches another by becoming a fertility goddess; a "castrating," decapitating Queen in "Alice in Wonderland" (199), who manages to chop off her own as well as other heads; and, preeminently, a Robber Bridegroom/Fitcher/wolf to double Marian's fiancé Peter, his pal Trigger, and witless "lady-killers" such as Len, who may be trapped and cooked in their own boiling cauldrons.

Presiding over the excessively protected home from which our fairy-tale heroine travels (Heuscher 74) is the paradoxical "lady down below," whose modern realm has degenerated into the "lower regions" of a rooming house, in a district not as good as it used to be. Ironically, Marian fears the landlady's "heavenly thunder-bolts" and generally conforms to her "law of nuance" forbidding everything (274, 14). Like many of Atwood's witch or evil step-mother figures, including *Life Before Man's* Auntie Muriel and *The Handmaid's Tale's* Serena Joy, the woman down below wears symbolic gloves protecting her from touch. Obsessed with cleanliness and "the child's" innocence, she seems to burrow through the woodwork, ironically seeking evidence of what she considers evil.

In contrast to the woman in Atwood's poem, "The Landlady," who is "a slab/ of what is real,/ solid as bacon" (*Animals in that Country* 14-15), the lady down below is the dark and gothic side of the fairy-tale godmother. Like the other characters in this and any fabulation, she represents part of Marian. A "Rapunzel" enchantress who removes "the child" from others' hungers, she blocks Marian's escape from her "tower," which is also Marian's conditioned self (See Atwood, *Survival* 209-10). Resembling the old fairy in Perrault's "Sleeping Beauty," the lady down below embodies a sleep-inducing curse.

Unlike the warnings of "The Robber Bridegroom's" old woman in the cellar, those of the lady down below deny the existence of a cellar as well as the sustenance of life. Apparently covered with "an invisible plastic coating" impervious to dirt, she wears spotless gardening gloves, causing Marian to wonder "who she'd been burying in the garden" (93, 11). Although part of Marian is already swallowed and buried, she will emerge, like the Robber Bride, Little Red-Cap, and Alice in Wonderland, from underground as well as background.

Avoiding Sleeping Beauty's spinning wheel, on which Len later becomes snarled (10, 220), Marian leaves "home" and journeys through the forest of Toronto to encounter a voice like cold oatmeal porridge and several other nursery-rhyme or fairy-tale figures. She enters the occupied house of the three bears (45, 50). The cadaverously thin baby-bear Duncan, who ironically fears cannibalism but is always ravenous for real and narcissistic food, also plays the mock turtle in *Alice in Wonderland*; the hairy papa Fish, who is in search of a Venus-womb, is eventually "caught" by a matrimonial angler; and the gourmet cook mama Trevor, who is a coconut-cookie king, also doubles as a contemporary "Prince Charming" (275). Marian next visits her friend Clara, whose doorway is marked with a nearly decapitated doll and a teddy-bear leaking stuffing (29). In addition to playing the pig-holding Duchess from *Alice in Wonderland* (212), Clara is a parodic mother-goddess/beauty queen. Resembling Atwood's watercolor of a pin-headed Termite Queen (Published in Wilson, "Sexual") when Marian presents roses to her, the eternally pregnant Clara is "being dragged slowly down into the gigantic pumpkin-like growth...enveloping her body." As Atwood says, "If you think you're a watermelon, you don't have to do anything, you can just sit around.... Life is very much simplified" (Gibson 26). Already consumed by her house-wife role, Clara causes Marian unconscious worry that her own Peter is a "pumpkin-eater" (117).

Other important figures Marian meets on her archetypal fairy-tale journey include Joe, cannibalistic pumpkin-eater, who is also the worm-prince invading Clara's apple-core self (242); and the three office-virgins, Cinderella's step-sisters, who unsuccessfully trail themselves "like many-plumed fish-lure[s]" for men "ravenous as pike" (114). In this fairy-tale Canada where pioneers journey through arborite-surfaced coffee shops, even the "wilderness" has been touched by "the knife and fork of man" (262).

The Robber Bridegroom's knife and fork are everywhere apparent in Toronto's urban "wilderness." To Marian, the pipes, boards, and blocks at Peter's uncompleted apartment building are part of the same system in which she and everyone around her participates: the "raw materials" disappear and are "transmuted by an invisible process of digestion and assimilation" into something else (231). As Marian enters this twentieth-century Bluebeard's castle, even the nearly empty building with its shining skin and orange-pink walls seems cannibalistic.

Marian first met Peter, who resembles a cigarette ad and is rising "like a balloon" in his law firm, while eating ice cream in the shade. Since Peter is attracted to Marian's absence of "filling" (he sees her "as the kind of girl who wouldn't try to take over his life" [57, 62]), this appropriately chilled environment sets the tone of their relationship for Marian's transformation into the puff pastry of the book's epigraph. Later, their dates continue to center on eating, a circumstance of some relevance to Marian's gradual renunciation of food. Consistent with *The Edible Woman's* gothic parody, Peter, a hunter who displays his collection of guns and camera-guns in his "murderer's den," flashes polished teeth while discussing fears of women predators (67). He begins to turn into a parodic and comic Robber Bridegroom, with touches of Fitcher, the wolf, and the pumpkin-eater, even before Marian meekly assents to marry him. Initially "disguised" as a bachelor-prince, Peter transforms first into a provider of stability and later a home-movie man. As Robber Bride, Marian begins to distrust him but ironically fails to heed genuine inner warnings because she listens to the socialized voice of her lady below. Drinking gin-and-tonics rather than the Robber-victim's wine or Alice's size-altering beverage, Marian experiences heartbreak, hides in passivity, and begins to turn into the victim who will be symbolically chopped apart and swallowed. Peter's authoritative touch, like Fitcher's, seems to enthrall her; and his matrimonial tests and secret or hidden identities seem to stain, "amputate," and consume similarly hidden facets of her personality.

Having dreamed that her feet are dissolving like jelly, Marian is surprised to find them moving after Peter brags about shooting a female rabbit through the heart and Ainsley unveils her pitcher-plant sex trap. Like Beatrix Potter and Lewis Carroll's rabbits, Marian runs while there is still time, away from the villain, the "killer," who stalks, traps, and touches her near the bed-"burrow" where she becomes stuck (43, 72-73, 77, 79, 82-83). The morning after her engagement to this eight-eyed ogre who has been "eating her," her skull feels scooped out like a cantaloupe (79, 84). Previously, Peter had bitten her during bathtub sex and, after imagining a naked woman in a bathtub coffin, she had bitten back (61-63). Later, as Peter's steak disappears into his mouth (154-55), Marian, who has been feeling anemic for some time, identifies with a cookbook cow born with lines and labels for cutting. She symbolically serves him her heart, a stale and belated token Valentine, as a cake (213-14). Continuing to find her delicious, he approves her decorated-cake hairstyle (214), says "yum yum" about her perfume (234), and, now that she's "been ringed," serves her to friends (180).

For one of these parties, a kind of pre-nuptial test, Marian endures a beautician's "operation" on her head in order to play the Russian Cinderella, Wassilissa, and her doll. Earlier, she gnawed on her own finger while looking at the doll whose fingers and toes she had once chewed off (105, 225). As a child, Marian had not only operated on her sawdust-filled doll, but, like Wassilissa, whose doll protected her from being eaten by the Baba Yoga, ritualistically served it food (In Von Franz 143). Ironically, although the doll's teeth and tongue are still intact (105), she, like the doll Marian becomes, is unable to consume the food; in addition to her amputated extremities, the doll's face "is almost eroded." After Marian is given another face for her Robber Bridegroom's party and imagines opening secret doors at his "castle," she discovers Peter the chef, holding a meat cleaver: she is no longer visible (228, 250). Although Marian is more than a victim of even a comic Robber Bridegroom, at this point she resembles the first and second sisters of Fitcher's Bird, who will always bear the lines where they have been cut apart and reassembled (Atwood, *BE* 159): she is unable to become the conscious and clever bride or fiancée of either the Robber or Fitcher as long as she identifies with slaughtered rabbits, eaten cows, and amputated dolls.

In addition to Marian's consciousness of the forbidden chamber, her ambiguous relationship with Duncan "stains" her engagement to Peter and follows many of the same "Robber Bridegroom" patterns. Duncan, too, is disguised: a wolf in baby bear's clothing, he seems to project his emotional cannibalism (Woodcock 315) onto Marian. A "changeling" from the underground who continuously changes "truths," his "identity" seems to spread out like an uncooked egg (144, 101). Fearing that his mirror might one day reflect nothing, he smashes it, diagnosing his own narcissism. Even his "bear" protectors feel Marian will "gobble [him] up" (190), and she occasionally wonders if her Florence Nightingale role has that dimension (102). Nevertheless, feeding on endless preoccupation with self, a closed circle of meaningless words, and the nutriment of others, he characteristically feeds Marian limitless supplies of nothing, licks his lips after she kisses him, and says, "I'm hungry" (263). Near the end of the novel, after gnawing his thumb and being alarmed by refrigerator sounds, Duncan jokes that Marian is "full of good things": perhaps he *has* tried to destroy her (286-87).

Like many of Atwood's other protagonists, however, Marian plays the Robber Bridegroom as well as the Bride: she participates in "the mutual games of disguise and sexual politics which hack off parts of the other in creating her/him as Bluebeard." Unable, like the characters of *Power Politics,* to "peel off both projected and defensive false skins...and stop playing or casting parts," for most of the book Marian fears the void of self (Wilson, "Bluebeard " 391) as much as Duncan, and possibly Peter, does. Wondering whether Ainsley, another gender-reversed Robber Bridegroom, is brewing aphrodisiacs and practicing voo doo, she jokes about chopping Peter into bits, camoflauging him as dirty laundry, and burying him in a ravine (94). Giving out bits of information about her engagement like candies, she looks down at the knives and forks on plates when asked how she caught Peter. Even Peter accuses her of "biting his head off" when he breaks a date (115-16). Although he doesn't make a believable Peter Rabbit and does try to assimilate his Cinderella when she's not in use as an ashtray stand (279, 213), he, too, is forced into shoes he cannot fill.

In *The Edible Woman* the fairytale intertext establishes a tone both comic and gothic, not only parodying the influence of popular culture and the reliability of Marian's vision, but our expectations of "plot" in sexual relationship: our simultaneous anticipation of "Cinderella" "true romance" and fear of "Bluebeard" amputation. We are by no means assured that, for either male or female, it is possible to marry anyone but the Robber Bridegroom or death. Atwood has said that, unlike a traditional comedy, *The Edible Woman* is a "circle": it is more pessimistic than *Surfacing,* which, like *The Circle Game* (Tape), "is a spiral," because "the heroine of *Surfacing* does not end where she began." The social order is not reaffirmed (Sandler 13-14), and we have observed all the characters' "circle games" of sexual politics. As in "Hesitations Outside the Door," we are again left outside, in the room where Marian began, but it is with a possibility if not a resolution.

In fairy tales, being eaten is not usually the end of the story. True, the Gingerbread boy does not return from the fox's stomach, but he, unlike Marian, is nothing but food (278). Like Gretel, Marian tricks the trickster, finding a substitute victim and escaping the oven. As in true fairy tales, this kind of transformation and rebirth are still possible for the edible woman if not her partners. In the Grimms' "Little Red-Cap" and "The Wolf and the Seven Little Kids," the wolf is cut open: like the goat kids, Red-Cap springs intact from his belly, reborn and no longer either victim or food. Rather than the Robber Bridegroom's real destruction of Peter, Marian, or Duncan, the novel ends with a "comic parody of ritual cannibalism" (Onley 195-96): Marian's conscious swallowing of the cake woman.

Like Fitcher's bride, Marian tricks the prospective groom and his kind with a decorated substitute victim and leaves Bluebeard's castle, disguised as a marvelous "bird" who may still appear but no longer be edible. She rejoins the severed pieces of her former victim self as she molds and joins the "separate members" of her cake woman (276). Marian even reverses the power struggle and has a revenge of sorts by confronting both Peter and Duncan with her own test. When faced with the smiling, "doll-like" pink sponge, Peter leaves in alarm (277-79); and Duncan, himself a "universal substitute," absorbs the substitute woman without either expression or pleasure (149, 287).

Like the Robber Bride, Marian returns to society, presents an emblem of her victimized self, and tells her story, acting to reclaim swallowed pieces and to regain identity. Unlike Goldilocks, she doesn't even leave a mess. Thinking of herself in the first-person singular again, no longer trapped in a tower, burrow, or forbidden chamber, she faces the "horrors" of both disordered life and apartment and penetrates through layers to discover another "floor" to reality (283-84). By baking, decorating, serving, and consuming the cake-woman image she has been conditioned to project, Marian announces, to herself and others, that she is not food.

Notes

[1]See Scholes, c.f. 145, for an explanation of intertext. This essay is based on a shorter paper of the same title delivered in the Literature and Culinary Arts section of the Popular Culture Association, Montreal, Canada, 28 March 1987.

[2]*Bodily Harm* was originally entitled *The Robber Bridegroom*. See the Margaret Atwood Papers c.f.

[3]Goddard c.f. offers a useful discussion of a few Atwood "tales within tales," but she does not discuss *EW;* MacLulich c.f. compares *EW* to "The Gingerbread Man" and "Little-Red-Cap" 111-19.

Works Cited

Atwood, Margaret. *The Animals in that Country*. Toronto: Oxford Univ. Press, 1968.

———. Art Work. 1958-1980. Margaret Atwood Papers, Thomas Fisher Rare Book Library, University of Toronto. Toronto, Canada.

———. Conversation. University of Northern Colorado, 30 Ap. 86.

———. *The Edible Woman*. New York: Popular Library, 1976.

———. Papers. Thomas Fisher Rare Book Library, University of Toronto. Toronto, Canada.

———. *Survival: A Thematic Guide to Canadian Literature*. Toronto: Anansi, 1972.

———. Tape-recording for Sharon R. Wilson. August 1985.

———. Telephone call. Placed by Sharon Wilson. December 1985.

Gibson, Graeme. Interview with Margaret Atwood. *Eleven Canadian Novelists.* Toronto: Anansi, 1973.

Goddard, Barbara. "Tales Within Tales: Margaret Atwood's Folk Narratives." *Canadian Literature* 109 (1986): 57-84.

Grace, Sherrill E. "Courting Bluebeard with Bartok, Atwood, and Fowles: Modern Treatment of the Bluebeard Theme." *Journal of Modern Literature* 11.2 (1984): 245-62.

Heuscher, Julius E. *A Psychiatric Study of Fairy Tales: Their Origin, Meaning and Usefulness.* Springfield, Ill.: Charles C. Thomas, 1963.

Hunt, Margaret, and James Stern, trans. *The Complete Grimm's Fairy Tales.* New York: Pantheon, 1972.

Jobes, Gertrude. *Dictionary of Mythology Folklore and Symbols.* 3 vols. New York: Scarecrow Press, 1962.

Leach. Maria, ed. *Standard Dictionary of Myth, Folklore, Legend.* New York: Funk and Wagnall, 1972.

MacLulich, T.D. "Atwood's Adult Fairy Tale": Levi-Strauss, Bettelheim, and *The Edible Woman.*" *Essays on Canadian Writing* 11 (Summer 1978): 111-29.

Magoun, Francis P., Jr. and Alexander H. Krappe, trans. "The Robber Bridegroom" (Der Rauberbrautigam). *The Grimms' German Folk Tales.* Carbondale: S. Ill. Univ. Press, 1960. 151-54.

Onley, Gloria. "Power Politics in Bluebeard's Castle." *Poets and Critics: Essays from Canadian Literature 1966-1974.* Ed. George Woodcock. Toronto: Oxford Univ. Press, 1974. 191-214.

Page, Sheila. "Supermarket Survival: A Critical Analysis of Margaret Atwood's *The Edible Woman.*" *Sphinx* 1 (1974): 9-19.

Rosenberg, Jerome H. *Margaret Atwood.* Boston: Twayne, 1984.

Sandler, Linda. "Interview with Margaret Atwood." "Margaret Atwood: A Symposium," *The Malahat Review* 41 (Jan. 1977): 7-27.

Scholes, Robert. *Semiotics and Interpretation.* New Haven: Yale Univ. Press, 1982.

Wilson, Sharon R. "Bluebeard's Forbidden Room: Gender Images in Margaret Atwood's Visual and Literary Art." *American Review of Canadian Studies* (Winter 1987): 385-97.

_____ "Camera Images in Margaret Atwood's Novels." *Margaret Atwood: Reflection and Reality.* Ed. Beatrice Mendez-Egle. Edinburg, Tx.: Pan American Univ., 1987. 29-57.

_____ "Off the Path to Grandma's House: Offred and the Wolf in *The Handmaid's Tale.*" Conference Proceedings, Ninth Commonwealth Literature Conference, June 1986. Laufen, West Germany.

_____ "Sexual Politics in Margaret Atwood's Art." *Margaret Atwood: Vision and Forms.* Ed. Kathryn Van Spanckeren and Jan Garden Castro. Carbondale: S. Illinois Univ. Press, 1988. 205-14).

Woodcock, George. "Margaret Atwood: Poet as Novelist." *The Canadian Novel in the Twentieth-Century:* Ed. George Woodcock. Toronto: McClelland and Stewart, 1975. 312-27.

Yearsley, Macleod. *The Folklore of the Fairy-Tale.* London: Watts, 1924.

Zipes, Jack, trans. *The Complete Tales of the Brothers Grimm.* New York: Bantam, 1987.

At Home on the Range:
Food as Love in Literature of the Frontier

Sue Hart

From the mid-1800s through the early decades of the 20th century, the population of the United States was involved in the migration from eastern settlements to the far western frontier. The westward trek was a great national adventure, both for those who made the trip by foot (the Mormon handcart pioneers), by covered wagon (in the 1800s), or by railroad coach or box car (in the late nineteenth and early twentieth century), and for those who stayed put and experienced the westering movement vicariously through letters from family members on the frontier, newspaper accounts of the pioneering experience (which focused mainly on the sensational or tragic) and fictional pieces chronicling heroic deeds and accounts of "taming" the wild land and its earliest inhabitants, be they human or animal.

While most readers of accounts of frontier life in whatever form were made aware of the hardships of trail life and the struggle necessary to survive on or beyond the western edges of civilization, they were generally given a rather one-dimensional view. Most literature of this period—both pieces written during the time of western expansion and those written after the frontier era had closed and had come to be looked upon nostalgically and romantically by most Americans—centered around the feats of men: mountain men, such as Jim Bridger; explorers like Lewis & Clark; hunters and scouts, such as Kit Carson and Buffalo Bill; the generic sheep*man*, cattle*man*, cow*boy*. If women figured in a frontier story, they were usually found in the background—doing the housekeeping, the childrearing, the cooking—or, occasionally, as a romantic interest of the hero whose main role seemed to be to applaud his exploits. Until recently, little attention had been given the struggles of the pioneer and homestead woman to deal with her new environment, no doubt because the battles waged in the kitchens or parlors of dugouts, soddies, log cabins, or weather-beaten frame houses pale in comparison to wrestling a grizzly bear or doing battle with savage Indians. And the kitchen was indeed where many of the frontier woman's hardest moments—and most rewarding times—were spent.

Authors who attempt to recreate the westering experience in their works have long recognized that the mention of certain foodstuffs can suggest an earlier time period or a specific region of the country. Thus a novel dealing with a wagon train might contain references to molasses, side pork, jerky, barrels of flour, and other items readers associate with the pioneer era. Careful readings of a number of first-hand and fictional accounts of this period suggest, however, that references to the preparation and offering of food can do more than evoke images of life in the 1800s or early 1900s; they can also speak to the emotional state of the women who do the cooking. In a time when provisions were frequently scarce and anything other than the simplest meal demanded foresight and extra effort on the part of the cook, what better way to illustrate a woman's love—or lack thereof—than through her culinary creations? (Today we hear the Madison Avenue version of this idea in the Pillsbury jingle: "Nothing' says lovin' like something from the oven." Long before this slogan became popular, authors were making use of that underlying theme to demonstrate the love or friendship—and sometimes the sexual tension—existing between characters.)

Both Elinore Stewart and Nanny Alderson, Southerners by birth and western homesteaders by choice, recorded their own experiences and speak frequently of the problems involved in planning for provisions to last between trips to town, preparing meals in less than ideal circumstances and surroundings, and the pride the western homemaker took in setting a good table. Their accounts and those of a number of other women who met the challenge of cooking with previously unknown ingredients, using methods that were primitive indeed compared to the kitchen facilities left behind in the towns and cities of the east and south, scrimping and saving to stretch the sugar or coffee or flour underscore the thesis that offerings of food made by actual people or fictional characters in literature of the frontier period are statements of love or friendship—or substitutions for sexual encounters forbidden the characters either by their own moral standards or through the conventions of the period written about or in.

"I don't think it will be necessary for you to bring food," Elinore Stewart, author of *Letters of a Woman Homesteader*, wrote in an unpublished letter to a prospective caller at her Burnt Fork, Wyoming, ranch. "No Southerner worthy the name or blood thinks it a trouble to prepare their very best for visitors; that is their pleasure." She might have been voicing the sentiments of every western homemaker, for visitors at ranch homes and homesteads, whether expected or not, were never sent away hungry. The fare may have been plain, but it was filling—and fulfilled a Code of the West that was just as ingrained as a cowboy's chivalry where womenfolk were concerned or the notion that a man's word sealed an agreement as effectively as his signature.

Nanny Alderson soon learned that western hospitality—the friendship aspect of food offerings—was extended not necessarily by invitation, but whenever a guest arrived at her eastern Montana ranch home. "I would often have to get a meal at odd hours, for one of our own boys or for a visitor who might arrive in the middle of the afternoon after riding fifty miles since breakfast," she recalled in *A Bride Goes West*. "He'd be hungry and would have to be fed without waiting for supper" (40-41).

While her Southern blood might have made it easy for Alderson to understand that hospitality included food, her Southern upbringing, in a household that featured not only the finest ingredients, but a kitchen staff to prepare them, did not. Her early attempts to "get meals" required the assistance of the men on the ranch (who were more accustomed to cooking than she was)—and some patience and good humor on the part of her guests. "Before I left Union [West Virginia] a dear old lady had taught me how to make hot rolls, but except for that one accomplishment I knew no more of cooking than I did of Greek," she confessed. "Hot rolls, plus a vague understanding that petticoats ought to be plain, were my whole equipment for conquering the West" (19).

"Conquering the West." For a good many of the women who came into the western territories in pursuit of a husband's or father's dream that conquest occurred on a smaller—though no less significant—scale than those words imply. There were new lessons to be learned, hardships to be endured, and methods of communication to be discovered. As will be seen, an extra sprinkle of sugar could speak of love in a world where sugar was not an ordinary commodity found in substantial quantities in every larder. A generous serving of a favorite dish could speak volumes about the cook's feelings for the recipient of the laden plate. But before such expressions could be made, the Nannie Aldersons on the western frontier had to use their heads as well as their hearts in learning what and how to cook, how to make the most of what was available, and how to "make do" when many of the foodstuffs they were used to were not.

Fortunately for Alderson—and for diners at her table—she was instructed by grizzled old cowboys and seasoned roundup cooks not only on how to cook, but what in her new surroundings could be cooked; "these hardy Western men were nearly all bachelors, and so cooked in self defense, but they did know how," she wrote. "One of them...taught me that the tops of young beets, which I'd been throwing away, make the most delicious of all greens" (41).

Alderson's first frontier meals were prepared and served by males— and if the cooks were not what she was used to at home in the South, neither were the menus. At a way station between Miles City, Montana, and the ranch home to which she was traveling, she was fed buffalo steak, boiled potatoes, dried fruit, and sourdough bread. The first meal at the ranch consisted of hot biscuits, venison and bacon, Saratoga chips (an early version of the potato chip, similar to pommes frites), evaporated fruit, and coffee. "It was one of the best suppers I ever ate," the bride exclaimed. "That men could cook was something new under the sun to me, but the men in Montana could and did, and most of what I learned during my first years as a housewife I learned from them" (29-30).

She learned quickly, as frontier women had to, for the demands of outside work meant that the kitchen became the responsibility of the wife (or housekeeper, as Elinore Stewart was before she married her employer), and it was not only a responsibility not to be taken lightly, but one which allowed a good cook to garner a following: "...with a loyal and uncritical group of supporters to cheer me on, I soon built up an undeserved reputation as a wonderful cook. But I cooked for hungry men, and because a woman had prepared the food they thought it tasted better" (68).

The woman's touch helped, certainly, but ingenuity was often the primary ingredient in frontier cooking and baking. The foodstuffs most frontier women were accustomed to had often been left behind, somewhere east of the Missouri River, as had familiar utensils, cooking pots and pans, and even stoves. Fresh fruits and vegetables were replaced by the canned or dried variety, regular baker's yeast was discarded in favor of sourdough starter or the more easily transportable baking powder, and a multitude of new foods and new preparation methods waited to be discovered.

It did not take long for these differences in "kitchen" techniques to surface. Pioneer women relearned cooking beginning with their first nights on the trail when they used an iron pot hung from a tripod above—or simply resting in—a campfire to prepare the family's meals. A.B. Guthrie, Jr., in the Pulitzer Prize winning *The Way West*, describes women "wiping smoke tears from their eyes while they tried to settle their cookalls in the flames" (51). Later in the novel, a serious shortage of wood for cooking fires is encountered; the men of the wagon train meet to consider an important question: Was it right and proper for women to cook over buffalo chips? Such fuel may not be "a lady-like thing" (92) to cook over, but starvation hardly seems a reasonable alternative, and so the unorthodox fuel is approved by the men, although it is decreed that the youngsters, not the women, will collect the chips.

Even when pioneering women reached their destinations, they frequently had to deal with less than ideal kitchen arrangements. Many a frontier family's meals were one-dish concoctions, cooked in kettles hanging in a fireplace, and even those women who were fortunate enough to have stoves cooked with wood—a feat demanding physical and mental stamina.

And the provisions! A grand-daughter of Montana pioneers recalls, "At one time my grandfather paid $100.00 for a sack of flour as his family had been without any for a long time. Early pioneers hoarded their supplies of sugar and flour, for sweets were for special occasions....People now take so much for granted. I do not think they realize what it was like to be a pioneer. Of course, there was gold dust and gold, but that didn't mean you could buy things with it in the Territory" (*First Ladies* 86).

For some, money may have been more plentiful than food, but for most homesteaders, who came to plow the land, not to mine it, such was not the case. Homestead families made sparing use of staples, not just because they knew that their flour, sugar, rice, beans and molasses had to last through many months until the weather broke and the roads and paths to town were passable, but because they also often had to wait until a crop came in to have the cash to restock depleted supplies. In O.E. Rolvaag's *Giants in the Earth*, set on the South Dakota prairie, Beret, the immigrant woman whose husband's dream of prosperity won from free land has brought the family west, is pictured making a statement of love for her family by ignoring her own concerns about dwindling provisions when she answers Per Hansa's request for "an extra-fine dish of porridge, to bless what has been put into the ground" on the evening they finish seeding their field:

[At their wagon-home] she measured out half the milk that Rosie had given that morning, dipped some grits from the bag and prepared the porridge, adding water until it was thin enough. Before she served it up she put a small dab of butter in each dish, like a tiny eye that would hardly keep open; then she sprinkled over the porridge a small portion of sugar; that was all the luxury she could afford. Indeed, her heart began to reproach her even for this extravagance. But when she saw the joyful faces of the boys, and heard Per Hansa's exclamations over her merits as a housekeeper, she brightened up a little, cast her fears to the wind, and sprinkled on more sugar from the bag. (51)

This passage not only demonstrates the concern of the frontier housewife over husbanding resources, but rings true in the recounting of a typical Norwegian meal. Rolvaag makes it clear that porridge was the mainstay of the Norwegian immigrants' diet, appearing on the table for all three meals. Homesteaders in areas of Montana heavily settled by Norwegians recall the ever-present porridge pot on the tables of their neighbors.

It is clear that elegance or the exotic was not a usual (or important) ingredient in frontier cooking—and that foods we take for granted today were viewed as "treats" in an earlier era. In May Vontver's short story "The Kiskis," much of the plot centers around acceptance—and that acceptance is spelled out in culinary terms. The teacher in a one-room school, Miss Smith, is unable to incorporate three of her charges into the student group; the Kiskis not only fail to participate in school recitations, but they miss the companionship that comes of eating together when they insist on taking their lunches outside.

"They have only bread in their lunch-pail. That's why they won't eat with us," one of the other pupils explains. "Miss Smith made no reply. She suspected that the lunches of the group around the stove weren't very sumptuous either. She knew hers wasn't. The people with whom she boarded were homesteaders, too." (225)

Gradually Miss Smith is able to win the confidence of the Kiskis by reading to them on days when bad weather keeps the other students away, but although they warm up to their teacher, the youngsters remain isolated from their classmates—until a gift—a wonderful gift—is delivered to the schoolhouse through the efforts of an older Kiski sister who works in a nearby town, and the Kiski children "assume importance" as the providers of such exotic fare.

Candy—candy of any kind—was a rare treat to everybody. These chocolates were very fresh. They had soft creamy centers. Some had cherries in them. The children had not known that sweets like these existed. They took their time about the licking and nibbling. Delights such as these had to be given their just dues. There was no needless or premature swallowing. And to think that the Kiskis had provided it!
...That noon the Kiskis ate lunch in the school-house. (232)

Because food, even plainer fare than the candies described in "The Kiskis," was at times at a premium, there are frequent references to foodstuffs as gift items in frontier literature, Elinore Stewart speaks of a Christmas gift to a needy family of "a package of oatmeal, a pound of butter, a Mason jar of cream, and a dozen eggs" (210). And in Willa Cather's "Old Mrs. Harris," a neighbor brings the elderly woman an offering of friendship fresh from her oven (and then frets because Grandma Harris is uncomfortable with the gift cake, feeling that it should be saved for her daughter):

Mrs. Rosen had brought Grandma Harris coffee-cake time and again, but she knew that Grandma merely tasted it and saved it for her daughter Victoria, who was as fond of sweets as her own children, and jealous about them, moreover—couldn't bear that special dainties should come into the house for anyone but herself. Mrs. Rosen, vexed at her failures, had determined that just once she would take a cake to 'de old lady Harris,' and with her own eyes see her eat it. The result was not all she had hoped. Receiving a visitor alone, unsupervised by her daughter, having cake and coffee that should properly be saved for Victoria, was all so irregular that Mrs. Harris could not enjoy it. Mrs. Rosen doubted if she tasted the cake as she swallowed it—certainly she ate it without relish, as a hollow form. (79-80)

Sweet tooths may have gone unsatisfied, and palates may have had to adjust to new tastes and textures, but thanks to instructions from Native Americans on how to prepare unfamiliar roots and fruits and inventiveness on the part of frontier cooks, few went hungry. Familiar foods were replaced by what was available, although there were occasional (and sometimes disastrous) attempts to "treat" family and friends with a prize dish from more civilized parts of the country. Nanny Alderson planned her first Christmas feast on the ranch around a delicacy seldom found in nineteenth century Montana:

I doubt if there was a turkey in Montana that Christmas, but we had oysters! We had persuaded a neighbor, coming from Miles City several days before Christmas, to bring us several cans of these, frozen and packed in ice as a double precaution....I was really proud of myself as I took my seat at the head of the table, with the baking dish of scalloped oysters in front of me....While my husband carved the beef roast I helped everybody generously to oysters. I did not notice that after the first exclamation of 'think of oysters on a cattle ranch in Montana,' nothing was said....I fear some of the guests ate more than was wise, just to spare my feeling. I needn't report on how sick some of us were before morning, for the oysters evidently had been tainted before they were frozen. (89-90)

Ocean fish and seafood were extravagent delicacies that only the wealthy town dweller could afford to serve—and then only rarely, as shipments of the perishable commodities were not that frequent. Frontier food, like frontier folk, had to have staying power. One woman in western Montana baked a pork cake in "a large round pan" that reportedly would keep a year! The recipe called for a pound of fat pork, free of rind, ground fine, mixed with four cups of brown sugar. Five cups of flour, 2 tablespoons cloves, 2 tablespoons cinnamon, and one tablespoon allspice were added to the meat mix, and a pint of boiling water, mixed first with one tablespoon soda, was added. After the mixture was well stirred, a pound of raisins and a pound of currants were added, and the cake baked for an hour (*FL* 78).

Some ingenious methods of preserving foodstuffs were devised on the frontier. Because feed was frequently scarce and hen houses cold during the winter months, chickens did not lay as well and eggs were frequently in short supply. One early Helena, Montana, resident recalls "an old fashioned dirt cellar where we kept all our winter vegetables, milk, cream, and our homemade butter....Also our winter supply of eggs were [sic] rubbed with butter and then stored in salt in earthenware crocks—the small end always down" (*FL* 48).

Frontier cooks also had to experiment with ingredients—sometimes learning how to use foods they had never run across before, and sometimes substituting what was available for what was not. Julia Rock Above, a Crow woman, is credited with passing on her recipes for cooking with the Bitterroot plant (the Montana State Flower) to pioneer families, making it possible for the white frontier cook to serve Bitterroot soup (dried roots boiled in buffalo, elk or bear broth; served with pemmican patties) or Bitterroot pudding (roots cooked until tender, sweetened with wild honey, enriched with bone marrow and thickened with the scrapings from the inner side of a fresh skin) (*FL* 43). More common foods were put to some uncommon uses: baked beans were used as a sandwich spread, for example, or lima beans used in place of pumpkin for pie fixings; cooks sometimes used emptied lard pails as cooking vessels, and whatever was handy as measuring devices. Thus recipes from the frontier era might call for a "bowl" of one ingredient, two "bowls" of another, and the number of servings will depend on the size of bowl used.

Nannie Alderson, living on a cattle spread, had beef to build meals around, but other frontier cooks were not that fortunate. Native fish (trout, for example) could be caught if one had the time and inclination to fish—and lived near a good stream, and wild game was plentiful. A woman who might previously have fed her family on beef roasts, hams, chicken and lamb now had to experiment with seasonings, cooking methods, and condiments for venison, buffalo, or bear meat. Again, ingenuity was an important ingredient in getting a savory dish to the table. Hunters had to learn methods of cleaning game that would keep the meat sweet and safe from predators such as birds, which might attack and peck at a hanging deer or elk carcass unless its cavity had been packed with pine or fir boughs—and cooks had to devise ways of ridding meat of a "wild" or "gamy" taste, such as soaking a jackrabbit destined for the stewpot or spider (heavy, cast iron frying pan) in vinegar overnight.

Sometimes, too, despite the skill or willingness of the cook, attempts to make unfamiliar meat or fowl palatable failed. In a particularly moving passage of *Giants in the Earth*, Rolvaag uses food as a symbol of humanity, and speaks—through Beret—of what can happen when the amenities of mealtime (i.e, "civilization") are lost or forgotten in the struggle to survive. Beret's determination that her family will leave the God-forsaken prairie before winter sets in has been strengthened by a gift of food sent to her household by a neighbor who tried to pass off badger as bear meat:

...So it had come to this; they were no longer ashamed to eat troll food; they even sent it from house to house, as lordly fare!...[Per Hansa], too, ought to be able to see by this time that they would all become wild beasts if they remained here much longer. Everything human in them would gradually be blotted out....(182)

The more human aspects of food preparation and service are clearly shown in several works by Dorothy M. Johnson, whose stories of frontier life were always solidly grounded in historical fact. Thus when Johnson uses food as a way of expressing love, the reader can be sure that such expressions were part of life in the American West of the 19th century.

("I believe in love," Johnson once said in an interview. She also recognized the validity of physical nurturing as an outward sign of inner feelings.) In "A Gift by the Wagon," Johnson wastes no time in moving her "courting" couple from Sunday services at church to the more intimate surroundings of a kitchen where her heroine, Fortune, can serve a hearty meal to Caleb, the young romantic interest, much more easily than she could speak of her feelings for him. (And the domesticity of the scene is not lost on Johnson's reader—or on Caleb.)

Fortune tied on a starched apron and busied herself with Sunday dinner while Caleb watched. Watching Fortune mash the potatoes was as fine a sight as he'd ever seen, he thought. As pretty as a flake of gold showing yellow in a pan of gravel....[At the table] 'Shall I cut your meat, Caleb,' Fortune asked. 'With your sore arm, you can't.'

'You cooked it so tender it don't need a knife,' he said, and she looked pleased. (60-61)

The heroine of another Johnson short story, "Blanket Squaw," is Mary Waters, a young Indian woman who has been given the "advantage" of being educated in the Whites' school system. When she returns to her home in the west, she meets and falls in love with an engineer who is building a dam project. Their romance scandalizes the community, but before there is a public outcry disaster strikes when the dam breaks and several workers are swept away to their deaths. Steve Morris, the engineer, flees to the woods, intending to starve himself to death as reparation. It is Mary, however, who makes the sacrifice of her life, figuratively at least. She finds the dying Morris, and in a scene reminiscent of a communion, she mixes bread into a broth and offers it to him, claiming it is "medicine" in the Indian sense of the word. When the cup has passed from her hand to his, the reader discovers that this nurturing act has been accompanied by a vow; she has renounced Morris's way of life and promised never to touch him or see him again if his life is spared. She is true to her word; she returns to the reservation and becomes the "Blanket Squaw" of the title. The bread and broth indeed symbolize the sacrifice of Mary's life, a sacrifice made in love.

A more positive—or happier—account of the gift of food signaling love and acceptance is found in Willa Cather's "Neighbour Rosicky," a story in which the oldest son of the Rosicky family has married an "American" girl instead of a Czech woman. There has been some constraint and mistrust on both sides, but Polly, the young wife, begins to break down the barriers between the generations when she offers to fix a holiday meal for her in-laws.

[Rudolph's] heart leaped for joy when [Polly] said she thought they might have his family come over for supper on New Year's Eve. 'Let's get up a nice supper, and not let your mother help at all; make her be company for once.' 'That would be lovely of you, Polly,'

he said humbly. He was a very simple, modest boy, and he, too, felt vaguely that Polly
and her sisters were more experienced and worldly than his people. (56-57)

More worldly, perhaps, but Polly's family and Cather's readers can
take a lesson from Rudolph's mother when it comes to using her cooking
and baking skills as expressions of love and caring. Early in the story,
the doctor for the community where the Rosickys live praises their
mother's kitchen talents to the Rosicky children as he recalls the meals
she has fed him after he has spent the night with the sick, the dying,
or the birthing. There are frequent references to the fragrance of fresh-
baked kolaches lingering in the air in the Rosicky kitchen—and exchanges
that show the importance of food as a part of the Rosicky family life.
At one point, Mrs. Rosicky recalls a long-ago summer when the plum
trees on the property yielded abundantly, and she was making preserves.

'I noticed it was terrible hot, but it's always hot in the kitchen when you're preservin',
an' I was too busy with my plums to mind. Anton came in from the field about three
o'clock, an' I asked him what was the matter. "Nothin'," he says, "but it's pretty hot,
an' I think I won't work no more today....Ain't you near through? I want you should
git up a nice supper for us tonight. It's Fourth of July.' "

'I told him to git along, that I was right in the middle of preservin', but the plums
would taste good on hot biscuit. "I'm going to have fried chicken, too," he says, and
he went off an' killed a couple....

'He says: "It's too hot in here to eat comfortable. Let's have a picnic in the orchard.
We'll eat our supper behind the mulberry hedge, under them linden trees."

'So he carried our supper down, an' a bottle of my wild-grape wine, an' everything
tasted good, I can tell you. The wind got cooler as the sun was goin' down, and it turned
out pleasant, only I noticed how the leaves was curled up on the linden trees. That made
me think, an' I asked your father if that hot wind all day hadn't been terrible hard on
the gardens an' the corn.

' "Corn," he says "there ain't no corn."

' "What are you talkin' about?" I said. "Ain't we got forty acres?"

' "We ain't got an ear," he says, "nor nobody else ain't got none. All the corn in
this country was cooked by three o'clock today, like you'd roasted it in an oven."

"You mean you won't get no crop at all?" I asked him. I couldn't believe it, after
he'd worked so hard.

' "No crop this year," he says. "That's why we're having' a picnic. We might as
well enjoy what we got."

'An' that's how your father behaved, when all the neighbours was so discouraged
they couldn't look you in the face. An' we enjoyed ourselves that year, poor as we was,
an' our neighbours wasn't a bit better off for bein' miserable. Some of 'em grieved till
they got poor digestions and couldn't relish what they did have.' (46-49)

Rosicky relishes what he has because he can recall earlier times in
another country when there was little to be had. He is grateful for the
fact that since his marriage he has not been hungry. Sometimes, recalling
the scarcity of food in his youth, "Rosicky would put on his cap and
jacket and slip down to the barn and give his work-horses a little extra

oats, letting them eat it out of his hand in their slobbery fashion" (61). Thus he repays the animals which help him provide the plenty for his own table with a food reward of their own.

All was not always peace and plenty in frontier or homestead kitchens, though. The frustrations of preparing meals for men who do not recognize their symbolic—or actual—importance is also dealt with in literature. In "Waiting," from Elliott Lincoln's *The Ranch*, a wife waits impatiently for her husband's return:

> That steak'll be like leather in a minute.
> I wish he'd come: he said he'd sure be home
> In time for supper, but it's half-past six
> An' no Jim yet. Oh well, I might 'a' known it.
> Killin' myself to get his meals on time.
> An' not a once—except, o'course, for breakfast—
> But everythin' got cold before he et. (233)

For the most part, though, the efforts to demonstrate love through food are appreciated by the recipients—at least in retrospect. Edward J. Cooney recalls such an effort made on his behalf in a poem which was first published in the *Great Falls* (MT) *Leader* on Christmas Eve, 1929. In simple verse, it reiterates much of what other observers of the frontier era have commented on—the scarcity of certain ingredients, the ingenuity of the frontier cook, and the statements that are made by foods prepared with love.

> *Little Brown Gingerbread Man*
> The little wool stockings hung plump on the nails
> By the side of the chimney of rocks;
> And the little wood dollies, with painted pigtails
> Looked prim in their calico frocks—
> 'Twas the morn of a Christmas, in time long ago,
> After Santy had called with his van—
> And from each little stocking, with face all aglow,
> Peeped a little brown Gingerbread Man.
>
> He was not much for shape and his mouth, all agape,
> Was made from a large pitted prune;
> And his tight little eyes made of currants—like flies—
> Shone warm as the sunlight of June.
> His wide little belly was flat as a hake;
> His head was spread out like a fan—
> For his baker baked love, more than art, in the make
> Of the little brown Gingerbread Man.
>
> In each stocking was sugar, like candy pulled white;
> With doughnuts all sprinkled like snow;
> And a weazened red apple for each little tike,

On the morn of a time long ago.
It was cold—as the snow sifted in on the floor
And, in tiny drifts, twisted and ran—
But not cold, ice, or snow, could bring chill to the glow
On the face of the Gingerbread Man.

L'ENVOI
The joy bells of Santy ring sweetly today,
As he calls in his aeroplane van—
But memory drifts back to the old wooden shack
And the little brown Gingerbread Man!

While moving from such a tender expression of a mother's love remembered over the years to the subject of sexuality may seem quite a leap, in actuality it is very short step. Perhaps the only item in shorter supply for the pioneer or homestead family than the provisions which had to be hoarded to provide special statements of love was privacy. Hungers must be satisfied, however, and frequently the situation or circumstances of life on the trail or in a crowded soddie dictated the method by which the demands of appetites were met. In many instances, writers who deal with this period find it possible to speak of one human appetite while actually writing about the satisfying of a different kind of hunger.

In polite society at the time of the westering movement, reticence on sexual matters was the norm. Authors describing that period in American history have chosen, for the most part, to respect the prevailing attitude of the time and to couch references to sexual encounters or concerns of their characters in careful and concealing language. But despite the reluctance to talk about it, sex was a fact of life in the 1800s and early decades of the 1900s, and silence on the subject did not quiet sexual impulses. In Guthrie's *The Way West*, Curtis Mack, one of the men on the wagon train bound for Oregon, struggles with his feelings about his unresponsive wife: "Were the others cold? Did the other men have their troubles and go to sleep hungry and sore? Were [other women] just more obliging or really more ardent?" (67).

Beret, the wife in *Giants in the Earth*, was, in her youth, one of those "more ardent" women; as the madness which is fed by fear of the prairie existence her husband has brought her to grows, she sees her situation as retribution for her past. "Now had fallen the punishment which the Lord God had meted out to her; at last His visitation had found her out and she must drink the cup of His wrath" (216). The birth of a son, Peder Victorious, almost robs Beret of her life and remaining sanity. It is only when a minister visits the settlement and shares both physical and spiritual nourishment with the Per Hansa (now Americanized to "Holm") household that Beret begins to recover. The first step in righting her mental confusion is the resumption of normal daily activities, such as the preparation of food in answer to the minister's request: "I should like very much to have you cook us a good cup of coffee, if there is any in your house; I want to take supper with you" (371).

The honor of having her home chosen as the site of a Communion service for the settlement (a spiritual meal, for starved spirits)—while at first it concerns her—proves to be an important step in the healing process. The minister makes his request, and Beret, still agitated over her willingness to sin with Per Hansa in their youth, replies, "Oh no— that would never do—oh no! It's too filthy and dirty there....There's too much...it's *unclean!*" (385).

Her scruples are eventually overcome, and she seems to be mending, although the process has taken on a religious fervor that Per Hansa finds difficult to deal with. As she grows mentally and physically stronger, Beret finds—to her horror—that she is once again experiencing sexual feelings for her husband: "...Oh no, no! she caught herself, how can I be thinking of such things again! The sweet desires of the flesh are the nets of Satan....How deeply sin has besoiled all life!" (443). Before she "falls" again, a neighbor falls ill, and Beret dispatches Per Hansa to find a minister for him. As she watches him prepare to leave on the journey that will take his life, she seeks a way to show him her love in something other than a physical manifestation. She settles on offering him freshly-made coffee. That he refuses it and leaves without returning to Beret's kitchen for this last offer of warmth and nourishment is a tragedy she will have to live with.

She put the coffeepot on the stove and began to set the table....'I guess I'll put on a tablecloth to make things nice for him.'...In the kitchen window Beret stood watching him....Wasn't he coming in?...Surely, surely he would come. She had fixed things so nicely for him...he simply mustn't leave this way!...But he had already gone.... (450)

Another refusal of food which is offered in lieu of romance occurs in Isabella Bird's *A Lady Life in the Rocky Mountains,* an account of Miss Bird's visit to Colorado in 1873, during which she spent a great deal of time with—and obviously lost her heart to (even if she kept her head about)—the desperado known as "Mountain Jim." "We spent the afternoon cooking the Thanksgiving dinner," Bird writes.

I made a wonderful pudding, for which I had saved eggs and cream for days, and dried stoned cherries supplied the place of currants. I made a bowl of custard for sauce, which the men said was 'splendid'; also a rolled pudding with molasses; and we had venison steak and potatoes, but for tea we were obliged to use the tea leaves of the morning again. I should think that few people in America have enjoyed their Thanksgiving dinner more. We had urged Mr. Nugent ["Mountain Jim"] to join us, but he refused, almost savagely.... (221)

One of the most famous scenes in Jack Schaefer's *Shane* occurs near the beginning of the book and pits Shane and Joe Starrett against a tree stump. (Shane has taken on the task of removing the stubborn stump as a "thank you" for a meal, but the job soon becomes a struggle for both men, not only against the tree, with its roots sunk so firmly in the earth the Starretts have claimed as their own, but with each other. It is reminiscent of the jousting matches of old—knights who admire— even love—each other proving their prowess to win the hand of the fair maiden. The fair maiden in this case is, appropriately enough, Marian—the wife of the homesteader—who is defined throughout the novel as Nurturer; the reader sees her most often cooking, baking, or otherwise domestically employed.) While the men battle the stump, Marian brings them a plate of hot biscuits and returns to the cabin to make a deep-dish apple pie which she has promised Shane flirtatiously: "It would be wasted on [my husband and son]. They eat everything in sight and don't rightly know good from poor" (19).

When the stump is finally excised from the ground, Marian is called out to congratulate the warriors on their victory. She is so fixed by the scene, which fairly crackles with sexual tension, that the pie burns. What occurs next puzzles Schaefer's young narrator, but speaks volumes about the sublimation at work in the actions of the three adults:

Mother had the door open to let the kitchen air out. The noises from inside sounded as if she might be throwing things around. Kettles were banging and dishes were clattering....I thought maybe she'd been crying. But there were no tears on her face. It was dry and pinched-looking and there was no color in....'I was planning to have a deep-dish apple pie. Well, I will. None of your silly man foolishness is going to stop me'. (49)

Acting as though the two men and her son are not in the room, Marian sets to work reconstructing the pie. She refuses any offers of help from Joe and ignores everyone and everything, "sitting by the stove, arms folded, waiting herself for her pie to bake" (50). As soon as it is done, she lifts it from the oven and cuts four pieces.

'I'm sorry to keep you men waiting so long. Your pie is ready now.' Father inspected his portion like he was afraid of it. He needed to make a real effort to take his fork and lift a piece. He chewed on it and swallowed and he flipped his eyes sidewise at mother and back again quickly to look across the table at Shane. 'That's prime pie,' he said.

Shane raised a piece on his fork. He considered it closely. He put it in his mouth and chewed it gravely. 'Yes,' he said. The quizzical expression on his face was so plain you could not possibly miss it. 'Yes. That's the best piece of stump I ever tasted'. (51)

It is interesting, certainly, and also telling, that what started out to be Marian's pie becomes the men's pie when it is taken out of the oven. Marian is indeed giving herself to Shane in the only acceptable manner open to her.

The most intimate exchange that takes place between Marian and Shane occurs when "she was settled on the porch with a batch of potatoes to peel" (115). As she pares the protective skin away from the vegetables, she also reveals her inner feelings—feelings shown by Shane in the way "he always regarded her with a tenderness in his eyes he had for no one else" (115). She tells him that she knows he is thinking of leaving, and she asks him to stay—to carry her token into battle, as it were.

'Don't go, Shane. Joe needs you. More than ever now. More than he would ever say.'
'And you?' Shane's lips barely moved and I was not sure of the words.
Mother hesitated. Then her head went up. 'Yes. It's only fair to say it. I need you too' (116).

Willa Cather frequently utilizes mealtime metaphors in her works of fiction, and she often employs food references as a method of making statements about her characters. Admirable women, like Antonia Cusak and Mrs. Harling of *My Antonia* and Mrs. Rosicky of "Neighbour Rosicky," enjoy cooking and baking for their loved ones. (In fact, in *My Antonia*, Chapter Four opens with a rhyme which the narrator and the Harling children chant to "tease Antonia while she was beating up one of Charley's favourite cakes in her big mixing-bowl: 'I won't have none of your weevily wheat, and I won't have none of your barley,/ But I'll take a measure of fine white flour,make a cake for Charley'" (159).* Some other Cather females are not so nurturing, though.

Niel Herbert, the hero of *A Lost Lady*, has several opportunities early in the novel to dine with Captain and Mrs. Forrester. In fact, it is when she is gracing her own dining table that Marian Forrester appears at her loveliest—and worthiest, in Niel's eyes. Later in the story, Niel gets his first intimation that Marian Forrester's worthiness might be tarnished when he notes the name of Frank Ellinger on the hotel register when Captain Forrester is out of town on business. Ellinger does not appear in the hotel dining room, and Niel understands from his absence "that he was dining with Mrs. Forrester, and that the lady herself would get his dinner" (83). Niel's suspicions are confirmed the next morning when he hears Marian Forrester talking with Ellinger behind the closed shutters of her own room.

How far she falls in Niel's estimation—and that of the town—is shown near the end of the book when an older, but no wiser, Marian cooks a meal herself to entertain eight young men from the community, including the odious Ivy Peters, an unscrupulous attorney a few years older than Niel. Peters serves as host in the home that Niel associates with Captain Forrester and a finer era—and finer woman—than he finds

* NOTE   From "Willa Cather Pioneer Memorial Newsletter," Volume XXXI, No.4,
                   Fall, 1987.

Folk Song for the 1988 Year of *My Ántonia*

Stanza 1:

I won't have none of your weevily wheat, I won't have none of your bar... ley--

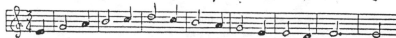

I want some wheat that's fit to eat to make a cake for Char... ley.

Stanza 2:
    O, Charley he's a nice young man, O, Charley he's a dandy;
    O, Charley loves to kiss the girls and feed them sugar candy.

NOTE:

The above folk song, one stanza of which is given (in somewhat variant text) in Willa Cather's *My Ántonia* (Book II, Chapter 4), was sung by my mother, Sarah Armitstead Crown (1883-1969), who I assume learned it from her mother, Alice McClellan Ford Armitstead (1849-1927). Grandmother Alice worked as a cook in a Red Cloud hotel in the latter '70s or around 1880. She had moved to Red Cloud after the loss of her first husband, and it was there that my grandfather, James Arthur Armitstead, met her. The coincidence in the time of my grandmother's residence in the town named "Black Hawk" in the novel and the setting in which the novelist uses the rhyme supports — whatever the rhyme's origin — its currency there in the 1880's.

The different phrasing in my mother's version (stanza one) hints that it is an older version: compare "I want some wheat that's fit to eat" with "But I'll take a measure of fine white flour" in Miss Cather's version. The term "sugar candy" suggests that candy made from refined sugar was a special treat to pioneer families, accustomed to the use of natural sweeteners such as sorghum and molasses.

Willa Cather's inclusion of part of a common rhyme (one perhaps set to an Irish tune, as my mother's song suggests) in her regional "memory piece" again reminds one of her art in preserving the glow of common pleasures girding the daily life of the settlers.

— Rachel Crown

there now. When Niel finally leaves his hometown, he does so with "weary contempt" (169) for Marian Forrester in his heart.

It happened like this,—had scarcely the dignity of an episode. It was nothing, and yet it was everything. Going over to see her one summer evening, he stopped a moment by the dining-room window to look at the honeysuckle. The dining-room door was open into the kitchen, and there Mrs. Forrester stood at a table, making pastry. Ivy Peters came in at the kitchen door, walked up behind her, and unconcernedly put both arms around her, his hands meeting over her breast. She did not move, did not look up, but went on rolling pastry. (169-70)

And Niel Herbert went away and "never went up the poplar-bordered road again" (170).

Cather's most explicit statement on food as a representation of sexual appetites and attitudes occurs in her Pulitzer Prize winning novel, *One of Ours*. Claude Wheeler, Cather's hero, has married a sexually frigid, politically active woman, whose interests often take her away from home. In a short chapter detailing the scene Claude's friend Leonard, married to the loving Susie, finds when he drops in on Claude at dinner time, Cather makes her point.

Enid's kitchen, full of the afternoon sun, glittered with new paint, spotless linoleum, and blue-and-white cooking vessels. In the dining room the cloth was laid, and the table was neatly set for one. Claude opened the icebox, where his supper was arranged for him; a dish of canned salmon with a white sauce; hardboiled eggs, peeled and lying in a nest of lettuce leaves; a bowl of ripe tomatoes; a bit of cold rice pudding; cream and butter. He placed these things on the table, cut some bread, and after carelessly washing his face and hands, sat down to eat in his working shirt. He propped the newspaper against a red glass water pitcher and read the war news while he had his supper. (173)

By contrast, the warm, busy kitchen waiting for Len on his arrival home and the attention to his needs as evidenced by Susie's "filling her husband's plate again" (176) seems bursting with life and with love. And, in case a careless reader has missed Cather's metaphorical descriptions of the two kitchens, there is an exchange between Len and his wife to drive the point home:

'Claude's wife keeps a wonderful kitchen; but so could I, if I never cooked any more than she does.'
Leonard gave her a meaning look. 'I don't believe you would live with the sort of man you could feed out of a tin can.'
'No, I don't believe I would.' She pushed the buggy toward him. 'Take her up, Daddy. She wants to play with you'. (176)

One of Ours closes on another kitchen scene, one that focuses on the two women who loved Claude the most, his mother and the family hired girl, Mahailey. It is surely no accident that their love for him

is most often recalled when they are working together in the kitchen—
nor that Cather seems to suggest the presence of Divine Love there as
well.

Mahailey, when they are alone, sometimes addresses Mrs. Wheeler as 'Mudder'; 'Now,
Mudder, you go upstairs an' lay down an' rest yourself.' Mrs. Wheeler knows that then
she is thinking of Claude, is speaking for Claude. As they are working at the table or
bending over the oven, something reminds them of him, and they think of him together,
like one person: Mahailey will pat her back and say, 'Never you mind, Mudder; you'll
see your boy up yonder.' Mrs. Wheeler always feels that God is near,—but Mahailey is
not troubled by any knowledge of interstellar spaces, and for her He is nearer still,—
directly overhead, not so very far above the kitchen stove. (390-91)

Whether the sharing of food is a commemoration (as in religious
ritual), a celebration (a wedding "feast"), or an acceptable way of speaking
of or demonstrating concupiscence, it deserves more attention when it
appears in literature than it has previously received. Indeed, in ignoring
the menu, the reader may be missing an important part of the author's
message.

Sources Cited

Alderson, Nannie T. *A Bride Goes West*. Lincoln: University of Nebraska Press, 1969.
Bird, Isabella L. *A Lady's Life in the Rocky Mountains*. Norman: University of
    Oklahoma Press, 1976.
Cather, Willa. "Neighbour Rosicky" & "Old Mrs. Harris" in *Obscure Destinies*. New
    York: Vintage Books, 1974.
———— *A Lost Lady*. New York: Vintage Books, 1972.
———— *One of Ours*. New York: Vintage Books, 1971.
Cooney, Edward. "Little Brown Gingerbread Man" in *Montana Margins*, ed., J.K.
    Howard. New Haven: Yale University Press, 1946,
Guthrie, A.B. *The Way West*. New York: Bantam Books, 1977.
Johnson, Dorothy M. "Blanket Squaw," *The Hanging Tree*. New York: Ballantine,
    1977.
———— "Gift by the Wagon," *The Hanging Tree*. New York: Ballantine. 1977.
Lincoln, Elliott. From *The Ranch* in *Montana Margins*.
Rolvaag, O.E. *Giants in the Earth*. New York: Perennial Library, 1955.
Schaefer, Jack. *Shane*. Boston: Houghton Mifflin Company, 1954.
Stewart, Elinore P. *Letters of a Woman Homesteader*. Boston: Houghton Mifflin,
    1976. Unpublished material from University of Wyoming collection.
Vontver, May. "The Kiskis" in *Montana Margins*.

Cookbook

Babcock, Mrs. Tim, ed. *First Ladies' Cookbook*. Montana Territorial Centennial
    Edition, 1963.

Recipes, Repasts, and Regionalism:
Marjorie Kinnan Rawlings's
Cross Creek Cookery and
"Our Daily Bread"

Michael P. Dean

In February, 1942, Scribners published Marjorie Kinnan Rawlings's *Cross Creek*, her "autobiography" of the remote hamlet in north Florida that she had learned to call home. This remarkable book cemented her place as one of the finest regional writers to emerge during the 1930s. Moreover, it showed her readers another of her talents, for the longest chapter in the book, "Our Daily Bread," revealed her skill as a cook and entertainer and demonstrated her flair for recounting the delights of dining. Indeed, "Our Daily Bread" proved so popular with readers that Rawlings determined to produce a cookbook that would provide recipes and menus as well as offer accounts of the delectable meals for which she had become justifiably famous among her friends. In August, 1942, just six months after the appearance of *Cross Creek*, Scribners published *Cross Creek Cookery*.

Cross Creek Cookery has been called "not a cookbook in the traditional manner, but...[rather] a mouth-watering, evocative, and charmingly conversational discussion of cooking at Cross Creek" (Rawlings, *Cookery*, back cover). An examination of "Our Daily Bread" and *Cross Creek Cookery* reveals Rawlings as a regionalist who uses food—its gathering, its preparation, and its ingestion—as a tool to explore the life and customs of her particular region. Together, these two documents show Rawlings's interest in filling more than empty stomachs. True, they offer food and drink, but the offering transcends the "mere intake of calories" (Rawlings, *Cookery* 2): within Rawlings's pages the reader finds something that "warms the being," something that conveys the "convivial gathering of folk of good will" (*Cookery* 2). The reader emerges with more than a mere taste of certain regional dishes; instead, she or he tastes deeply of a region's way of life.

Marjorie Kinnan Rawlings herself tasted deeply of a particular place. It is not exaggeration to state that she owed her career as a writer to the move she made in 1928 from Rochester, New York, to Cross Creek, a remote village in the interior of Florida. Rawlings responded immediately to her new surroundings, to the little clustering of black and white families at Cross Creek, "a bend in a country road, by land, and the flowing of Lochloosa Lake into Orange Lake, by water...four miles west of the small village of Island Grove, nine miles east of a turpentine still" (Rawlings, *Cross Creek* 4), and to the land east of Ocala, the scrub, a place where human habitation was scarce, a "silent stretch enclosed by two rivers," a place where the "timid and alien" (Rawlings, *Letters* 50) did not venture. Rawlings gave herself to this strange and unusual and little-known part of Florida with an intensity that bordered on fanaticism. Rawlings became the chronicler of these people, the crackers, and their ways, but she was not an outsider merely peering over their shoulders. On the contrary, she became part of this way of life. In a 1931 letter Rawlings recorded her growing attachment to and absorption in this intriguing land. She told her correspondent, "Possibly you wonder how I gain the confidence of these people without being a cold-blooded spy who intends to 'use' them. It is so easy for me to live their life with them, that I am in some danger of losing all sophistication and perspective. I feel hurried sometimes, as though I must get 'written out' in this country within the next few years, because so much is no longer strange or unusual to me" (*Letters* 50). It took Rawlings nearly a dozen years to get, as she put it, "written out," and the product of living this life that she termed "peculiarly right" (*Letters* 50) was some of the finest regional books of the 1930s and '40s.

Today, Marjorie Kinnan Rawlings is, of course, inextricably identified with the Florida frontier she recorded in *South Moon Under, Golden Apples, The Yearling, When the Whippoorwill, Cross Creek Cookery*, and in her masterpiece *Cross Creek*. The latter book contains chapters on a variety of subjects, on "toady-frogs, lizards, antses, and varmints," on the "evolution of comfort" (Rawlings, *Cross Creek* 144, 56), that is, the move from an outhouse to indoor facilities, on snakes, and on the seasons. The book is, by turns, funny, sad, charming, and evocative. In its opening and concluding chapters it is lyrical and poignant. It is, however, Chapter 17, "Our Daily Bread," that is, for many readers, the most memorable. For Rawlings herself the chapter was clearly an important one; she states at the beginning of it, "Cookery is my one vanity and I am a slave to any guest who praises my culinary art" (205-206). Rawlings goes on to declare that she recognizes cookery as "one of the great arts" (206), and she confesses that she thought she would be a great cook because her mother was a great cook. Next, she admits that her "instinctive cooking proved, in...maturity, a thing of horror," and that her mother-in-law rescued her with a gift of the *Boston Cook Book*, a book Rawlings studied as "a novitiate the prayer book" (206-207). Her devotion to Fanny Farmer was a success, and by the time she moved to Florida, she was clearly on the road to being the superb cook she eventually became.

Marjorie Kinnan Rawlings's life at Cross Creek honed her culinary skills and taught her the finer points of the art. She writes, "The new foods that I found in Florida were a challenge and I have learned more about cookery in my years at the Creek than in those that preceded them" (207). Then after a brief discussion of William Bartram's encounter with a cooked rattlesnake in 1773, Rawlings begins her cook's tour of north Florida with an examination of the various meanings and guises of bread in Cross Creek country. Cornbread in its several manifestations, hush puppies, biscuits, and ice-box rolls "baked by preference in a Dutch oven with live coals for heat" (211) constitute this category of comestibles. Rawlings's description of local vegetables follows, and such delights as pokeweed, mustard greens, turnip greens, and collard greens are scrutinized. In her paragraph on collard greens Rawlings introduces one of her quick and memorable anecdotes. Declaring collard greens and hog chitlings "an unhappy combination," Rawlings points out that "rural Florida is divided into chitling and anti-chitling camps and feeling sometimes runs high" with "man [standing] against wife and mother against child" (214). However, her friend Fred Tompkins overcame his difficulty with his wife's love of chitlings in an eminently reasonable way. " 'The Old Hen's a fool for chitlin's,' he said, 'and I don't believe in deprivin' another of anything they call pleasure. So when she cooks 'em, I just sell out and leave home for a day or two' " (214). This example conveys useful information about cookery in Florida while it also allows Rawlings to display her talents as a storyteller. In this same discussion of vegetables Rawlings also reveals her ability to turn a phrase when she calls okra "a Cinderella among vegetables," particularly when it is transformed by her "magic wand with which [she] waves it into something finer than mere edibility..." (215).

Now the pattern is established, and the remainder of the chapter conforms to it. That is, Rawlings introduces by turns "Florida fruits" (217) and meats prepared at the Creek—she calls these her "most exotic dishes" (225) and she includes turtles and crabs, blackbirds and limpkins in this category—and a few other dishes that do not fit into any clear classification. The chapter concludes with a long anecdote about Fatty Blake's "doings at Anthony" (240), an event which included the serving of squirrel pilau and Brunswick stew. In these sections of the chapter the reader must move carefully lest she or he miss something. For example, Rawlings declares, "Better men than I have written lyrically about the mango" (218); then she proceeds to provide an account that can, indeed, only be labelled as a lyrical one. She mentions the guava, that wonderful fruit that has the "rankness of odor of the tropics, deathly sweet and pungent" (220), and she tosses in as lagniappe the old canard about it: "the uncouth say that a self-respecting cat will bury a guava" (220). Rawlings introduces us to "an old man far off in the piney-woods who gave [her] cups of Scuppernong wine so dry, so fine, that [she] could not believe [her] palate" (223). Then she provides an account in dialect of his method of producing such wine. He begins by warning his pupil, " 'Now don't look to this not to fail you if you don't do like I tell you,' " and he concludes his lesson with " 'Now that ain't the way of a heap o' folks, but it's my way' " (223-224). Her section on the blue crabs of Salt Springs, a delicacy that should have "straws drawn for it by the gourmet elite" (230), concludes with these directions for cooking the delectable creatures: "stir in a tablespoonful, or two, of the finest brandy, and turn the Newburg into a piping hot covered serving dish...serve on toast points [with] a Chablis or white Rhine wine...as an accompaniment" (232). Then one must listen carefully, for, says Rawlings, "Angels sing softly in the distance" (232).

The description of the "doings at Anthony" is provided because Rawlings wishes to illustrate the "strong differences of opinion on the edibility of the [squirrel] head" (240). Fatty Blake, "a snuff and tobacco salesman, and Anthony's richest citizen," invites "the world," or two counties, at least, to a feast of squirrel pilau and Brunswick stew (240). Rawlings hears the invitation from Fatty's own lips when he stops at the village store. "Fatty couldn't likker folks, as he would like to do, but if you brought your own 'shine and were quiet about it, why he'd meet you at the gate for a drink, and God bless you" (240). On the great day, she tells us, "cars and wagons and lone horses and mules" began arriving in Anthony long before dark, and their occupants gathered around Fatty's house where in back "a Negro stirred rice in a forty-gallon iron kettle with a paddle as big as an oar" (241). Singing and praying and the passing of the hat preceded the crowd's convergence upon the heavily laden table. After this build-up Rawlings brings her story to its climax. She writes, "The passing hat reached a lean, venerable farmer just as he had completed a tour of exploration through his pilau" (242). Then,

"No!" he shrilled, with the lustiness of an old man with a grievance.

"No, I ain't going' to give him nothing'! This here was advertised as a free meal and 'taint nothin' but a dogged Georgia prayer-meetin'. Get a man here on promises and then go to pickin' his pocket. This food ain't fitten to eat, dogged Georgia rations, Brunswick stew and all. And he's done cooked the squirrel heads in the pilau, and that suits a damned Georgia Cracker but it don't suit me.

"I was born and raised in Floridy, and I'm pertickler. I don't want no squirrel eyes lookin' at me out o' my rations!". (242)

Rawlings refrains from telling us any more, leaving us the job of imagining the disintegration of the great "doings at Anthony."

It should be noted that "Our Daily Bread" is, for all its appearance of looseness and ramblingness, a carefully constructed chapter. It begins with a lengthy anecdote, the one about Rawlings's hope to be an instinctively great cook and her failure to achieve that status. It ends likewise with a lengthy anecdote, the one about Fatty Blake discussed above. In between, we hear shorter stories and read pithy remarks. And along the way, of course, Rawlings introduces us to the foodways of north Florida. It is an extremely effective narrative strategy, plying us with a substantial appetizer and a hearty dessert while letting us sample in small amounts any number of main course items in between. Moreover, it is a strategy that Rawlings will reemploy when she writes *Cross Creek Cookery*.

The immediate success of *Cross Creek* and especially its chapter "Our Daily Bread" was the impetus for the writing of *Cross Creeky Cookery*. Rawlings noted that "eight out of ten letters about *Cross Creek* ask for a recipe, or pass on a recipe, or speak of suffering over my chat of Cross Creek dishes" (*Cookery* 2). Clearly, there was a ready market for a book of recipes based upon "Our Daily Bread." In addition, the conditions prevailing in 1942 created a potential readership for such a book. Rawlings recounts the receipt of letters from American military men in many parts of the world. "Always," she notes, "there was a wistful comment on my talk of food; often a mention of a boyhood kitchen memory" (*Cookery* 2). When one adds to this apparent need for such a cookbook Rawlings's life-long desire to be a storyteller, one has all the ingredients needed to reconstruct the origin of *Cross Creek Cookery*.

The structure of Rawlings's cookbook is adumbrated in "Our Daily Bread." Rawlings begins and ends her new book with anecdotal chapters called "To Our Bodies' Good" and " 'Better a dinner of Herbs.' " However, she prefaces her book with an overview by listing what she calls "Cross Creek Menus." These enticing menus include breakfasts of "orange juice, very small crisp-fried Orange Lake bream, grits, cornmeal muffins, kumquat marmalade, strong coffee [and] Dora's [Dora was Rawlings's jersey cow] cream: and "camp dinners" consisting of "fried fresh-caught Orange lake fish (bream, perch, or bass), hush puppies, cole slaw, coffee [and] any dessert any wife has thought to bring along or send, preferably lemon pie" (xvi, xxi). The "recipe chapters" of the book move in an orderly way from soups through luncheon dishes, vegetables, and potatoes, rice, and grits to Florida sea foods, game and meats, and salads. The longest chapter, "Desserts," follows all of these, naturally, and the whole thing is concluded with a look at "Preserves, Jellies and Marmalades."

The opening anecdote, "To Our Bodies' Good," discusses in addition to the letters from military men and other readers of *Cross Creek*, life, and particularly culinary life, at the Creek. Rawlings ends this section with an account of the aftermath of a typical company dinner at Cross Creek: "My friend Cecil reported to an acquaintance that...the guests often wandered through the old farmhouse and fell here and there on the beds to sleep." The "horrified" acquaintance ventured that "such disappearances must be annoying to the hostess." Cecil's rejoinder apparently pleased Rawlings. " 'Oh,' said Cecil, 'the hostess goes to sleep, too' " (4). Rawlings's final word in this section is an apparent afterthought (but we quickly learn better) on Dora. Rawlings writes,

> Where I specify Dora's cream and butter, I am indicating that so generous a quantity, of so high a quality, is meant, that one's own Jersey cow is called for. This is not always practicable or possible. In all such cases, the recipes work very nicely with ordinary materials. I mentioned to my friend Edith that I was doing a practical Cross Creek Cookery. She said, with a trace of bitterness, "You should give away a Jersey cow with every copy of the book." (4)

Throughout the book the reader longs for Dora's oft-mentioned cream and butter, but now as then, no Jersey is delivered when the book arrives.

Each recipe section begins with a prose piece. Some are short and to the point. Others are fairly elaborate and relate fascinating narratives. An example of the latter is the beginning of "Florida Sea Foods." Here Rawlings tells on herself the story of the time she mistook electric rays for flounders. She concludes by saying, "No self-respecting starving dog has ever been known to eat them—" (79), and she leaves us the task of filling in the blank. Some of this material appeared in "Our Daily Bread," but Rawlings always reworks it slightly, and often extensively. In addition, much new material appears, and the reader who attempts to skip something she or he thinks is from *Cross Creek* will miss delightful new material. When Rawlings does introduce her recipes—the book contains over 250 of them—she does so in a very effective way, a way that keeps her reader's attention. As illustration of this method, consider her recipe for carrot souffle. First, Rawlings supplies the needed ingredients: "2 cups cooked carrots, 1 teaspoon salt" and so forth. Next, she gives the needed cooking information: "put the cooked carrots through a sieve," But watch what she does at the end of the cooking directions. "Pour into a buttered casserole and bake forty-five minutes in a four-hundred-degree oven. People like this who usually turn up their noses at carrots." And she concludes with this declaration: "As far as I know, this is my own concoction. It tastes almost too good to be true" (54). An inattentive reader could clearly miss much matter of great interest here. However, Rawlings works hard to capture her reader's attention, just as she worked diligently to capture her dinner guests' attention.

Surely, Rawlings had her narrative strategy in mind, and obviously was assured of its success, when she wrote her editor, the legendary Maxwell Perkins, in August, 1942, "I'm so glad you find the *Cookery* good reading" (*Letters* 226).

The title of the final passage of *Cross Creek Cookery* is based on a Biblical text, Proverbs 15:17, "Better is a dinner of herbs where love is, than a stalled ox and hatred therewith." The section revolves around a discussion of Rawlings's philosophy of cooking and eating. There are two elements necessary, she says, for "successful and happy gatherings at table." The first involves the food that, "whether simple or elaborate, must be carefully prepared, willingly prepared, imaginatively prepared" (217). The second element is the guests, who "must be conscious of their welcome" (217). With food and guests in place, one can begin the process of pursuing sustenance and fellowship. Here is the way Marjorie Kinnan Rawlings suggests it should go:

The breaking together of bread, the sharing of salt is too ancient a symbol of friendliness to be profaned. At the moment of dining, the assembled group stands for a little while as a safe unit, under a safe roof, against the perils and enmities of the world. The group will break up and scatter, later. For this short time, let them eat, drink and be merry. (217)

In the uncertain war-torn world of 1942, this was an appealing picture. In our own day, the appeal remains.

"Our Daily Bread" and *Cross Creek Cookery* reveal both an imaginative writer and an imaginative cook. That the two were merged as one in the person of Marjorie Kinnan Rawlings is to our benefit. Lovers of good prose, lovers of regional delineations, and lovers of good food continue to rejoice, more than forty years later, in these two documents and in this writer. Rawlings must be pleased at her continued appeal, for near the end of *Cross Creek Cookery* she tells us that "no greater offense can be given in the rural South than to refuse a meal" (218). Rawlings offers us meals for our minds—" 'Reckon 'taint what you're used to, but the greens are bound to be nice, for they're fresh picked.' " Or, " 'Taint much, but it's the best we got, and you're sure welcome' " (*Cookery*) 218)—and no one in her or his right mind will refuse the invitation to partake.

Works Cited

Rawlings, Marjorie Kinnan. *Cross Creek* New York: Scribners, 1942.

_____ *Cross Creek Cookery*. 1942; rpt. New York: Scribners, 1970.

_____ *Selected Letters of Marjorie Kinnan Rawlings*. Eds. Gordon E. Bigelow and Laura V. Monti. Gainesville: University Presses of Florida, 1983.

From Eggs to Stew:
The Importance of Food in the
Popular Narratives of Betty MacDonald

Delmer Davis

Forty years ago, in 1946, the most popular non-fiction book (over 1,000,000 hardbound copies sold) in the United States was *The Egg and I*, a rollicking narrative of life on a chicken ranch on the Olympic Peninsula in the late 1920s.[1] After this first-book success, Betty MacDonald produced three more narratives based on her personal experiences: *The Plague and I*, 1948, a seriocomic treatment of MacDonald's successful fight to regain her health in a tuberculosis sanitorium; *Anybody Can Do Anything*, 1950, a narrative of MacDonald and her family in search of jobs and entertainment during the depression years; and *Onions in the Stew*, 1955, a book about MacDonald's life on Vashon Island in Puget Sound in the 1940s and early 1950s. Although MacDonald's use of humorous irony and exaggeration doubtless helped push the books to best-seller status, certainly her preoccupation with food and her ability to render food experiences concretely and evocatively contributed to her success with the popular audience who seemed "starved" for her often food-centered prose. As the titles of the first and last of the books indicate, food and cooking are central MacDonald concerns and show themselves also in the handling of setting, characterization, and imagery.

That MacDonald loved food herself and could not help but write about it seems clear. The very first sentence of *The Egg and I* sets the tone for her other books: "Along with teaching us that lamb must be cooked with garlic" begins the narrative (11). Since the book is centered on carving a successful farm out of the wilderness, it is probably not surprising that throughout, food settings and backgrounds are rampant. The narrator, Betty, and her husband, Bob, plant and raise a lush and productive vegetable garden and cultivate an orchard (54-56). A complete chapter is devoted to harvesting and canning (182-185). Another chapter describes the available food in the surrounding Olympic Peninsula wilds, including "pheasant, quail, duck, cracked crab, venison, butter clams, oysters, brook trout, salmon, fried chicken and mushrooms" (82). The narrator gives special emphasis to how to dig, clean, cook and eat clams, especially the large variety known as Geoduck (86-89).

114

MacDonald's second book, *The Plague and I*, at first might seem some distance from food preoccupations, given its emphasis on recovery from disease, but, in truth, her second writing effort is, perhaps, more compulsively centered on food in its setting than any other of the works. As the narrator notes in the first paragraph of the book, like "being hit by a bus," getting T.B. sets new priorities. Now "what you will have for dinner" becomes important in the same way as "who is in the next bed" (11). The patient's progress towards health is charted in relationship to weight gain (83). Getting well depends on "rest, fresh air, good food" (73). The daily routine at The Pines sanitorium is anchored on meals and eating, which MacDonald describes in accurate and evocative terms (see, for example 68, 72, 78, 86). As the narrator, Betty, notes, all patients on the mend "had voracious appetites and took any and all food offered," and "letters home were always pleas for more food" so that "visiting days our ward looked like a delicatessen" (115).

MacDonald's humorous record of the depression years, *Anybody Can Do Anything*, is perhaps her book least food-oriented, but even in this narrative, the woes of the down-and-out are evoked against a persistent backdrop of eating well, if simply, in spite of poverty, even though eating well in those years might consist of "stretching the meatloaf, macaroni and cheese, spaghetti, chili, tuna fish and noodles, vegetable soup" plus "gallons of coffee which was seventeen cents a pound," and simple sweets such as "cinnamon toast" (130). In these tough times, fallen on hard luck, Betty, as narrator, tries to dignify the fact that she must economically carry a lunch to work by buying a "straw envelope" to hide things in, but the device ruins the sandwiches and makes "everything taste like mothballs and incense" (112). In contrast, other people with few funds "boldly" use "paper bags" or "briefcases" for their lunches, and Betty's sister Mary, never a victim of false pride, often wraps the food with "old printed bread wrapping" or "newspaper tied with a string" (111). The depth of hardship in the depression is revealed in the streets of Seattle by the "musty choky smells of...rancid grease, fish, doughnuts and stale coffee" with a whole meal selling for fifteen cents and including "stew, bread and butter and all the coffee you can drink" (114).

Because of its island setting, MacDonald's last narrative, *Onions in the Stew*, more naturally includes generous portions of descriptive food passages. With their house located on a beach, the MacDonald family relishes, in particular, seafood. Clams figure prominently, with precise recipes for clam chowder and clam fritters (80-81). MacDonald also suggests how to fix and eat more exotic delicacies: squid, sea cucumbers, shrimp, and scallops (84-85). Besides seafood, however, Vashon Island boasts "red currants, pie cherries, peaches, strawberries, gooseberries, boysenberries, loganberries, raspberries, chickens, eggs, goat's milk" (12). Food feasts with the neighbors on the beach are regular occasions as are holiday celebrations with family and friends (110, 114-121). Visitors are so many and fixing enough food so important that MacDonald devotes one whole chapter, "Triple That Recipe," to handling such problems (175-189).

So central is food to her books that MacDonald often ties characterization to eating, cooking, and culinary tastes, with characters categorized as superior or inferior in relationship to the food abilities and preferences of Betty as narrator and of her family. The character most idealized by her cooking abilities and food tastes is Betty's mother, "a marvelous cook" (*Egg* 33), whose tastes set the tone for all would-be cooks. Throughout the depression, while her daughters and son are out trying to earn livings, mother is home keeping the family together and cooking well on very little. On Saturdays, she makes a huge kettle of chili while the family listens to football on the radio (*Anybody* 131), and, on Sundays, she provides "an enormous meatloaf" (*Anybody* 131), a dish the family enjoys sixty-three straight weeks (*Anybody* 228), but a meal mother ingeniously varies on Thanksgiving by shaping it "like a turkey" (*Plague* 165).

Good motherhood, indeed, for the narrator, Betty, seems to be intimately connected with cooking skills and food tastes. Especially is this relationship emphasized in *The Plague and I*. Betty remembers childhood happiness as partially characterized by "Mother's delicious cooking" (27), and Mother had contributed to the children's health "in the form of good food" (18). Betty reveals that on her last weekend at home prior to her stay in the sanitorium, her mother made her comfortable and provided "chicken soup, fresh gingerbread and hot tea" for lunch (43), while later creating supper "smells of woodsmoke, garlic, and baking potatoes" (46). When her mother visits the sanitorium, she always brings good things to eat—on her very first visit, "hot fresh cookies" (87). Betty learns later that all such food which a patient cannot eat by bedtime must be shared with the other patients. The cart for sharing already has lots of inferior food brought by less effective cooks than Betty's mother. To Betty, it is "a sacrilege to put mother's cookies on the cart" with "dry cupcakes and choke cake" (89).

All the female members of Betty's immediate family strive to achieve the mother's goal of "good food, simply prepared, well seasoned and beautifully served" (*Onions* 179). Many other characters in MacDonald's books do not measure up as cooks and are recipients of varying degrees of ridicule, however. It must be understood, of course, that much of MacDonald's humor results from making fun of people. In her defense, one cannot help but notice that she generally makes as much fun of herself as narrator as she does of other characters. Self-deflation is, perhaps, MacDonald's most characteristic method of portraying the inept narrator for humorous effect whether it be as an ineffectual and unhappy frontier woman in *The Egg and I*, as an uncooperative patient in *The Plague and I*, as an inefficient and unskilled employee in *Anybody Can Do Anything*, or as a beleaguered mother to teen-age girls in *Onions in the Stew*. In all these books, though, no matter how much fun MacDonald makes of her narrator self for her stupidity, her lack of skills, her human weaknesses, she rather carefully exempts cooking and food tastes from her persona's long list of foibles. Although Betty is somewhat modest about her other traits as mother, she brags that she herself is "sometimes a very good cook" whose "weakness is 'if a little is good a whole lot is better' " and whose "leftovers are often carried from the table in tubs" (*Onions* 179). The implication is that the leftovers are well-cooked and tasty, if overabundant. This family pride in good food and motherhood explains Betty's concern with a balanced, well-seasoned diet which often puts her at odds over food with others in her books—people with less taste and fewer abilities.

In *The Egg and I*, Betty as narrator abhors the food practices of her country neighbors who eat repetitiously and unhealthfully in the midst of plenty. She cannot understand why only she uses fresh vegetables and serves salads. The neighbors feed such things to their livestock and chickens. For the neighbors, meat is always "fried and boiled." The typical diet is "sowbelly, fried potatoes, fried bread, macaroni, cabbage or string beans boiled with sowbelly...day in and day out" (90). Mothers feed this indigestible fare to their children from infancy. Betty, on the other hand, a more enlightened mother, gives her baby Anne "sun baths, vegetables, meat and cod-liver oil" and scorns the neighbor babies who are "fed pork gravy, mashed potatoes, beer—and had 'fits' " (221).

Similarly, in *Onions in the Stew*, Betty as narrator makes fun of the dishes served by well-intentioned neighbors. She pictures herself at a baby shower staring at "a large lumpy salad" which turns out to be "tuna fish and marshmellows and walnuts and pimento (just for the pretty color, our hostess explained later when she was giving us the recipe) and chunks of pure white lettuce and boiled dressing. I almost gagged," Betty notes (177). The narrator goes ahead to list other abominable recipes she has been served, among which are "a ring mold of mushroom soup, hard-boiled eggs, canned shrimps (that special brand that taste like Lysol) and lime Jello," "creamed tuna fish and peanuts over canned asparagus," and finally "a salad of elbow macaroni, pineapple chunks, Spanish peanuts, chopped cabbage, chopped marshmellows, ripe olives and salad dressing" (177-178). Then Betty as narrator, growing somewhat strident, in a general condemnation of all the cooking of her American neighbors throughout the country, says, "I don't know what is happening to the women of America but it ought to be stopped" (178).

Given this general MacDonald framework for evaluating people by their relationship to food, one is not surprised to see how individual characterizations are partially developed by attention to cooking abilities and culinary tastes. Not even all family members can escape MacDonald's narrative censure if cooking is not their forte. Gammy, Betty's father's mother, is part of the family household during Betty's growing-up years. Idiosyncratic in many ways, Gammy is characterized as a horrible cook who fixes "dreadful food" in contrast to mother (*Plague* 27). Gammy basically does *not believe* that "eating was healthy" (26) and specializes in two choices for breakfast, either "mush or batter cakes" (21). Her oatmeal mush is "gray and gluey" and her batter cakes taste "as though they had been basted together over a wool batt" (21). Betty marvels that her father grew up "tall, handsome, and vital in spite of Gammy's cooking" (19). Gammy's cakes and cookies are notorious repositories of anything handy in the kitchen while Gammy is baking, and only some odd, tasteless neighbor children who regularly eat dog food find the cookies edible (*Egg* 32-33). When Gammy makes jam, she uses a similar inclusive method, "dumping together all left-over fruit, jams, jellies, applesauce, honey, peanut butter and candy and boiling it into a dark brown gummy mess," which the children refuse to eat and call "Gammy jam" (*Plague* 23).

Gammy's ineptness in the kitchen can partially be forgiven by the narrator because she is, after all, a relative, indeed a colorful and funny woman whose cooking is just one of her unusual traits, and also because she is a pessimist. As a pessimist "who gives every cloud a pitch black lining" and for whom pessimism "was a twenty-four-hour proposition" (*Plague* 13), Gammy is characterized as one for whom cooking efforts are inevitably useless since life will turn out badly no matter what one eats or how healthily one lives (*Plague* 13-15).

Other characters in MacDonald's books cannot be easily redeemed from their abominable cooking and food tastes by family ties and philosophical outlook. Such characters suffer varying degrees of the narrator's censure in relationship to their personality traits and culinary abilities. One who comes off surprisingly well is the memorable Maw Kettle of *The Egg and I*. Maw is the matriarch of a huge, sprawling, lazy, dirty, vulgar, rude family (112-119). Maw, however, becomes Betty's closest mountain friend, this in spite of differences over cleanliness and diet. Betty finds all the Kettles interesting, but she finds in Maw, behind her rough exterior, a considerate, good-hearted and amusing companion (123, 204-209). MacDonald's mixed attitudes towards Maw Kettle are mirrored in the way she relates Maw to food. Like all the neighbors, Maw cooks the typical diet of food boiled or fried (121, 206), and her method of fixing steaks makes them "gray and chewy like pieces of a thick wet blanket" (226). Yet, to offset these negatives, Maw, even in the middle of a smelly, fly-infested kitchen, serves up exquisite bread and cinnamon rolls better than any Betty has ever eaten (113-115).

Another neighbor, Mrs. Hicks, Betty likes less than she likes Maw Kettle, and her picture of Mrs. Hicks and food shows this distaste more one-sidedly. Mrs. Hicks keeps the Hicks farm compulsively clean and neat in contrast to how Maw keeps her house (124-128). But Mrs. Hicks loves to control her neighbor's activities and to recite community gossip in her own "pure" and highly judgmental manner. Mrs. Hicks' organized control of the lives around her extend to the kitchen. At a supper for Betty and Bob, Mrs. Hicks efficiently serves the usual boiled fare, but in large quantities: "a huge, standing rib roast boiled, boiled potatoes, boiled string beans, boiled corn, boiled peas and carrots, boiled turnips and spinach" along with "cheese, pickles, preserves, jam, jelly, homemade bread, head cheese, fried clams, cake, ginger bread, pie and tea" (125). One can see how far this complicated menu departs from the MacDonald women's ideal of simplicity! Betty shows her disapproval of Mrs. Hicks by her comments on her culinary results. Although Mrs. Hicks gets blue ribbons for her canning and preserving at the county fair and in spite of the uniformly beautiful appearance of her canned goods, to Betty her canned peaches "tasted like glue" and her canned tomatoes "tasted like nothing" (184).

Characters in *The Plague and I* are similarly characterized in relationship to food. Betty as narrator constantly gives The Pines, the T.B. sanitorium, high marks for its food which she describes in terms of her mother's goals as a cook: "well-seasoned" and "very good," even though often too cold (68, 72). Such reviews take on forceful meaning as characterization contrasts when Betty finds patients who do not like the food, people such as Beryl, a new bath mate, "a gray-faced girl with toothpick legs" who thinks "the food at the Pines stank" and who refuses to eat anything but what her male friend brings and intends to survive a week on his recent gift of "a whole roasted chicken and twelve chocolate eclairs," which she hides from the medical staff by wrapping in her pajamas in her night stand (135-136). Beryl is so stupid that she has worked for years at her food-related job, dipping chocolates in a candy factory, while ignoring the telltale signs of her cough, until she literally hemorrhages on the job. Betty, of course, worries about "all those chocolates she had dipped and sprayed with germs" (136).

Food also helps to characterize one of the worst nurses at the sanitorium, Miss Muelbach (the coined surname itself suggests stubbornness and thick-headedness). Betty and her roommates nickname Miss Muelbach, Gravy Face, in honor of her repulsive complexion and habits, including her "gray hairy legs" (107-108). Gravy Face falls into that category of nurses who must have gotten "their vocational training kicking cripples and hitting small children" (124).

In *Anybody Can Do Anything* MacDonald devotes one complete chapter, " 'Let Nothing You Dismay,' " to narrating her experiences with the most threatening and weirdest character in any of her books: Dorita (182-209). All of Dorita's mysterious and suspicious attacks on Betty, her eerie laughter, her veiled threats to Betty's children and to Betty's sister Mary's boss, are played out against the building excitement of the coming Christmas holiday and the gigantic party that Betty and her sister Mary are planning in order to advertise a trucking company. Dorita fulfills Betty's worst fears by turning out to be deeply emotionally disturbed and ends up sending terribly obscene letters to the boss of the trucking company, signing Betty's and her sister's names. The two sisters are falsely arrested and luckily can explain their innocence.

Betty, however, has suspected from the beginning that Dorita has an aberrant personality because of the way she eats everything with *her gloves on*, from "sticky sugary doughnuts" (191) to a "tuna fish sandwich" (196). Does she, in some twisted way, believe she must hide her fingerprints, even on the food she eats, Betty wonders (191). Regardless, the book's narrator has forever been changed by the experience. Now every Christmas season, amid holiday festivities, Betty thinks of Dorita "eating sugar doughnuts with her gloves on" (209).

Some characters in *Onions in the Stew* are also developed in relationship to food and cooking. Lesley Arnold, for example, moves to the island beach community during World War II and immediately poses a threat as a husband-stealer. Says Betty, Lesley is so beautiful she "made me [Betty] slightly sick at my stomach" and feel "like a hygiene teacher...in an ugly tan knitted suit, the wrong shoes...[with] no husband" (117). Lesley begins to work her wiles on Betty's husband, Don, and insists on his helping her, walking her home, fixing broken items, while Betty plays the martyred housewife who cooks the food for family and new neighbor Lesley. Betty's jealousy cools when she and Don eat at Lesley's house, however. Lesley proves to be a rotten cook who serves "one of those revolting ripe olive, macaroni, Brussels sprouts, chestnut casseroles so dear to the heart of the bum cook" (120). As Don picks at this casserole and "the raisin-stuffed prune salad," it is clear that he "still preferred" Betty's "cooking" (120).

Another character in *Onions in the Stew* developed by MacDonald in relationship to food is Elizabeth Gage, who receives a full chapter treatment (199-218). Although a graduate of Smith College and the daughter of a wealthy Texas attorney, Elizabeth is pictured as very inept as a mother. Her four children are dirty, ill-mannered, and wear wet pants. She keeps herself no better. "Elizabeth Gage was wearing a pair of faded jeans with enormous legs and a broken zipper, a dirty T-shirt of Everett's [her husband's], no brassiere and red satin mules" (201). Not surprisingly, Elizabeth's inadequacies as a mother are relayed by means of food-related details. The children presumably survive on junk food (201), even though their father, Everett, makes lots of money and owns a yacht. At first, Betty is sympathetic to Elizabeth and her tales of drunken mistreatment from her husband, but after Betty meets Everett (who looks like Gregory Peck) and she and Don join the Gages and friends for a day on their boat, she soon begins to realize that Elizabeth Gage is herself responsible for most of her problems as wife and mother. As Don observes, Elizabeth " 'is one of those women who like to be pitiful' " (213). Key to Betty's change of heart is her surprise at discovering that Elizabeth is, of all things, "a superb cook" (208). Elizabeth demonstrates these culinary skills effortlessly in difficult kitchen conditions aboard the yacht and, importantly, away from her children.

Periodically, during the day at sea, she hands out "loaves of hot French bread hollowed out and packed with fried chicken," "strawberry shortcake," and "tiny hot meatballs" (208). Betty clearly cannot really fathom how a good cook can be such a complaining and careless mother and housewife. Elizabeth does not change, however, inspite of Betty's attempts to help her. After a five-year break in their friendship, Elizabeth again demonstrates her glaringly inconsistent character to Betty by saying she would ask Betty "to lunch, but all they had in the house were graham crackers and honey" (218). Given the narrator's commitment to good food and cooking, Elizabeth Gage's irresponsibility seems nearly unforgiveable.

Although MacDonald's interest in food is clearly shown by her pervasive use of settings and characters steeped in culinary details, perhaps her most evocative and fascinating compulsion to use food and cooking in her narratives is her continual reliance on food-related imagery and figures in order to describe phenomena that on the surface of things have nothing at all to do with food. Again and again, MacDonald projects reality by means of food-related word pictures. These comparisons, usually similes, sometimes metaphors, suggest how deeply ingrained food and cooking were in MacDonald's very thought processes and how naturally food words and ideas emerged from MacDonald's mind as she tried to project her imaginative reconstruction of experience.

One can see MacDonald's culinary imagination at work first in *The Egg and I*. Muscles are pictured as squashing "back to jelly" (29); cold at night, Betty's "blood turned to sherbert" (92); rhododendrons are "as big as cabbages" (95); Betty is so anxious for company that when relatives visit she "clung to them like the smell of frying" (188); a baby looks "as if he had been molded out of dough" (223); a logging victim "cracked" his "head like an egg" (229); and Maw's "large white breasts bobbed to the surface like dumplings in a stew" (268).

MacDonald really hits her stride with food images in *The Plague and I,* however. The food-related word-pictures for non-food-centered events almost overwhelm the reader and make one wonder what it is about having tuberculosis that turns one's mind to food. As a child, Betty looks unhealthy and is "olive green" (13); the young girls wear woolen leggings that have "little slippery black buttons like licorice drops" (16); Betty's children, Anne and Joan, "come boiling into the room" (37); a nurse at the clinic is "about as friendly as a halibut" (39); Betty sees "milky windows" her last day at home (47); the bark on madrona trees is "cinnamon brown" (49); a patient has a hoarse whisper "that sounded like walking on spilled sugar" (56); when Kimi takes a soapy bath in "two scant cupfulls of water" she must feel as if she "had been dipped in white of egg" (64); some sad people have voices "like whistling teakettles" (64); patients in Betty's ward are "all as immobile as blobs of dough in rising pans" (68); chrysanthemums are described as being "as big as grapefruit" and "butter yellow" (87); a black patient, Evalee, has a voice that is "deep and soft as melted chocolate" (9); Minna's husband, "Sweetie-Pie," is "old, bald, fat and doughy-faced" (106); Betty gets rid of depressing thoughts by brushing "them off the day like a crumb off the bedclothes" (107); Kimi taunts Minna by telling her that Indians stake an informer to the ground and "pop out his eyeball like a grape" (112); Minna is "apparently about as complicated emotionally as a bowl of mashed potatoes," and watching her wake up is "like watching a sluggish white worm poke its head out of an apple" (114); Kimi has "cheeks as plump and ruddy as winter pears" (126); in occupational therapy, Betty notices that a pillow with "green yarn...tied in knots...looked like a sea of old parsley stems" (178); going to a movie at The Pines is accompanied with so many rules it is "like being given a present of one smelt wrapped in the New York Sunday *Times*" (184); when Eleanor flirts with her escort to the movie, she looks "like an eager brown moth about to eat lunch" (185); and Betty's face is "a mottled tomato red" when she gets excited about a possible move to the Ambulant Hospital (201).

In *Anybody Can Do Anything,* food figures continue. The children's bodies against Betty are "warm and soft like dough" (41); Betty's "hands trembled like Jello" as she goes to her first day on the job (46); Betty feels that her boss' continual reaction to her meagre secretarial skills might be similar to "that of a hungry man who day after day opens his lunch box and finds it empty" (50); when one boss gets angry, his face is "pomegranate-colored" (62); two dates for Betty and her sister are characterized by head problems—"one with a tiny head like a shriveled brown coconut" and "one with a huge white melon-shaped dome" (74); employment offices have an "old-lunch-baggy" odor (84); Betty goes to a job interview "feeling as soggy and unappetizing as a leftover salad"

(92); bad singers are described as "thick mashed-potato contraltos" (135); a house has "peach plaster" (137); a speech teacher at nightschool enunciates in such a way that "she looked like a red snapper" (141); and a photo of Mr. Ajax as an infant shows "a doughy-looking little baby" (196).

In *Onions in the Stew*, Vashon Island is described as "green, the intense green of chopped parsley" (10); Mt. Rainier looks " 'just like a dish of ice cream'—strawberry or vanilla depending on the time of day" (11); Scotchbroom is pictured as "pouring in over the hills like a flood of melted butter" (13); houses are "made of banana-colored stucco" (15); "riding in a car without doorhandles on the inside made me [Betty] feel like a canned peach peering out of its jar at the landscape" (28); after a soggy Christmas walk, the family members' "spirits...were like yesterday's dumplings" (68); a rough ride makes one daughter " 'feel like a milk shade' " (164); Lesley Arnold's "skin was the color of good bourbon" (117); and at the peach orchard water for the pickers is meted out "as if it were vintage champagne" (170).

The titles of two MacDonald books epitomize her concern with food items as figures for reality itself. With *The Egg and I*, the choice of the word *egg* is key. Clearly either chicken or egg could have nicely referred to the chicken-ranching experiences around which the book is organized. However, chicken would have limited other suggestive possibilities available with the choice of egg. Eggs cross the boundaries of species and have come to represent fertility in an almost universal sense. Much in MacDonald's first book centers on fertility; the fertility (often frightening) of nature; the prodigality of the garden and orchard; the teeming woods; the large families of the neighbors; even Betty's own pregnancy and motherhood. Egg in the title helps to sum up all these narrative reverberations.

Similarly, the title *Onions in the Stew* becomes an apt and fitting expression for MacDonald's island life. The frontispiece of the book gives the whole quotation from the minor poet and dramatist Charles Divine: "Where hearts were high and fortunes low, and onions in the stew." The MacDonald fortunes are low as they start island life with no down payment yet with high hopes (33). The book itself mirrors a stew-like existence made up of a variety of ingredients almost randomly mixed together. MacDonald organizes her book topically more than chronologically, mixing the narrative into a highly-seasoned whole, each chapter flavored with wit and humor and some pathos, the onions in the stew of island family life.

In an early photograph of MacDonald that accompanies a *Time* review of *The Egg and I*, the newly-famous author is pictured in her island kitchen flanked by her two teen-age daughters as they wash and dry dishes after a meal (99). Betty smiles graciously, almost beatifically, in this mother-daughter culinary role. With MacDonald, the pose was seemingly not merely a publicity gimmick, as a reading of her books underscores. From titles to settings, from characters to figures, the popular narratives by Betty MacDonald reveal her considerable interest in and artistic use of food and cooking.

Note

[1]See Alice Payne Hackett, *70 Years of Best Sellers* (New York: R. R. Bowker Company, 1967) 172-180. The book was on best-seller lists for three years: 1945, 1946, and 1947. *The Plague and I* also made the list of the top ten non-fiction works for 1948.

MacDonald's last two books, *Anybody Can Do Anything* and *Onions in the Stew*, did not sell as well, but both reached a large readership as *Readers' Digest* condensed books.

Works Cited

Hackett, Alice Payne. *70 Years of Best Sellers*. New York: R.R. Bowker Company, 1967.

MacDonald, Betty. *Anybody Can Do Anything*. Philadelphia: J.B. Lippincott Company, 1950.

———. *The Egg and I*. Philadelphia: J.B. Lippincott Company, 1945.

———. *Onions in the Stew*. Philadelphia: J.B. Lippincott Company, 1954, 1955.

———. *The Plague and I*. Philadelphia: J.B. Lippincott Company, 1948.

"Scrawk." *Time* 18 March 1946: 99-104.

Main Course
Part Two

Recipes for Reading:
Pasta Salad, Lobster à la Riseholme, Key Lime Pie

Susan J. Leonardi

I had planned to begin by giving you my recipe for peach upside-down cake, but it's 100⁰ out, and advising readers to turn on their ovens, even if only for half an hour (which is all it takes to bake) seems a bit of gratuitous nastiness. Although I realize that it's only 65 in Chicago, that readers in Dallas all have air-conditioning, and that you may be reading this in Minneapolis in mid-January, I have decided to give you instead my recipe for the only dinner besides green salad and sourdough bread which sounds good to me on hot summer nights. Pasta salad. Don't be put off. This bears as much resemblance to the old macaroni-salad-dressed-with-miracle-whip as Fettucine al Alfredo bears to macaroni and cheese. Pasta salad is lovely, delicious, and takes only twenty minutes from start to finish because you can assemble the "sauce" while you boil the water and cook the pasta.

In a large bowl put a third a cup of good olive oil; a teaspoon of salt; some freshly ground pepper; a handful of fresh basil, oregano, and parsley, chopped (or use half a teaspoon of the same herbs dried); two cloves of garlic, crushed; a bit of finely chopped onion, half a pound of lightly cooked asparagus in bite size pieces (if you have some around. If not, don't worry about it); a couple of tablespoons of wine vinegar; a handful of cheese—parmesan or chopped, skinned brie; and a quarter cup of olives of any sort, capers, marinated artichoke hearts or mushrooms, and/or a combination of these. A few slices of marinated dried tomatoes is a nice addition, too. Cook a pound of linguine, fettucini, or other pasta (just be sure it's imported) until you can bite into it without crunching (al dente), drain, pour into bowl, and toss until the cheese melts. Let it sit for a few minutes, if you're not in a hurry, toss again, and serve. You can leave anything out of this recipe except the pasta and the olive oil.

The remainder of this essay is an attempt to explore the nature of the act I have just performed—the giving of a recipe—which seems to me to have some interesting relationships to both reading and writing. The "nature" I'm exploring here is that of the-giving-of-the-recipe and not simply of the list of ingredients and the directions for assembling

Reprinted by permission of the Modern Language Association of America from *PMLA* 104 (1989): 340-347.

them. Such a list is, in fact, surprisingly useless, even for a fairly experienced cook, and surprisingly seldom encountered. Occasionally one finds this sort of recipe on a rack next to its main ingredient in a supermarket. Sometimes I get offers in the mail for a whole recipe box filled with such lists and directions. But I have never been tempted to buy them, and although I may pick up one from the supermarket rack, I never try it. I think I can safely claim that a cookbook which consisted of nothing but rules for various dishes would be an unpopular cookbook indeed. A recipe needs a recommendation, a context, a point, a reason-to-be.

A recipe is, then, an embedded discourse, and like other embedded discourses, it can have a variety of relationships with its frame or its bed. I want to consider here several examples of such relationships in order to make some claims about the significance of this discourse as a narrative strategy. One example will be my own pasta salad, but at the risk of rushing you through the first course (it serves four, by the way), I would like to consider first a possible dessert, red devil's food cake.

This recipe comes from a widely-used American cookbook, *The Joy of Cooking*, by Irma S. Rombauer, and I begin here because it seems easier to account for a recipe in a cookbook than a recipe in an essay, even an essay in a book about cooking and narrative. *The Joy of Cooking*, first published in 1931, has gone through numerous revisions and reprintings. Bookstores carry the latest edition in three different formats— a cloth bound book, a regular paperback, and a spiral bound paper back. The variety attests to its popularity. The fourth edition, the one I am using here, mostly because it is the one I use at home, came out in 1951. In the "Introduction" to this edition, Rombauer credits her daughter Marion, beginning to be acknowledged as co-author, with the demand for an Introduction. Without one, the younger woman says, how will readers know "that an ingredient in parenthesis means 'optional' and 'chocolate' means the bitter kind unless otherwise stated?" To her mother's concern that readers won't bother with an Introduction, Marion Rombauer Becker suggests, "Perhaps they will if you tell them a story."

The story that Irma Rombauer tells to entice the reluctant reader has nothing to do with cooking. An old handyman with a wooden leg almost drowns in a farmer's ditch and says after his rescue that what terrified him most was the thought that his wooden leg might warp. Rombauer uses this narrative to point out that "correct preparation, cooking and time of food" should be of more concern to the cook than a "decorated cake or a fancy salad." The narrative does not, however, serve the purpose which the daughter is claimed to have had in mind. It does not, that is, tell us that parenthesis means optional and chocolate means the bitter kind. But, although this story fails to do what it was supposed to do, the story's frame—the dialogue between mother and daughter—does tell us that parenthesis means optional and chocolate means the bitter kind. Still, we see that this information has come to us indirectly, perhaps as a sort of compromise between the daughter, who asked originally for a straightforward exposition or definition of conventions, and the mother, who presumably assumed that her readers would realize these things without having to be told. The canny mother, of course, believes no such thing, but by attributing to her daughter the less flattering view of the reader—in need, that is, of explanation— Rombauer manages to impart the information while seeming to think it unnecessary and creating in the process personae for both herself and her daughter. The literality of these personae is borne out in a later, much revised edition of *The Joy of Cooking*, published after the mother's death. In *this* introduction, renamed here "Forward and Guide," Marion Rombauer Becker does away with her mother's coy indirections and explains directly that parenthesis indicates that an ingredient is optional (she continues, some what redundantly, that "its use may enhance, but its omission will not prejudice, the success of a recipe") and that "milk means fresh whole milk; chocolate means bitter baking chocolate . . . [and] condensed canned soup . . . is to be used undiluted."

The daughter thus significantly alters the context of the recipes which follow by removing the dialogue and the "story" (like the recipe itself a mark of relationship between mothers and daughters) and replacing them with straight exposition. This is not to imply that the 1963 edition completely deletes all narrative elements—it would be a much less popular cookbook if it did—but it significantly reduces them, to the detriment, I claim, of the appeal and usability of the recipes in the book. The case of the red devil's food cake is a good illustration of this. In the earlier edition, Rombauer includes this recipe in a subsection called "Chocolate Cakes," which is, in turn, in the section called "Cakes and Cookies," which begins with the enticing and punning claim, "If you wish to be glamorous, become a cake baker. It is a simple accomplishment, rewarding beyond its desserts!" The same section, with an expanded title, begins in the later edition with the more prosaic and obvious, "At weddings and birthdays, a cake can become the center of interest. . . ." But an even more noteworthy change is that in the later edition there is no subsection, "Chocolate Cake," and the number of recipes for chocolate cake has been reduced from fifteen to five. One of the victims of this elimination is "Red Devil's Food Cake."

I lament this not because I am fond of red devil's food cake. In fact, although I have made ten of the fifteen chocolate cakes (plus a couple of others which are, for various reasons, in different sections of the book), I have never been tempted to try the "Red Devil's Food." The reason is important and will become clear with the description of the subsection "Chocolate Cake." It begins with the personal reflection, "After entertaining I often wonder whether it is worth while to bake anything but chocolate cake. What unusual quality gives this particular food such an overwhelming popularity?" Rombauer's enthusiasm for chocolate cake is obvious and contagious. The recipes which follow are, then, all embedded by and embued with this enthusiastic introduction and framed by the assurance that each recipe in the section has been "very carefully chosen...[and is] distinctive in flavor and texture" (608). In addition to the general information about cakes, in addition to the comments about chocolate cake, each recipe begins with a further comment. Of "Red Devil's Food Cake," Rombauer remarks, "Generally popular—but not with me, which is not to be taken as a criterion, 'likes' being what they are" (612).

One assumes that the daughter agreed with this judgment and therefore left the recipe out entirely of her revised edition. What has happened here, however, is that the omission of this recipe has, along with the deletion of the subsection, again significantly altered the context of every other recipe. Such remarks as "not popular with me" establishes the author as an identifiable persona with whom the reader not only can agree or argue but is encouraged to agree or argue. The inclusion of recipes which she herself would not bother with enhances the value of the recipes she does bother with. Each recipe in the subsection helps establish the criteria for the reader's decision about which recipe is, under present circumstances, most appropriate; each recipe thus comments on every other recipe in the section. This embedded discourse, then, elicits reader response in the adventure of cooking in a way that the less thoroughly embedded and commented on recipes in the second edition cannot. This pattern persists. Attempts to include the reader as an active participant are systematically eliminated in the later edition. The earlier edition, for example, has a recipe heading "Open-Faced Apple Pie with Crumb Topping," followed by an atypical format: "A Montana fan writes that she concocted a sure-fire, he-man pie by baking by my rule an open faced apple pie...topped with the crumb mixture given under Apple Paradise" (569). This suggestion encourages the reader to modify and combine and it offers a reward for such modification: inclusion in the next edition of the book. Not only is the modification itself included, but something of the persona of the modifier is included as well—"sure-fire," and "he-man" are, the reader knows by now, not words that Rombauer would use of her own work. Daughter Marion eliminates all this encouragement and fun by eliminating such modifications.

Rombauer even argues with her readers and concedes defeat, though not particularly graciously. Of her inclusion of "Hard-Cooked Egg Cookies," she writes, "I am tired of hearing from friends who felt injured when they failed to find it in an earlier edition" (691). The sense of the cookbook as a cooperative effort, belonging as much to the reader as to the writer is reduced when Marian Becker skirts this controversy over hard-cooked egg cookies by not even mentioning the offending recipe.

Reduced too in the revised edition are references to literary texts and authors. Rombauer describes "Cottage Pudding" as something "Jane Austen would probably have pronounced...only 'moderately genteel'..." She quotes Fielding, rather gratuitously, tells anecdotes of famous cookbook writers and cooks of the past, and refers to Willa Cather's *Death Comes to the Archbishop*. Marion Becker retains only the last mentioned reference but replaces the mother's "kindly prelate"—a rather friendly and familiar phrase—with "the archbishop," thus distancing herself from her mother's fond familiarity with the text. With these omissions and alterations the recipes become, again, less embedded and the implicit claim to literariness established by the intertextual references is almost gone.

Finally, and perhaps most importantly, the shift away from recipe as highly embedded discourse akin to literary discourse moves the recipe away also from its social context. In the earlier *Joy* there is, as in more literary discourse, a cast of characters. Besides the famous cooks, historic personages, and authors illustrated above, we meet in its pages Mary, Jane, Adele, Mrs. Nina Mayer, Ruth Buchan, Faith, and the Rombauer household cook. All these women and more contribute comments and recipes or variations on recipes. Adele, for example, consents to share her children's favorite Christmas cake. The "Foreward" introduces the illustrator, Ginnie Hoffman, as a friend of Marion's, and introduces Marion herself. It repeats the dedication of the former edition to a friend who helped with the work from the beginning and who compiled the "admirable index," Mary Whyte Hartrich. And, as already claimed, the author herself becomes a palpable personality in the earlier edition. She jokes, cajoles, condemns, informs, and reflects—and in the process creates a persona who approaches the first-person narrator of a fiction or autobiography, with faults and failures as well as charms. She says, for example, to introduce the section on sauces, "Having once been asked my opinion of a newcomer I gave it unhesitatingly. 'She is the kind of person who serves *gray gravy*.' " I read this anecdote as a neophyte cook, took it to heart, and have been scrupulous ever since about the color of my sauces. How I would hate to be the object of that sharp tongue. Needless to say, Marion Becker does not reproduce the comment. Nor does she tell us, as her mother does, that the "JellyRoll" is the first cake her mother ever attempted. In fact, one cannot imagine the reviser of this book ever having made either a first cake or cutting remark.

In the earlier *Joy*, the establishment of a lively narrator with a circle of enthusiastic and helpful friends reproduces the social context of recipe sharing—a loose community of women which crosses the social barriers of class, race, and generation. Many women can attest to the usefulness and importance of this discourse: mothers and daughters—even those who don't get along well otherwise, old friends who now have little in common, mistresses and their "help," lawyers and their secretaries— all can participate in this almost prototypical female activity. I will discuss shortly some of the possible nuances of this activity, but first I want to note the dissolution in the Becker edition of this female community. The "foreward" now thanks—in place of various friends—home economists, consultants, and male chefs. The dedication mentions Irma Rombauer but primarily acknowledges Becker's husband John for both support and, interestingly, "crisp creative editing." While I don't mean to imply that Mr. Becker is the villain of the piece, I am suggesting that the intrusion of males into the heretofore women's world has significantly altered the context of the recipes. The embedded discourse which is so clearly gendered discourse as well has a bed of complex, female meanings. The entrance of the male into the bed cannot help but alter those meanings if not drive them out altogether.

Since I so quickly snatched away the pasta salad, you must by now be hungry again, so I will explore those female meanings in two literary texts, one of which, *Mapp and Lucia* by E.F. Benson, will provide the promised main course, Lobster a la Riseholme. You may wonder why, after my sinister implications about John Becker's "crisp creative editing," I have chosen here a male-authored text; I can only say that Benson knows something about recipe-sharing, or, to be more accurate, about recipe-withholding, and that perhaps his gender-confused background made this knowledge possible. His father, holder of that eminently patriarchal position, the archbishopric of Canterbury, married a cousin who he had educated to the role of churchman's wife from her twelfth year; but she, according to Stephen Pile, who wrote the introduction to the new Hogarth Press editions of the Benson books, "shared the last thirty years of her life and a large four-poster bed with Lucy Tait, daughter of the previous Archbishop of Canterbury." Pile adds that "Of Mrs. Benson's [four] children none married, none reproduced..., and all were happier in the company of their own sex." I think Pile's phrasing here is not quite accurate. Benson may not have been physically attracted to women but the only three friends of his whom Pile mentions are all women. These details perhaps reinforce the notion of the constructedness of gender. Like Georgie in the Lucia books, Benson was, on the basis of his writing, surprisingly free of masculinity, a comment which my readers must take in the spirit of the male critics who proclaim a woman writer surprisingly possessed of masculinity—that is, as a compliment. At any rate, the lobster à la Riseholme sequence displays admirable accuracy in ferreting out some of the meanings of the recipe.

When Lucia rents a summer house in Tilling, prior to her permanent removal there, she proposes to treat Tillingite society to her famous luncheon dish, Lobster à la Riseholme, the reputation of which has presumedly proceeded her. Miss Mapp, Tilling's heretofore reigning presence, tries unsuccessfully to anticipate the dish and produces "something resembling lumps of India rubber...swimming in a dubious pink gruel" (553). Lucia refuses to reveal her secret; when Miss Mapp asks for the recipe Lucia changes the subject "without attempt at transition." The narrative continues, "This secretiveness was considered unamiable, for the use of Tilling was to impart its culinary mysteries to friends, so that they might enjoy their favorite dishes at each other's house" (553). The text makes clear, however, that "unamiable" is an understatement. Lucia's refusal is clearly tantamount to a declaration of war. At the Tilling premier of the dish, Miss Mapp takes an extra large helping in order to have a better chance at guessing the ingredients. But the attempt, though it starts out well enough, ends up in Mapp's further frustration. "There was cheese; there were shrimps; there was cream; there were so many things that she felt like Adam giving names to the innumerable procession of different animals" (555). Here the text teases the reader with a partial list of ingredients, just as Lucia teases Mapp with her refusal to reveal anything that Mapp cannot infer from the food in front of her.

Soon, however, the issue fades, and Mapp and Lucia make an uneasy peace, though Elizabeth Mapp has a "chronic grievance against Lucia for her hoarding the secret of the lobster" (561). Another request for the recipe ends in another abrupt change of topic. While the reader is lulled into forgetting about the incident, however, getting the recipe becomes "a positive obsession" with Mapp, and she one day thinks of stealing this "apple of Desire" (588). She sneaks into Lucia's kitchen, takes down a titleless volume, turns the "leaves," and finds "the pearl of great price." The recipe begins with the "luscious words": "Take two hen lobsters."

The diction of these passages is revelatory. First, the dish and the recipe for it take on religious qualities, both good and evil, alternately the animals of Eden, the forbidden apple which leads to the fall, and the pearl of great price for which readers of the gospel are advised to sell everything else. Mapp's quest, then, becomes a religious one: the recipe will give her power (like Adam's), knowledge, and salvation, that is, restoration of her status as Tilling's queen. What female readers of this text already know, that the recipe's social context give it far more significance than a mere rule for cooking, the religious diction provides for readers less aware of the many nuances of recipe sharing.

Another important implication of the diction is the conflation, effected by the phrase "luscious words," of the embedded discourse that constitutes the recipe, and its literal result. This conflation, like the religious language, expands the signification of the recipe and the significance of recipe sharing. Like a narrative, a recipe is reproducible and, further, its hearers/readers/receivers are *encouraged* to reproduce it and in reproducing it to revise it and make it one's own. Folk tales, ghost stories, jokes, and recipes willingly undergo such repetition and revision. Unlike narrative, however, a recipe's reproductibility has, like human reproducibility, a literal result.

This, in addition to the social context, may contribute to the gendered nature of this form of embedded discourse. Margaret Homans in *Bearing the Word* suggests that women may value the literal more than men, because a daughter "retains the literal or presymbolic language that the son represses at the time of his renunciation of his mother." Unlike men, whose entry into the symbolic or figurative order, is, according to Freudian/Lacanian theory, a crisis, womens "entry into the symbolic order is only a gradual shift of emphasis" (13). Men thus privilege the figurative and assign the literal a place as devalued as the place assigned women themselves. Homan's argument is too complex to reproduce (can one reproduce an argument? How literally?) here, and she acknowledges that literal literality (my term, not hers) would hypothetically destroy any text it actually entered. But the relative literality of a recipe is clear, and if we accept Homan's and Chodorow's myth of women's language acquisition, such literality, in part by its analogy to women's own reproductive capacity, which can be both figurative and literal, resonates more significantly for feminine readers and writers.

Elizabeth Mapp becomes, in Benson's text, a kind of map for the reading of the feminine significance of recipes. From the untitled (and therefore relatively non-figurative) cookbook, she quickly copies the rule for Lobster à la Riseholme. Lucia walks in just as Miss Mapp has finished. Instead of the incident's ending as a result of the ensuing confrontation, instead of, that is, the victory of either Mapp or Lucia, the theft of the recipe takes a bizarre turn. The two women suddenly hear "a terrific roar and rush as of great flood waters released" (589). And flood waters they are, right outside Lucia's kitchen. Lucia turns the kitchen table upside down, the two women step into it, and the flood "eddying fiercely round the submerged kitchen, took them out the doors that it had flung wide, and in a few minutes they were floating away over the garden and the hornbeam hedge" (589). The two women, archrivals for the kingdom of Tilling, the instrument of power between them the recipe for lobster à la Riseholme, sail off on the kitchen table in a comic parody of the end of *Mill on the Floss*.

Literally, of course, the flood has nothing to do with Mapp's theft, but juxtaposed so deliberately in the text, the two incidents cannot but seem causally related. Stealing the recipe is not a harmless deed, the text implies, albeit comically, but a matter of concern to Nature herself. The two women who break the feminine code, one by withholding the recipe, one by lusting after it and stealing it, bring in the flood waters and undergo a ritualistic death, together. Mapp and Lucia are gone for weeks. Assumed dead they are given a memorial service, and Georgie erects a cenotaph—on which is inscribed, "In death they were not divided" (602). While the deaths of Tom and Maggie in *Mill on the Floss* imply perhaps the impossibility of the earthly reconciliation of male and female, the unexpected return of Mapp and Lucia implies the possibility of female reconciliations. And not only do the women survive but the purloined recipe as well. In fact, the first Tilling gathering after the miraculous "return of the lost" (617) is a luncheon hosted by Elizabeth Mapp to celebrate her engagement to Major Benjy. The main course is, of course, Lobster a la Riseholme. The rivalry between the woman has thus by no means been lessened by their weeks at sea, but once back the rivalry assumes an established place in Tilling society; Tilling residents in the absence of Mapp and Lucia having realized how much they have come to depend on the rivalry for the life of their town. At the luncheon Lucia urges Elizabeth to come by and look at the recipe again. "Never mind," she says, "if I'm in or not...you will find the recipe in a book on the kitchen shelf. But you know that don't you?" Lucia has, of course, no alternative now but to pretend to generosity (while revealing the theft to all of Tilling). The recipe here, now finally, if reluctantly shared, anticipates the new relationship between the women, no less rivalous, but rivalous with rules, and "rule" used to be a synonym for recipe— a kind of archetypal and model rule, which allows for infinite variations while still maintaining almost complete reproductibility and literality.

Before we leave the main course, however, I would like to call attention again to the scene of the theft. Mapp opens the titleless book, sees the heading Lobster à la Riseholm, and reads "Take two hen lobsters." While the text, then, allows Mapp to copy the rest of the recipe, it withholds the recipe from the reader. We know that there is cheese, shrimp and cream. We know it begins with two hen lobsters, but this recipe is, for us, forever fiction—like Mapp and Lucia (the "two hen lobsters" of the narrative) forever fiction, nonreproductible, nonliteral. And its being withheld calls attention to the fictionality of the narrative itself and establishes thereby uncrossible boundaries between Tilling and real life.

The final text I will consider here, a woman's text, has no such boundaries. Not only does the text invite us to see it as literal but the author herself made clear that the novel, an account of the breakup of a marriage, is a thinly disguised account of the breakup of her own marriage. And since both the author and the erring ex-husband are persons of some national recognition, the text itself not only refuses to decide whether it is cookbook or narrative, cookbook or autobiography, autobiography or novel, but also whether it is journalism or auto-biography or novel—or mudslinging. Key to the confusion is our dessert here: Key Lime Pie. In the film version of *Heartburn* the scene which is the book's climax, is less than climactic. Rachel, having had enough of her husband's infidelities, hits him in the face, in company, with a pie she has brought to the gathering. Critics complained that the old pie-in-the-face routine was only moderately amusing and not particularly dramatic. In the novel, however, the scene really is climactic—and the reason is in the recipe.

Rachel Samstatt, the pregnant heroine and narrator, writes cookbooks, and the cookbooks "do well," in part because "They're very personal and chatty—they're cookbooks in an almost incidental way" (17). We have seen that this "personal and chatty" style was characteristic of the earlier edition of the *Joy of Cooking* and such a style continues to be popular in contemporary cookbooks like Alice Walker's *Chez Panisse* cookbooks. Readers, Rachel knows, like their recipes embedded, so she writes "chapters about friends or relatives or trips or experiences and work[s] in the recipes peripherally" (17). Not only does this description describe her cookbooks, however; it also describes the task in which she is presently engaged, the narrative of the breakup of her marriage. She writes chapters about friends and relatives and trips and experiences— and works in recipes. And these recipes, mostly given, occasionally withheld, assume great significance in the narrative, significance of the sort with which we are now familiar. Rachel has just discovered that her husband is having an affair with Thelma Rice, and although she is upset by his infidelity, "the most mortifying" (6) part of it is that she has just sent Thelma, in response to Thelma's request, her recipe for carrot cake, a recipe that, further, Rachel has worked on after serving it to Thelma, among others, and deciding that it had too much crushed pineapple. To share a recipe—both to request one and to give one— Rachel implies, is an act of trust between women, a trust which Thelma has clearly betrayed. Interestingly, the recipe for carrot cake is one of the two withheld recipes in the narrative, withheld perhaps because, ineffective as a sign of trust between Rachel and Thelma, it could not be expected to carry the weight of recipe sharing between narrator and reader.

There are fifteen recipes in this text, from the sorrel soup touted on the bookjacket to the perfect four-minute egg. The last recipe, the key recipe is, of course, the recipe for Key Lime pie. At this point in the story we have met Rachel's friends, we have shared, step by step, the discovery of her husband's affair with Thelma Rice, and we have in our possession fourteen of Rachel's recipes. The second to the last chapter, in which we also share the "complicated Caesarean" (160) delivery of her second child, ends with a friend's invitation for Rachel and Mark to come to dinner. Betty asks her to bring a Key lime pie. The last chapter begins: "If I had it to do over again, I would have made a different kind of pie. The pie I threw at Mark made a terrific mess, but a blueberry pie would have been even better, since it would have permanently ruined his new blazer, the one he bought with Thelma. But Betty said bring a Key lime pie, so I did. The Key lime pie is very simple to make" (166). The recipe follows.

Rachel then describes shopping for the ingredients, in the course of which she discovers that Mark, after assuring Rachel that his affair with Thelma is over, has just bought his lover a necklace that cost thousands of dollars. Every aspect, then, of this pie has now been revealed to the reader. We have heard the request, accompanied Rachel on the shopping trip, and most important of all, we have been given the recipe. The paragraph in which she actually throws the pie begins, "I looked at the pie sitting right there in front of me and suddenly it began to throb" (175). Since we would expect Rachel's head to begin to throb at this conversation about people's true natures and their infidelities, attributing the throb to the pie reinforces Rachel's identification of herself with the literal result of her recipe. As the child to whom she has just given birth embodies the fiction of the happy marriage of Rachel and Mark, columnist for the *Washington Post*, so the Key lime pie embodies the fiction of the narrator herself. Like Mark Feldman who steals all his friends' experiences as material for his column, Rachel turns event into story and food into recipe. The difference, however, is that with Rachel's recipes, she, and we, can turn it back again. In the end, the narrative itself becomes a kind of recipe—how to survive a disastrous marriage. And the recipe is this: turn it into a story,

Because if I tell the story, I control the version.

Because if I tell the story, I can make you laugh, and I would rather have you laugh at me than feel sorry for me.

Because if I tell the story, it doesn't hurt as much.

Because if I tell the story, I can get on with it (176).

But a story, unlike a recipe, cannot be literally turned back again, or can it? Nora Ephron, by letting us know that this is her version of the story of her disastrous marriage to Bob Woodward, a journalist for the *Washington Post*, hero of Watergate, does in a sense make it literal. Like the recipes, the story is first embedded in fiction, then literalized in the text, then given the possibility of literalization outside the text, not simply as advice but as Nora Ephron's version of real life. The Key lime pie is both dessert and dessert of this story—to modify Irma

Rombauer's pun—dessert for the dinner, Mark's dessert as an unfaithful husband, and the dessert of the text itself, coming as it does to both end and climax. And it is a dessert to which we as readers *have the recipe*. No wonder then that the scene doesn't work in the film where the pie is just a pie like any other pie and not a dessert to which the viewer has access, not a point of trust and inside knowledge between narrator and reader, not a wink from author to reader, not, that is, a pie that can be either eaten, read, or thrown into anyone's face.

The Key lime pie is dessert also to this text, a happy consequence of my decision to give you pasta salad instead of peach upside down cake. But by way of conclusion, however, I want to return for a moment to the pasta salad. It has been this process of thinking about the meaning of recipes and recipe giving that made me want to begin this text with a recipe, to embedd a recipe with a text that meditates on the recipe as embedded discourse. I wanted to begin with a recipe in hopes of doing something of what Irma Rombauer does in the *Joy of Cooking* and what Nora Ephron does in *Heartburn*, in hopes, that is, of creating a persona readers could identify and trust, in hopes of creating readers who would, therefore, willingly suspend for a few pages not to much disbelief as academic skepticism. What importance, after all, can recipes have to the reading, writing mind?

I was interested, too, in my recipe sharing as gendered discourse. Would women readers more easily see my methods and my meanings? Would they more easily appreciate the literality of the discourse, more easily enter into the context of Ephron's narrative, Benson's Tilling, Rombauer's cookbook, and my own reflections? Would the tensions that academic women face between the domestic and the professional make it more or less difficult for them to extend credibility toward a writer who begins with a recipe? A character in Mary Gordan's *In the Company of Women* claims that women professionals who can cook should never let on if they want to maintain professional credibility. Is she right? Do I erode my credibility with male academics by this feminine interest in cooking, cookbooks and recipes?

I also wonder if, like Irma Rombauer, I can prompt you, the readers, to respond; if by speaking the language of the recipe, I can invite answers to these questions for inclusion in subsequent revised editions. Will you, as a result of my attempt at recipe sharing, find it easier to argue with me, to point out better examples than the ones I have used, to send me stories, heartwarming or otherwise, about recipe sharing?

Since the use of the "you" is a convention of recipe giving, I have used it freely here, although I have never directly addressed my readers in any other writing. Do you mind? Will you try my recipe for Pasta Salad?

Who Deserves a Break Today?
Fast Food, Cultural Rituals, and Woman's Place

Kate Kane

Gender differences in culture are usually visible around food. In fast food advertising we can see some of those differences played out as fantasies of consumption. How fast food advertising mediates the real experience of taking a meal, and what that says for symbolic constructions of the body is the subject of this essay. A McDonald's commercial is a text rich in cultural information. I shall argue that McDonald's positions itself as the new Mother in a social order determined by the conditions of contemporary American culture.

When anthropologist Mary Douglas says "Food is not feed" (1977 7), she refers to the conjunction of the social and the culinary. Food is "a blinding fetish in our culture..." of which "our ignorance is explosively dangerous" (*ibid.*). Our ignorance is particularly dangerous for women, since feeding is a primary part of women's role in our culture. It is a problematic but central element of femininity, and as such plays a part in the current crisis in gender roles.

Introduction

Food is also an indicator of social status, according to Douglas (1975). This paper examines a McDonald's biscuit commercial for its messages about women's social status. First I shall analyze the commercial itself, and then discuss the issues it raises from the perspectives of history, anthropology, and psychoanalytic theory. Throughout, a recurring theme is alienation.

It is a commonplace among Marxist scholars that workers are alienated from the products of their labor. I am arguing that alienation also operates in the symbolic economy, the system of ideas and values that circulate in the mass media. In regard to women and food, alienation is multiply coded. Fast food signals a double alienation of women from food (displaced as Mothers) and from our own bodies.

Coming from a tradition in which previous generations of women were indoctrinated with the mysteries of home economics, women today confront a profound ambiguity about our gender role as we renegotiate our place in the productive sphere. As Kim Chernin argues in *The Hungry*

Self (1985), this ambiguity centers on women's relationship to their mothers (and thus to food and separation). The current proliferation of eating disorders is a manifestation of this identity crisis. Corporate solutions to working women's problems, such as fast food, may momentarily alleviate time pressure. But in the long run, they do little more than that, and may compound women's identity crisis in the following way.

As media scholar Michèle Mattelart observes, "liberal media accept several different ways of conceiving women's role and image, but demand some kind of feminine specificity" (1986 23). In food commercials, that specificity is an "eternal" feminine that defines women as primarily maternal. Definition of the feminine as essentially maternal underpins an entire edifice of female stereotypes. At base is the virgin-mother-crone (or whore) dialectic. At end is the Child Molester School of Femininity, in which the adolescent female body and mind are held up as models for all women. The pursuit of this false idol distracts women from confronting the injustices done in her name. This is mental alienation.

In the social discourse on gender roles, many voices argue for their definitions of womanhood. In the television commercial, the interests of particular social institutions converge. Those who have the most to gain from the status quo—the corporate sector, the state, the mass media—continue to argue for the "naturalness" of woman's place in the home. Women participate in the workforce outside the home, but in subordinate positions. Further, domestic labor remains "women's work," whether we do it ourselves or see that it is done. This arrangement generates huge profits for corporations and stability for the state. It also perpetuates and legitimates a mode of consciousness based on sexism. Constructions of the feminine in television commercials are used to sell more than products—they are selling cultural values.

Iconography of a meal

I shall consider in detail one commercial that is a particularly good example of alienated labor, "Your Biscuit Makers." A twenty-one-shot, thirty-second spot, "Your Biscuit Makers" celebrates alienated labor and its social relations (lyrics and shot breakdown are in the appendix.) This commercial presents biscuit-making as a labor of love, not profit.

Description of the commercial. Three young women (two white, one black) sing and dance with rolling pins in a McDonald's restaurant. They stand in formation, salute, use the rolling pins as though they were guns. The song is in the style of the Andrews Sisters. The women dance in the spaces where customers are allowed—in front of the counter, in the "dining room." These performance shots alternate with close-up shots of biscuits in various stages of production. Biscuit production is performed by a pair of white hands and takes only four shots, three of which occur in sequence. Two white male customers in a pick-up truck come to the drive-through (excuse me, drive-thru), where a perky, dimpled, white teenage woman proffers the bag. The older man salutes as he drove off; the woman salutes back.

This commercial masks labor with fun, alienation with social interaction. An army of women makes breakfast. We don't see the generals; the troops are well trained. Eggs marching in formation underscore the "naturalness" of this hierarchy (shot 7). Indeed, eggs are a double code for women and for nature; thus, feminine nature. Men are on their way to work; women are in their place in the kitchen. Not only is there perfect order in this universe, but because everyone is in her/his "natural" place, it is not labor they are performing, it is fun. The harridan wife with a rolling pin weapon has become three cheerful, energetic, nubile teenagers.

While the military metaphor asserts an invisible pecking order, social relations in the workplace here are celebrated as non-hierarchical. Everyone in the place is a private—that is, equal. There is racial "equality" in the makeup of the dancers. The commercial also uses the familiar "you" form of direct address. "We're making biscuits every morning at McDonald's for you." The announcer invites an implied you to "Take breakfast by the hand with a fresh biscuit sandwich," that is, to treat the biscuit as a friend, or perhaps even as a child. In the former sense, McDonald's suggests that "you" the parent solve your breakfast problems at Ronald's house.

McDonald's is a neighborly mother substitute, a friendly place where you get social satisfaction with your meal. Indeed, it is the interpersonal interactions that promise satisfaction. However, there are no interpersonal exchanges among workers. The commercial's social moments mask the alienation of worker from food, worker from consumer, worker from worker. In addition, only food and smiles are exchanged; money is conspicuously absent. McDonald's positions itself as the Mother by association. Who else performs such labor for free? Who else does "it all for you?" Who else "deserves a break today"?

There are some interesting uses of time here. The production of biscuits occurs in close-up, leaving the actual labor off-screen and foregrounding the fun and socializing. Time is of the essence in fast food. Fast service is the obvious motive, but other elements conspire to render fast food an atemporal (=universal=democratic) experience. In its ideal form, fast food is always the same, and so each burger is indistinguishable from any other. The ritualized/standardized procedure, established to minimize time, destroys time. As if to eradicate evidence of one's presence, the fast food consumer throws away empty food containers.

Fast food translates industrial modes of production to the production of food. There is social alienation between the server and the consumer—imagine complimenting the lady behind the counter for the delicious meal, or asking if you can help with the dishes. Indeed, any conversation outside the ritual exchanges ("Is this for here or to go?") would be counter-productive, for it would interfere with the promised speed of service. Industrial values such as efficiency and interchangeability determine the alienated social relations, even though the commercial works to mask alienation. Everyone in the production-consumption equation is interchangeable, except of course Ronald McDonald.

How industrial values made their way into women's education about food is the subject of the next section.

Rationalization of Domestic Labor and the Capitalist Mode of Production

Many of the beliefs we have about food are traceable through the development of the home economics movement, as Laura Shapiro posits in *Perfection Salad: Women and Cooking at the Turn of the Century* (1986). Fast food is the fulfillment of that movement, which sought to rationalize domestic labor, just as assembly-line methods in the workplace were transforming labor. With the growth of industrialization, women were negotiating a new relation to food, setting new boundaries in the kitchen and concomitant ones in the public sphere.

The middle-class women who formed the domestic science movement took as their cause the democratization of American taste. They emphasized nutritional value, predictable results, economy, and appearance in food. Quantification became the order of the day: science had given the calorie as a unit of measure; Fannie Farmer extolled the virtues of level measurement. Armed with scientific analyses of bleach, starch, and baking powder, the new ideal American homemaker was to be a critical consumer. Sanitary kitchens were to produce attractive meals loaded with protein, and working men would be grateful, invigorated, and treat their families properly.

The social formation imposed by industrial society was changing women's relation to men from one based on productive alliances to one based on economic dependence and affectional ties (Ewen 1976). Industrialization split production from reproduction, and assigned gender roles to each. Men exchanged their labor for wages. Women exchanged their bodies in reproductive labor (babies, housekeeping, social maintenance); food was a commodity to exchange in the home. In this sense women stood in the same relations to the products of their labor as did the assembly line laborer—except of course that women had no one at home maintaining them.

Urbanization, a companion to industrialization, further alienated people from their families, creating a void in cultural authority that corporations were eager to fill. Labor-saving technology required new information that grandma could not have provided. Advertising could and did serve as the teacher, in the process creating the role of the consumer "...and establishing a new function for the household in the world of mass production and mass distribution...." (Strasser 1982 245). Home economists taught classes and wrote advice on how to consume. Industrialization's agenda wrought a new scientific approach to domestic labor.

Fast food signals the absolute acceptance of rational cooking. It is efficient, economical, sanitary (one hopes), and—above all—standard. It also signals the absolute marginalization of discourse on the relationship between food and social relations. Fast food is American taste industrialized and democratized. "Democratic" is used here in its vulgar sense, in which it refers not to egalitarianism but to sameness. Not only are hamburgers and fries standardized, but those who produce them are interchangeable parts. See for example the following recruitment flyer from the Evanston, Illinois McDonald's:

McDonald's pay mothers for serving breakfast and lunch. If your family doesn't need you to serve breakfast and lunch anymore [sic], we do!
Come work with us, arrange your hours to fit your schedule and earn extra money. See our manager.

The Mother in the home and the McDonald's server are interchangeable. The flyer implies that the skills women use at home are transferable to the fast food industry. By conflating the mother-at-home and the Mother-server, McDonald's buys the appearance of home cooking. The triumph of form over content is another example of alienation: the illusion masks the slippage between real mother labor of love and McDonald's employee wage labor. This Mother is also a consumer: note that the money she earns is "extra"—not enough to live on, but enough to spend, perhaps taking the family out to eat because she has worked all day and "deserves a break." Her identities as server and as consumer are interchangeable.

So far I have discussed alienation and definitions of the feminine in the text of the commercial and in the historical development of mass production. Next I shall argue for the centrality of gender difference in cultural thought at the mythic level, and finally how that positions this specific commercial within a larger discourse on women and food.

Food, culture, and gender difference

Anthropologists have noted the close relationship of a culture's food practices to the larger social context. While Mary Douglas (1975) emphasizes the symbolic connection of the body human to the body politic, Lévi-Strauss (1983) speaks to the inner workings of language and consciousness. In his analysis of South American myths about the origins of cooked food, he identifies patterns of thought in the stories tribal peoples tell to explain the universe. The myths work on structures based in symbolic oppositions. "The function of signs is, precisely, to express the one by means of the other" (Lévi-Strauss 1983 14). About food, for instance, he notes a universal distinction between the raw and the cooked. Other basic oppositions, such as gender difference, are interwoven to form symbolic patterns that myths represent on several simultaneous levels.

One such pattern that Lévi-Strauss (1977) identifies is a sub-distinction between roast food and boiled food, which invariably revolves around gender difference. The food's relation to the fire is a structuring difference—food that meets fire directly carries one load of signification, food cooked over, but not in, fire carries another. These differences in signification are further coded along gender lines. Men roast and women boil. In some cultures it is the other way around. This opposition is visible in our present-day culture, as in the traditional division of labor that assigns barbequing to men, while women's cooking involves kitchen (indoor, domestic, private) tools that separate food from fire (boiling). The "cave man" myth obtains in associating the masculine with the outdoors (external, public) and an unmediated conjunction of fire and meat.

In American mass culture the roast:boiled distinction appears in the "Burger Wars," ad campaigns for fast food. Burger King, the second-place company in the market, argues that its hamburgers are superior to McDonald's because Burger King "flame broils" its beef. Burger King commercials emphasize the difference between the broiled and the fried. Health considerations aside, this attack is at base a gender difference argument. Symbolically, Burger King positions itself as the masculine player in the competition for fast food dollars. Already coded as masculine by virtue of its name, Burger King seeks to distinguish itself from McDonald's, and does so in the name of "masculine" cookery.

Burger King's campaign is an offensive against the already-positioned first-place McDonald's. McDonald's has achieved its dominant market position in part by constructing itself as a purveyor of social, as well as gustatory, exchange. "We do it all for you" aligns McDonald's with the self-sacrificing eternally nurturing "feminine."

Sexual difference is arbitrary and must be constantly reconstructed in social practice. Commercials are cultural storytelling about food, and their ideological significance touches the very essence of social control—the body. As dominant film practice inscribes woman's body, the male-identified feminine image stands as a sign for male dominance. In this inscription we can see the rhetoric of food as discourse on feminine specificity. No matter how "modern" the times may be, feeding the family is still woman's work. Thus, in its current incarnation, food advertising insists on an "eternal" feminine even as it counsels that women's "equality" is a reality.

Commercials code fast-food restaurants as havens of nourishment, but the emphasis is not on nutrition, it is on fun. Food rituals revolve around excitement and individual identity, not sharing or interacting. What that means for the role of women is impoverishment of the food relationship. No longer a privileged one (with all problems that carries), food relations for women are emptied of sanctity but still loaded with hierarchy. This is precisely the crisis point that Kim Chernin (1985) identifies as women's present gender-role confusion.

Commercials exploit the ambiguity inherent in reformulating gender roles to account for women's necessity to participate in the workforce (like our fathers) and at the same time develop a mature female persona (like our mothers). The mass media continue to identify that mature (sexual) female with the adolescent body, thereby maintaining a constant state of tension that can never be resolved. As Chernin says:

...we are in urgent need of a ceremonial form to guide us beyond what may well be the collective childhood of female identity into a new maturity of female social development. (Chernin 1985 169).

As long as the global conditions of food production require that women perform more than their share of unpaid labor, however, it is doubtful that the mass media will provide any support for a "new maturity" for women. The mass media, and the industries whose interest they represent, must continue to insist on a female identity that is fundamentally domestic and dependent. Otherwise we might realize that our labors of love are underwriting their profits.

References

Chernin, Kim. 1985. *The Hungry Self: Women, Eating, and Identity*. New York: Harper & Row.

Douglas, Mary. 1975. *Implicit Meanings: Essays in Anthropology*. London: Routledge & Kegan Paul.

———— 1977. "Introduction." In *The Anthropologists' Cookbook*, ed. J. Kuper. London: Routledge and Kegan Paul.

Ewen, Stuart. 1976. *Captains of Consciousness*. New York: McGraw-Hill.

Lévi-Strauss, Claude. 1977. "The Roast and the Boiled." In *The Anthropologists' Cookbook*, ed. J. Kuper. London: Routledge and Kegan Paul. 221-30.

———— 1983. *The Raw and the Cooked: Introduction to a Science of Mythology* Vol. 1. Trans. J. Weightman and D. Weightman. Chicago: University of Chicago Press.

Mattelart, Michèle. 1986. *Women/Media/Crisis*. London: Comedia.

Shapiro, Laura. 1986. *Perfection Salad: Women and Cooking at the Turn of the Century*. New York: Farrar Strauss & Giroux.

Strasser, Susan. 1982. *Never Done: A History of American Housework*. New York: Pantheon.

Appendix

"Your Biscuit Makers"

Lyrics
We're making biscuits at McDonald's every morning for you
we're up at dawn
shoopoopydoo
get our aprons on
we're making up the dough
we roll it out
put it in a pan
nobody makes biscuits
like we can
with bacon or sausage
the eggs are fresh
if you say (unclear)
ours are the best
Announcer: take breakfast by the hand with a fresh biscuit
sandwich
Song: it's a good time for the great taste of Mcdonald's

Shots
1. wide shot outside building, sign turns on
2. three women salute
3. open biscuit close up
4. three biscuits close up
5. women spin
6. eggs in formation
7. hands pat dough close up
8. women in dining room flip rolling pins
9. hands roll dough close up
10. cut dough close up
11. biscuits bake
12. women dust hands
13. bacon flips to sausage
14. close up eggs
15. crack egg close up
16. hands take biscuits from oven

17. three-shot through guys in truck to drive-thru window
18. two biscuits
19. hand pats one biscuit
20. older guy salutes, truck drives off
21. girl salutes, smiles

Mourning Among Plenty:
Eating Disorders in the Shadow of the
Persephone Myth

Andrew Stubbs

And still she slept an azure-lidded sleep,
In blanched linen, smooth, and lavender'd
While he from forth the closet brought a heap
Of candied apple, quince, and plum, and gourd
With jellies soother than the creamy curd,
And lucent syrops, tinct with cinnamon;
Manna and dates, in argosy transferr'd
From Fez, and spiced dainties, every one,
From silken Samarcand to cedar'd Lebanon.

(John Keats, *The Eve of St. Agnes*)

Reader, I married him. A quiet wedding we had:
he and I, the parson and clerk, were alone
present. When we got back from church, I went
into the kitchen of the manor-house, where Mary
was cooking the dinner, and John cleaning the
knives...

(Charlotte Brontë, *Jane Eyre*)

A serious house on serious earth it is,
In whose blent air all our compulsions meet,
Are recognized, and robed as destinies.
And that much never can be obsolete,
Since someone will forever be surprising
A hunger in himself to be more serious,
And gravitating with it to this ground,
Which, he once heard, was proper to grow wise in,
If only that so many dead lie round.

(Philip Larkin, *Church Going*)

Analysing the "Snow White" fairy tale as an emblem of the fate of female energy which has become attached to, or closed inside, a male text, Sandra M. Gilbert and Susan Gubar (in *The Madwoman in the Attic: The Woman Writer and the Nineteenth-Century Literary Imagination*, 1979) observe that the warfare between "the two women" ("the one fair, young, pale, the other just as fair, but older, fiercer; the one a daughter, the other a mother; the one sweet, ignorant, passive, the other both artful and active; the one a sort of angel, the other an undeniable witch")

is fought out largely in the transparent enclosures into which, like all the other images of women we have been discussing here, both have been locked: a magic looking glass, an enchanted and enchanting glass coffin. Here, wielding as weapons the tools patriarchy suggests that women use to kill themselves into art, the two women literally try to kill each other with art. Shadow fights shadow, image destroys image in the crystal prison, as if the "fiend" of [Aurora Leigh's] mother's portrait should plot to destroy the "angel" who is another one of her selves. (36-37)

Let us begin with this image of a "glass world" within which women's "creativity" would seem to be both configured, illuminated, and at the same time trapped, and see where it leads. The first question which might be asked concerns the nature of the prison itself. For this trap is characterized not by its being "seen" but by its being seen *through*, not by its appearance, in other words, but by its immanence. Gilbert and Gubar elaborate on a theme which is tied to this: the problem, as they see it, of "the absence of the king from the [Snow White] story as it is related in the Grimm version":

The Queen's husband and Snow White's father (for whose attentions, according to Bettelheim, the two women are battling in a feminized Oedipal struggle) never actually appears in this story at all, a fact that emphasizes the almost stifling intensity with which the tale concentrates on the conflict in the mirror between mother and daughter, woman and woman, self and self. At the same time, though, there is clearly at least one way in which the King *is* present. His, surely, is the voice of the looking glass, the patriarchal voice of judgment that rules the Queen's—and every woman's—self evaluation. He it is who decides, first, that his consort is "the fairest of all," and then, as she becomes maddened, rebellious, witchlike, that she must be replaced by his angelically innocent and dutiful daughter, a girl who is therefore defined as 'more beautiful still' than the Queen. To the extent, then, that the King, and only the King, constituted the first queen's prospects, he need no longer appear in the story because, having assimilated the meaning of her own sexuality (and having, thus, become the second Queen) the woman has internalized the King's rules: his voice resides now in her own mirror, her own mind. (37-38)

To start here, with a more or less archetypal presentation of female conflict, as it is constituted by and in a structure of masculine will, points us in two directions at once. The first is towards the "metaphysical." The other involves language—and we will deal with this aspect in due course. It is not too much of an inductive leap from the notion of an Absent King to that of a Philosopher King or Magician King (such as Shakespeare's Prospero—who dreams himself an island once inhabited by a witch and now by a loving daughter). Underlining the *conceptuality* of this mythical situation allows us to see that the woman inside it is in the position of student, either actually or potentially. The embracing or imbibing of male defined "rules," her interiorization of his desire, is nothing other than the consummation he devoutly desires. Literature is full of examples of women marrying their instructors, "beginning" (perhaps) with Heloise and Abelard and including such diverse figures as Jane Austen's Emma, and Margaret Laurence's Morag Gunn. In these cases, the dialectical tension distributed between mother and daughter is resolved *via* the supremacy of the husband/father. Synthesis, therefore, might be called the bedroom of the whole dialectical process. Philosophy may be nothing other than an elaborate epithalamion, half of whose story is, nonetheless, suppressed. What, though, is the nature or "content" of masculine instruction? In instances such as "Heloise and Abelard," the woman, ultimately, finds her "true" or "authorial" voice by asserting soul over body, the afterlife over the "here and now." Contained within this drama of "which came first" (heaven or earth?) which it is critical that the woman as pupil answer properly is another drama: one of renunciation (of the flesh). Consider Wordsworth's "Laodamia." In this poem, the title character mourns her absent lover, the first Greek to be killed at Troy. (He is slain by Hector in accordance with the oracle's prophecy that "the first Greek who touched the Trojan strand/Should die" [11.44-45].) He is allowed to return to her for three hours, due to the fervency of her prayers. When she tries to touch him, however, he tells her "to control/ Rebellious passion: for the Gods approve / The depth, and not the tumult, of the soul" (11. 73-75).

> He spake of love, such love as Spirits feel
> In worlds whose course is equable and pure;
> No fears to beat away—no strife to heal—
> The past unsighed for, and the future sure;
> Spake of heroic arts in graven mood
> Revived, with finer harmony pursued;
>
> Of all that is most beauteous—imaged there
> In happier beauty; more pellucid streams
> An ampler ether, a diviner air,
> And fields invested with purpureal gleams;
> Climes which the sun, who sheds the brightest day
> Earth knows, is all unworthy to survey.
> (11. 97-108)

If the paradisaical world which Protesilaus is advertising, here, is the glass cage which carnal woman "must" become attached to, we are freed to suspect the duplicitous character of his self-declared spirit-state. What is *revealed* is its sublimity, pomp, heraldry. What is unstated (which has to do with his own self-definition as absence, as spectre) is that it is founded on a death, a mutilation, a castration. The very transparency of the woman's prison is, then, the signature of a lack, a sign pointing nowhere. The closed, privacy of this world is a symbol of the non-ness of its exterior reference: in other words, its powerlessness to regenerate. Its language, which is also its landscape, is caught in a web of inwardly directed significations. But if this verbal system is only capable of situating *itself* (tentatively) and that which it points to is already under erasure, then to speak at all is to invent a disappearance (which the plot of the story afterwards commemorates). This vanishing act is also an act of self-annihilation: a re-creation of one's own death, or suicide (as in Tennyson's "The Lady of Shalott"). One point to be drawn from these speculations is that the woman who dwells in such overly and overtly stylized or, as we might say, "emaciated" worlds as we are describing, seeks not forward (to a new lover) but backward to the recovery of a previous (and therefore predestined or "legitimate") bridegroom (Penelope, Dido). The overwhelming remorsefulness of her story results from its having been violently truncated. The woman exists in the gap between a forgotten (almost) opening and an uncertain end. She tells her story in the interval (womb, wound) of another story, her lover's story, which both sanctifies and incriminates her, unravelling it (Penelope, again, or consider the Maenads' dismantling of Orpheus) as she goes along. Female memory is, possibly, always the memory *that she is* remembering, and subsequently, the memory of loss, from a male point of view (as in Joyce's story, "The Dead"). It is the absoluteness of the interior spacing which she inscribes, or which is inscribed for her, which makes her, ostensibly, two things at once: a new woman (child-bride) who instigates the romantic poet's lyrical effusions, and also the woman he has known before (mother, witch). The woman who exists purely as a conception, as art, as imagination, not reality, is the "bride" of Frankenstein's monster. The network of anxiety surrounding the girl who must be "had" for the first time, *again*, underlies the stories of Fitzgerald's Gatsby and Hemingway's Jake Barnes, incidentally.

Let us see where we are. If a woman's prison is characterized by her inability to procreate (all the while the male is demanding that his wife be the carrier of his memory, his seed, the bearer of his word/scar), in some sense it is an emblem of child-sacrifice. Though it is a landscape crowded with archetypes, omens, foreshadowings, it in fact sets out to deny futurity. Under masculine impulsion, the woman must deny the progeny which most resembles or monumentalizes herself: her daughter.

This is the motif behind Richard Adams' extraordinary novel, *The Girl in a Swing*, and, of course, William Styron's *Sophie's Choice*, both of which depict a woman bound in a rococo world of vanishing, libidinal forms, a kitsch world in which there is no longer any distinction between (mere) symbols and (real) objects.[1]

I have been insisting, somewhat ruthlessly, on the metaphysical/ metafictional dimensions of my subject, here, with a fairly specific object in mind, which will become clearer as we go along. Let me say now, though, that the *abstractness* of the above observations raises a very particular problem: namely, how to translate metaphorical patternings into "reality," how to "ground," as it were, the individuality, the ephemerality of psychic formations in language. I want to show, ultimately, that food itself is such a system of meanings, under certain conditions, and that the whole uncertainty as to whether food is an iconography or a (physical) commodity is an extension of the doubleness and duplicity which binds words themselves. It is probable that the whole attraction/repulsion dynamic investing food as a kind of intelligence, as bridegroom, is linked to its status as communication: one asserts *and* denies the truth-telling or self-mirroring powers of the word. We need, first, though, to retrace our earlier path through this cloudy and, perhaps, forbidding philosophical territory before launching, precipitately, into a more exact consideration of food as text. The key point is that the very restrictiveness of the term "metaphysics" also suggests its opposite: opulence. The banquet which Porphyryo prepares for Madeline in "The Eve of St. Agnes" signifies a contraction of the whole world (as extended in time and space) into the miniature framework of a few lines of verse. Something similar, we might note, takes place with respect to Belinda's *Toilet* (in Pope's "Rape of the Lock"), which also shrinks the wealth of nations to the inner space of an image.[2] (This failure to achieve perspective is taken as a symptom of the error in judgment practiced by the parties to this poem's titanic, yet trivial—entirely interiorized, psychologized—battle of wills.) It is insofar as "metaphysics" is an emptiness masquerading as a plenitude that it lures the female principle into its folds. It completes her in the act of cancelling her out. Or, she fills it herself by becoming absent to her own body, invisible to her outward eye, replaced by another, cleaner, smaller version of herself. We come back to the motif which Gilbert and Gubar designate as the woman's killing of herself "into art." Such an elaborately ritualized (like cognition itself) self-slaying is carried out in such works as Muriel Spark's *The Driver's Seat*, or Margaret Atwood's *Lady Oracle*. Let us, however, take another instance of a woman/girl trapped in the con-game/space of a male-initiated textual intervention into her psyche: Cordelia. Remember that Lear as outcast is himself located between the onset of madness (conceived as a self-dismembering) and his longing for immortality: to have his kingdom returned to him as words. But his daughter, in reply to his measuring, systematizing query ("Which of you shall we say doth love us most?") answers: "Nothing" (I, 1). This "command- obedience couplet," verging, as it does, on silence, prefigures another event later in the play: Lear on the heath, mastering the elements ("Blow, winds, and crack your cheeks! rage! blow!" (III, 2)). Is Lear in charge, though, or is it nature "herself," prior to his presence, independently of his commands, conserving its own silence? Michel Serres adopts a scenario akin to this as a founding myth for scientific thought itself:

If we define nature as the set of objects with which the exact sciences are concerned at a given moment in history, viewed synchronically (which is a restrictive but operational definition), the emergence of physics, in particular, can be thought of only in the global framework of our relations to nature. Now, ever since Francis Bacon's work, these relations have been described, from the heights of his social situation, by the command-obedience couplet. One commands nature only by obeying it. This is probably a political ideology— betrayed by the prosopopoeia—which implies practices of ruse, and subtlety: in short, a whole strategy. Since nature is stronger than we are, we must bend to its law, and it is through this subterfuge that we dominate it. We are under its orders and turn its forces back against order. This is the circle of ruse and productive hypocrisy: nature is a majorant; we try, ourselves, downstream, to majorize ourselves in relation to it. Here one finds again, intact, an ordered structure, a game, its rule (and how best to implement it), the struggle to seize power, and the closed cycle outlined by these moves.

Descartes, after Bacon, picks up the precept: he calls for us to become the masters and possessors of nature. *The impulse to obey has just disappeared.* Baconian physics made science into a duel, a combat, a struggle for domination; it gave it an agonistic model, proposing a form of ruse for it so that the *weak one* would triumph. It transformed science into a game of strategy, with its rules and its moves. But Baconian reason is a weak reason which loses on the first round, because it first resigns itself to obedience. Descartes rejects this, and, consequently, he suppresses the loss. In the relationship of agonistic forces between ourselves and the exterior world, he seeks the means that will permit us to win at every move. "The reason of the strongest is *always* the best." The best reason always permits a winning game. The foundation of modern science is in this word, *always*. Science is a game, an infinite game, in which we always win. Reason is an absolute and constant "optimization." (267-68)

The metaphors overlying Serres' argument resemble our own in curious (perhaps) ways. The dominance of the weaker partner in transactions between mind and nature is tantamount to that of the male principle which attains its majority over the female *by means of* its "own" (i.e., self) wounding. The feast which this "majority" presents to the suppressed component, to the woman as emblem, as bearer of the "loss" (and as *object*), corresponds to the set of objects which are opened at any given time to the scientist's inspection. The issue, here, is whether it is possible, or, indeed, desirable, that one be able to distinguish "symbolic" objects from what we might call, for lack of a better term, "natural" phenomena (which is not a distinction between types of objects so much as a designation of priority). To turn the world into an appearance (a language, a mythology) however, is a tactic which can lead to disaster. For we notice that the palace of art which is so constituted by this transformation, notwithstanding that it seems to denote a timeless structure of meanings and values, is in fact a place of ever-shifting forms: a world not quite alive, but never utterly dead, either. This is, in effect, the world of Blake's "Thel" (which, as Frye tells us, can be derived from Acrasia's Bowerof Bliss in Spenser's *The Faerie Queene*). It is possible to say, that the very "truth" of words is a revelation that nature is absent—or defeated; language captures the world at the instant of its (i.e., nature's) disappearance. This sense of being ambiguously alive in an environment whose placements are always about to die may remind us of scenes in the fiction of Alice Munro, as a matter of fact.[3] With this notion of a world whose death we keep remembering, we enter the realm of magic once again: Circe's, say, or, again, Prospero's. The former envisions the beast in men. The latter, for purposes he is always *preparing* to reveal as the future time of the ending of the play advances to meet him, starts by inventing the world into magic, in order, ultimately to (re)constitute a human community to which Miranda gives the name of "brave new world." But is this not the structures of Cartesian rationalism? Descartes, in his *First Meditation*, reduces the sensible world itself to a fraud, trick, delusion as a preamble to the freeing, in his *Second Meditation*, of the *cogito*. The more open, flexible, grounded, the constructed world of the *cogito* appears to us, the more we are haunted by, at the same time we are subsumed under, its promise of eventual liberation (Ariel). This contract, or binding (depending on what angle we view it from), leads definitively to Kant's categorical imperative in which, as we might say, freedom becomes entirely the property of reason: it is "unsexed," to use Lady Macbeth's word (as is the phenomenal world, or world of "Generation," as Blake called it, itself, once it is made the projection of the human faculty of comprehension). We might be reminded of Geoffrey Hartman's offering, in *Saving the Text*, that Kant's noumenal world (a world without a history, constituted *via* a negation) may in effect be a sublimated form of female energy: still another version of the crystal palace.[4]

Once we adopt Serres' conflictual presentation of the transactions between mind and nature certain terms may be clarified. One of these is the way in which the instruments of thought fail to arrive at that pure denotation of actuality which they so exhaustively and ravenously seek. This situation may engender in us a sympathy with NFL Commissioner Pete Rozelle in his search for a camera angle which will enable him to see, so as to judge, action in football games exactly as it is taking, or has taken, place. The means by which a system of laws is implemented within a random field of events is in fact highly problematic; every metaphysics, it would seem, requires something akin to Kant's "schema" or Jung's "archetypes": i.e., a device which partakes both of the universal order of cognition and its rules, and of the concrete as well. It is not too much, perhaps, to say that this is one of the functions of the feminine, or the female as phallus, by which her status as bearer of inscription, and as prisoner, is cemented. There is, as we may imagine, a paradox here. The archetype, insofar as it designates a point of intersection, prescribes the meaning of a conflict, threatens to resolve the conflict, thus ending the game which can theoretically be played to infinity. Once the intention of a game, and its execution, are brought into alignment, so that the outcome can be predicted, the chance factor in the contest is cancelled, and the game ends, or it is won. The point of all this is that the rules of application of a language to phenomena are not different from the procedure just outlined. Language requires a colonized feminine principle so that the "seed" of meaning may be transferred to a new ground. This process is expansive, fruitful. Any symbolism, to survive, would be required to nourish itself by absorbing into its (organic) structure, its own marginalia: whatever it has initially cast out. Food, since it is that which is both proffered and denied, is the possibility of such a language: woman's "fruit" being the receptacle of signification itself, as well as the manifold of objects which make up "nature." The question is: who is the maker of the rules—in effect, the maker of language? For it is this language which the "player" must accept or reject, if the game, seemingly, is to remain intact.

Thus we come to a consideration of the role of language itself in neurosis. Once a word is seen as the centre of a conflict, operated on by contradictory forces, the very adoption of speech, of writing, of thought, becomes defined as an entry into a game. The crucial choice is one of sustaining the structure of the game, of playing by the rules. Pope's Belinda, we might conjecture, could end her struggle at any time, simply by refusing to play; she chooses to continue, thus delaying the ending of the contest more or less indefinitely. The effect she achieves is that the "epic" she is taking part in (epic being a "giant" form, a form containing all the possibilities of human knowledge and action) is unclosed; through parody it is caught up in an endlessly repeating performance. The *mockery* of the heroic becomes the infinite poem of the infinite game; the "rules" are infinitely applicable to a historical situation through the mediation (vessel) of a woman who rejects, at critical points, the possibility of consciousness that it is all just a game. In a remark which could be a gloss on Belinda's predicament, Marion Woodman notes:

The obese and the anorexic are fighting their battles for consciousness through food—the acceptance or rejection of it. Food in our culture is a catalyst for almost any emotion—a positive way of expressing love, joy, acceptance, or negatively, a way of expressing guilt, bribery, fear of rejection. Food and the quality of the food are at the center of every festival. To share the food is to be a part of the festival; to reject it is to be left out of life. (22)

Belinda's trial opens with a rape, however "trivial"; but the "designifying" process itself signifies a politics—it is a move in the game, even before the game begins (like the *cogito*). There is, in other words, a capitulation, right from the start, without which the game could not be carried forward to its "transcendent" conclusion, which is the woman's reward in heaven. Now, the paradox of all this is that the scarring of the female has no name in itself. It is not important enough to be a "violation" as such. It is, we ought to say, a misnaming. It is, at least, a carving up, a hollowing out. It is also, though, a lesson, a lesson, particularly, in fidelity: Penelope's rejection of the suitors, say. We become aware of woman as the critical mid-point of myth itself, imbibing rules from without which must be enacted in "reality" i.e., in relation to external nature, though the form of action is not affirmation but rejection. Emptiness becomes plenitude becomes withdrawal from the world in a mad version of the birthing process itself as encapsulated by Persephone's history of innocence, abduction and appointment as queen (of the dead).

Woodman cites the comments of an analysand whose very language reflects this dialectical incarceration:

My man once decided to cut my fingernails. I resisted. We fought but he cut them. I felt I could commit suicide. I felt if I couldn't defend myself I would destroy myself. Cutting my nails was an invasion of my person. I cut off my hair. I felt powerless and dead. Then I had to feed myself, I felt so destroyed. (63)

We veer towards an observation made by Angelyn Spignesi regarding the whole interconnection between the anorexic and the world of death.

Spignesi's thesis embraces the realms of recognition as well as treatment of the disease in such a way that both processes become in their way extensions of metaphor, in effect, counter-epistemologies. Of the anorexic she states:

The doctors claim that her frigidity appears through her literal body, her emotional pattern, as well as her sexual response, in terms of absence: no body, cold body, absent emotion, asexuality. Certainly she shows us that she comes from a place beyond personal entanglement and passionate sexuality. From an underworld perspective we would try not to bring her back to life or warm her up but instead could ask what kind of body she lives within. What sort of connections do bind her? Where is the place of blood and heart, in her cold connections? Hillman suggests meeting the cold at its own level in an underworld perspective instead of trying to heat it from above.

Here [citing James Hillman, *The Dream and the Underworld*] is a soul figure who is neither flighty, nor sensuously rippling, nor brooding moods and emotions. Instead the glitter of ice reflects perfection; nothing but crystallized insights and sharp-edged truths are good enough. Desire for absolutism in perfection. The ice-maiden is a terrible taskmaster, frigid and unresponsive; but since her region is on the map of psychic geography, polar coldness is also a place one can be. Therefore the urge to warm the cold and melt the ice (oppositionalism again) reflects a therapeutic effort that has not been able to meet the ice at its own level. The curative urge conceals the fear of the Ninth Circle, of going all the way down to those depths that are so quickly and surely called psychotic.

This [Spignesi comments] allows us to see that perhaps here we have a soul figure living in the house of death, a Persephone who brings the realm of the dead to waking life. Instead of attempting to follow the lady into soul and to see her coldness in terms of its ancient connection to the soul, since 1874 with Gull and his hot packs doctors have been trying to poke, pry, and even, with electroshock, fry her out of her frigid nature. The fact that she has been seen for a century in terms of negatives, absence, and loss indicates more than anything else the culture's neglect of death and the failure to recognize the relation of the female to death. (11-12)

I quote these passages at length in order to dramatize the ontological aspect of the problem. The body (of the anorexic) as the literal yet vanishing trace of an entire cosmos of signification.

Blake had a name for the married state (tripartite, dialectical) which could also be an entrance to the place of death: Beulah. Derived, as Frye tells us, from Homer, this side had two entrances, a southern and a northern one, one for the gods and one for mortals. The married state, it would seem, participates in two orders; the supernatural on the one hand, and the (merely) "carnal" on the other. Meaning and its "generation" may be a completion to be strived for, perfected, but it could easily turn out to be just another commodity, a propaganda, as it were. "Knowledge", in the most absolute, religious, sense of the term, may not be a *true* home (after all), but rather a substitute for that home, which must always be defined *elsewhere*. This is what any language reveals to us, once we swallow it. Beulah, at any rate, that garden of earthly delights, is also a landscape planted with symbols: trees of knowledge of good and evil which, if they are chosen at all, can only be chosen in the flesh. This leads us, perhaps, to a kind of *felix culpa*; but it is worthwhile to remember that to the remorseful gaze of the twentieth-century thinker, whose bondage to language is history, the other name of the earthly garden, as *Sophie's Choice* would teach us, is Auschwitz.

Notes

[1]An analogue to these fictions is William Blake's "The Book of Thel", in which

a female voice is trapped in the "garden" of her own mortality. Thel's garden is "Beulah" and as Northrop Frye situates this place in Blakean symbolism (*Fearful Symmetry: A Study of William Blake* (Princeton: Princeton University Press, 1947, rep. 1969).:

"...Beulah is a place of perilous equipoise, being as it is the region of the imagination which falls short of the disciplined unity of art. Eden is "human"; Beulah is "sexual", the region of passive pleasure, a Freudian land of dreams in which all images are erotic. Like its prototype in Spenser, it is a world where forms dissolve and substance does not, in contrast to Eden, where the reverse is true. As such, Beulah provides only a temporary escape from the world, not a permanent creation out of it. Wonder that does not stimulate art becomes vacuity: gratifications of appetite that do not build up a creative life become destructive. Everything that enters Beulah must quickly emerge either by the south or the north door; up to Paradise, or back again to this world. Bunyan includes Beulah in his vision, but there is also in Bunyan an "Enchanted Ground," a place of great spiritual danger. Spenser, too, has both a Garden of Adonis and a dangerous Bower of Bliss. In the latter we can see the perils in the state of imaginative passivity that led to the original Fall" (pp. 233-235).

[2]See Alexander Pope, "The Rape of the Lock":

And now, unveiled, the toilet stands displayed,
Each silver vase in mystic order laid.
First, robed in white, the nymph intent adores,
With head uncovered, the cosmetic powers.
A heavenly image in the glass appears;
To that she bends, to that her eyes she rears.
The inferior priestess, at her altar's side,
Trembling begins the sacred rites of Pride.
Unnumbered treasures ope at once, and here
The various offerings of the world appear;
From each she nicely culls with curious toil,
And decks the goddess with the glittering spoil.
This casket India's glowing gems unlocks,
And all Arabia breathes from yonder box.
(I, 121-134)

[3]Consider the following passage, from "Marrakesh," *Something I've Been Meaning to Tell You* (Toronto: McGraw-Hill Ryerson, 1974):

"She saw what beauty was, all right; she acknowledged the dappling shadows on the grass, the gray sidewalk, but she saw that it was, in a way, something to get round. It did not matter greatly to her. Nor did familiarity. Those houses across the street had been across from her for forty years, and long before that, she supposed, they must have been casually familiar to her, for this town had been Town to her when she was a child, and she had often driven along this street with her family, coming in from the country, on the way to put the horse in the Methodist Church shed. But if those houses were all pulled down, their hedges and vines and vegetable plots and apple trees and whatnot obliterated, and a shopping centre put up in their place, she would not turn her back" (p. 162).

[4]See Geoffrey H. Hartman, *Saving the Text: Literature/Derrida/Philosophy* (Baltimore and London: The Johns Hopkins University Press):

"Derrida's interest is chiefly in this phantom mother, or her discourse, which he prefers to call a *calcul* because it is at once complex and mute. The only words we have are Genet's own and perhaps the fact so determining in Sartre's eyes, that Genet as a boy was accused of being a thief and took his identity from that. Derrida agrees that the insult, literalized, allowed the child to give himself back to his "true" mother, to identify with what is really her condition, that of having to draw an identity out of being abandoned. Abandoned in the absolute sense: *verworfen* or *geworfen* without husband, father, father in heaven.

Derrida projects her image as a person without "Eigentlichkeit" and therefore also without a sense (and certainly not a bourgeois sense) of "Eigenschaften" or properties: "The mother is a thief and a beggar. She appropriates everything because she has nothing that is her own [*en propre*]" (170b). He makes her, wittily, a Heideggerian 'Thing,' even a 'Ding-an-Sich.' This vastated being, however, is not filled with grace, like the Virgin, but with ersatz; she is immaculate because she can't be stained by any gift, wound, or word. These are mere fillers of her nonessence, decorative substitutes, votive nothings. Like certain phantoms she has the capacity of incorporating all the names, abusive or exalted, magnifying or mourning, her son bestows until she becomes, in this double function of identity-vamp and muse, what is called, untranslatably, a 'bourreau berceur' " (pp. 105-106).

Does Kant's noumenal world become that world of the muses which Nina Auerback designates as the female in *Communities of Women: An Idea in Fiction* (Cambridge and London: Harvard University Press, 1978):

"As the Muses determine a hero's ultimate survival through their control of the mind, another group of sisters determines the pattern of his life: the three Fates run human and divine destiny through their fingers, at one with an unspecified power Zeus cannot controvert. In this vision of the world, solitary women together are both beyond the pale of human experience and at the heart of it. Their exclusion from civilization seems at one with their control of mind, life, and immortality. A triad of sisters begins as an image of maimed and outcast pathos and ends as a unity of force neither god nor hero dare invade" (p. 5).

Works Cited

Frye, Northrup. *Fearful Symmetry: A Study of William Blake.* Princeton: Princeton University Press, 1947.

Gilbert, Sandra and Susan Gubar. *The Madwoman in the Attic: The Woman Writer and Nineteenth-century Literary Imagination.* New Haven: Yale University Press, 1979.

Hartmann, Geoffrey H. *Saving the Text: Literature/Derrida/Philosophy* Baltimore: The Johns Hopkins University Press.

"Marrakesh," *Something I've Been Meaning to Tell You.* Toronto: McGraw-Hill Ryerson, 1974.

Serres, Michel. "The Algebra of Literature: The Wolf's Game," in *Textual Strategies: Perspectives in Poststructuralist Criticism*, ed with introduction by Josue V. Harari. Ithaca: Cornell University Press, 1979.

Spignesi, Angelyn. *Starving Woman: A Psychology of Anorexia Nervosa.* Dallas: Spring Publications, 1983.

Woodman, Marian. *Addiction to Perfection: The Still Unravished Bride.* Toronto: Inner City Books, 1982.

Creation and Annihilation:
Uses of Food in Contemporary French Narrative

Lynne L. Gelber

It is possible to trace writings on food and its relation to literature to the earliest civilizations from which we have written records. In fact, food was likely the cause of the rise and demise of most cultures. Samuel Kramer proposed that the first civilization to invent an alphabet, Sumer, arose because of the need for fertile land on which to grow barley, the staple of the Sumerians' paste, bread, and beer. And these people provided the first writing on food, a Farmers' Almanac.

The geography of France has always fostered an unusually wide variety of food in the diet. The richness of resources became the subject of many narratives and at least since the 18th century France has enjoyed a reputation for having the finest cooks in Europe. What has happened to that reputation? Contemporary French narratives reveal the contradictory nature of that reputation just as they reveal the contradictory impulses of society and the creative process. This study explores how food, that which sustains living creatures, and cuisine, the transformation of food, serve as metaphors for both creation and annihilation. Culinary texts for the mass market, the essays, short stories and novels of Marguerite Duras and Marguerite Yourcenar, and two contemporary films will demonstrate how, as metaphors for creation and/or annihilation, narratives derive from paradoxical sources which are at once 1) complex and simple, 2) communal and individual, 3) poetic and scientific.

Analysis of the culinary mass market is one way of examining the contradictory nature of society and the creative process. Narratives such as we find in *L'Express* or in cook books produced for the middle class provide examples. Louisette Bertholle, known for her collaboration with Julia Child and Simone Beck, wrote recipes in *French Cuisine for All, (Une Grande Cuisine pour Tous)* and in her columns for the daily paper, *France Soir*, which try to simplify older, classic dishes. She promotes the scientific by suggesting new techniques using food processors and other modern machines. She also promotes the simple by frequently using words like "alléger," "simplifier," "pas trop," or "pas tout" to express the need for moderation in the use of seasonings or the arrangement

159

of food on a plate. "Lightening up" for her means removing animal
fat which liquefies in the cooking process or avoiding garnishes which
are not useful (edible). She appears to be balancing on a tightrope,
avoiding the fall which leads to destruction. The negative tonality reminds
the reader of the dangers of eating and of the spell the successful chef
must cast. Her role thus becomes that of magic maker helping the reader
and cook to create illusions, to be poetic. For example, she explains
the decorative effect desired in the presentation of slices of roast beef,
artfully displayed on a heated metal oval platter using garnishes with
parsley carefully arranged along the outer edges of the plate. She also
promotes maintaining the integrity of food as much as possible through
preservation of its original nature. Consequently, she prefers grilling
fish, so that we can 'rediscover' the flavor, or poaching fish, whereby
salted water resembles the natural habitat of the live product. She also
calls for the simplification of menus and recommends a hostess focus
on the main course, omit dessert, and serve a good cheese afterwards.
To justify this simplicity she appeals to the communal. It is acceptable
to be simple in presentation because, she notes, desserts, like first courses,
are done less and less often (397). While recommending "not too much"
sugar or salt, "not too many" spices or condiments, she nevertheless
insists that they be carefully chosen, that creativity come in the choice,
that the personality of the dish or of the cook become manifest in the
choice. She complains that excessive use of spices and careless mixing
of flavors are the bane of modern cookery. Still, she includes recipes
for the classic sauces which, however, she tries to simplify by providing
helpful hints for successful preparation or by the inclusion of recipes
using the products of science, prepared products like canned fruit for
a dessert topped with a Sabayon sauce or frozen peas for vegetable puree.
Finally, although simplicity is the effect she desires to create in the end
product, beneath the ease of preparation and the light effect she tries
to create, the theory of the techniques, she insists, is not easy, except
in appearance. It is complex and based on scientific principles,
technologically advanced methods of preservation, packaging, and
efficient delivery to the ultimate consumer.

Louisette Betholle's work is typical of the contemporary mass market
narratives. They continue to use the special vocabulary of the cooking
world inherited from the 18th-century writings of La Chapelle, their
cookbooks are still arranged in the diachronic sequence of the meal with
separate chapters for basic techniques fashioned after Francois Marin's
Les Dons de Comus ou les délices de la table printed in Paris in 1739,
where there is discussion, meant for the amateur cook, of the chef's tools
and frequently used sauces. And, like the Jesuit priests Brunoy and
Bougeant, who wrote the preface to Marin's work, masters of "nouvelle
cuisine" since the 1960s profess a desire to make simple, attractive recipes

available for the ordinary home. In fact, the narratives of the last twenty years only admit to inspiration reaching back to just before the second world war with Fernand Point, the gray eminence of nouvelle cuisine who owned La Pyramide in Vienne (Isère), and whose immediate disciples in the 1970s include such chefs as Paul Bocuse, the Haeberlin brothers, Roger Vergé, Claude Peyrot (the only one of this group from Paris), Alain Chapel, and the Troisgros brothers, as well as Michel Guérard. It was these chefs who declared war on heavy sauces bound with flour or other starches passed down from Taillevent, ritual decoration of plates and camoflage or prepared food influenced by the architectural creations of Caréme in favor of what, in their mind, was a return to the nature of the ingredients. They admit to borrowing heavily from provincial and from home or "women's" cooking. They also abjure the Escoffier-style division of labor in production or the finishing of a dish at the table in favor of uncomplicated platters presented as finished products for which the chef would take complete responsibility from start to end. They prefer the apposition of contrasting colors and textures rather than the subtle blending of flavors and nuances of colors of earlier methods. The insistence on simplicity demands freshness and high quality of all ingredients, they declare. Yet this kind of cooking also demands precise timing and delicate sauces which enhance without masking. "In becoming simpler and lighter, the cuisine of the chef has made a 'rapprochement' to that of 'ménagère', the French home cook," state Jean and Pierre Troisgros (10). There are of course the obvious excesses of this style of cooking which Rudolph Chelminski calls "interior decorator silliness of the 'new' cooking" (268) or "a wolf in sheep's clothing, an apotheosis of sophistication disguised as common fare" (84). Yet Michel Guérard calls himself a poet, making marriages between unexpected food products, using simplicity and imagination (Leby 54). But as Jean-François Revel points out, Carême's cuisine at the beginning of the 19th century was also a complicated process whose result was meant to be "very simple and immediately obvious" (258).

Since the individual skill of the cook or chef depends on the appreciation of the diner who consumes and ultimately annihilates the creation, the person or group for whom the poetry is created is enormously powerful. Consequently, both the individual cook and the mass producer rely on the written record where the poetry can be preserved. Although the written recipe is not synonymous with the food eaten, the creator can depend on his or her own written skill or that of the community to save the product, the creation, and the artistry of the chef from annihilation. Publicity thus becomes paramount and, used successfully, it has helped bring about the development of McDonald-type fast food outlets with their limited menu and economic efficiency. Production of this kind of food relies on quick appeal. Its recipes use food processors and other "modern" conveniences. Its quality depends on modern production like that of the French company Davipêche whose ads proclaim it to be "le spécialiste du poisson surgelé en mer" (Chevalier, 152-153).

Current consciousness of caloric and nutritional values in recipes and techniques which insist on the use of fresh vegetables, chicken, and fish, and which strive to retain the flavor of their basic ingredients by replacing heavy starch-based sauces of constructed dishes are nevertheless based on complex procedure and are creations destined for annihilation. Still, with the internalization or universalization of food due to forced migrations, tourism and desire for variety since at least the 19th century with "exotic" influences in France from Asia, America, and North Africa, one can easily see the coexistence of the complex and the simple, the communal and the individual, the scientific and the poetic.

The works of Marguerite Duras reveal similar existents. They are particularly expressive of the annihilating strain of modern life, and food is among the many metaphors she uses to depict this. *La Douleur* offers examples of the struggle, as Julia Kristeva says, "to rediscover the vital forces of life" (144). When D, the chief Resistance fighter, would have the female narrator participate in life, he makes her go to a restaurant with him but she cannot eat. The restaurant is full, but everyone around her talks of the end of the war and German atrocities. "Je n'ai plus faim. Je suis écoeurée de ce que mangentles autres. Je veux mourir. Je suis coupée cu reste du monde" (55). She considers herself a part both of the race of victims and of the race of torturers, "de la faim des fosses communes de Bergen-belsen..." (57). When Robert L. returns from Dachau, his first direct statement is a reference to food. " 'Qu'est-ce que c'est?' On le lui avait dit. A quoi il était? Aux cérises, c'etait la pliene saison. Je peux en manger?'..." (65). Rejoining society and life becomes for him solely a question of eating, but society withholds, it interposes its science, it prevents uncontrolled eating in this war hero, this poetic symbol of a fighter for creative forces, "Parce qu il y a déjà eu des accidents dans Paris à trop vite faire manger les déportés au retour des camps" (66). As a result, he stops further verbal communication, he stops trying to make connections between the past and the present, he stops seeing those around him. "Son visage s'était recouvert d'une douleur intense et muette parce que la nourriture lui était encore refusée, que ça continuait comme au camp de concentration. Et comme au camp, il avait accepté en silence" (66). The profound contradiction is that he must eat to live but eating is annihilation. "S ll avait mangé dès le retour du camp, son estomac se serait déchiré sous le poids de la nourriture,..." (67). Thus eating becomes a metaphor on an individual scale for the war fought on the societal level. As the battle between life and death mounts, his temperature rises, and, as long as death is winning, his hunger disappears. His friends first feed him a bouillie, gruel for an infant, and then when the fever abates, meat juice. As he recovers they add more and more solid foods, "Il mangeait. C'était une occupation qui prenait tout son temps. Il attendait la nourriture pendant des heures. Il avalait sans savoir quoi" (72). He loses all identity. He becomes Hunger. He is a void to be filled and an existent filling the void. He becomes the mysterious function of the universe. He exhibits no preference for any particular kind of nourishment. "Il avale comme un gouffre" (73) with no connection to those around him. And as Robert begins to eat, the narrator's hunger reappears as well (79).

In *Waiting for Godot*, Estragon and Vladimir eat in order to assuage their hunger, but they discuss what they eat in order to pass the time and to give order to their lives. At the end of *La Douleur* in "L'Ortie brisée," the stranger and the child observe Lucien eating white beans from his mess kit with bread and wine. His gestures have "la lenteur réguliere d/un spectacle,... celle d'une lecture insidieuse et vaine" (188). When the noon siren sounds, a signal to stop work for lunch, Lucien stops eating and addresses the stranger for the first time. He states the hour as he consults his watch. He remarks how, "Ca fait toujours peur, un sale bruit" (189). The text has already alerted the reader to the link between siren and war, between eating and annihilation, with the characterization of the sound of the siren as "très triste, pareille à celle des alertes de la guerre" (189). The war is decay and dying. Its indications are all around these people as they sit in the road amidst the stench and debris. The mechanical, slow eating is barely a signal of life, yet it is closely observed, but does not suffice to remove the pain of life and the memory of war, suffering or alienation. Shared words become, then, the only means to deny death. "L'étranger ne pense pas à ce qu'il dit, il parle machinalement, mais à la place de se taire, à la place de mourir...Il retient enfermé en lui une chose qu'il ne sait pas dire, livrer...Il ne sait pas comment on parle de la mort.... Tous ces efforts sont faits pour éloigner le silence" (191). The only thing the stranger and Lucien share is the act of smoking in silence, of occupying adjacent spaces at the same time. But the pain of their existence is in their inability to create meaningful conversation or to share food or positive emotions.

This contrasts dramatically with "Ter le milicien" where sharing food is the most positive value in any individual. In this story, food links everyone in the community, collaborators and resistance fighters alike. Tuna is the main food available since D and Beaupain have recovered a thousand cans of it from a German P.C. to serve all the centers where suspected collaborators, among them Ter, are being held by their French captors during the first days after the liberation of Paris. The Spanish are characterized by their habit of eating tomatoes with their tuna. The French Resistance fighters are, ironically, the least heroic or communal. They complain because there is no wine and a major fight erupts among the men when a round of Gruyere cheese found in a German truck disappears. The pettiness of the resistance fighters squabbling over food, cheating the prisoners out of their rations and torturing their captives contrasts dramatically with Ter who had joined the militia to obtain a gun which he used to go hunting in the country, not to combat his countrymen during the Occupation. When he asks for extra bread and cards, he shares all with his fellow prisoners. He is the favorite of his captors with his lust for life, his naive acceptance of the justice of society, the complete lack of individual pride, a true "coeur simple," "rien que de l'enfance" (181).

Whereas the food metaphors in *La Douleur* deal mainly with the conflict between the individual and society, the collected articles in *Outside* extend to the contradiction between the communal and individual, the scientific and poetic. Duras characterizes these articles as "alimentaires." Food in these essays reveal national character, social class, and individual alienation. The brittle syntagmas of "Le Sang bleu de La Villette," for example, demonstrate the sharpness of the butchers' instruments and the mercilessness of the process. The essay points out the centrality of slaughter to individual and communal life. All can derive nourishment from the slaughter. After work the butchers drink the blood they have let us a delicacy and the aristocracy, says Duras, after a night on the town, joins them at dawn. Duras also points out how the violent process becomes acceptable. The meaning of the word for those who evoke tender emotions and for the instruments used for tenderizing meat are both implied in the French, 'attendrisseurs,' which appears in a sign over the door of a knife and cleaver manufacturer which reads, " 'La maison fait les attendrisseurs' " (47). The pun actually dulls our senses to the pain of the violence of this trade. "Et puis la S.P.C.A. qui sommeille en chacun de nous se réveille. On s'attendrit. Et le second degré de l'attendrissement nous verse à la littérature" (47). Duras further shows the murderous violence is regulated by the State to dull the sense of reality. The structure of the passage reinforces this sentiment. It is veal, not the butcher, which is isolated. It deserts Paris and La Villette as a result of the decentralization of transportation, of the widening group of people engaged in the slaughter, preparation and sale of foodstuffs, isolated by scattered economic corporate trusts striving for material efficiency. Food preparation and dislocation in the narrative both reflect a society striving for simplicity in complex organizations inspired of the provinces where foodstuffs sell for higher prices and where the distributor has greater freedom from state control.

The narrative structure of "La Soupe aux poireaux" also reveals through food and cuisine the contradictory nature of society and the creative process. Duras shows how lightness, clarity, and health, fostered by the provinces and middle class, are signs of individual alienation and suicide. The essay begins under the sign of doubt. The first verbs are "croit savoir" and "paraît" (275). In order to retain the flavor of the leeks, the basic nature of the soup, and the simplicity of the preparation, the essay recommends against the overcooking and reheating common in restaurants. It speculates on the middle class origin of a soup that could nourish and warm, yet be light and tasty, green and evocative of its health-giving qualities. The images become rawer, more suggestive of the hardships of life, "vulgaire comme le manger pauvre, le travail des femmes, le coucher des bêtes, le vomi des nouveau-nés" (276). Making the soup becomes, finally, the statement of life and human activity between two annihilating alternatives, between doing nothing and suicide.

Moderato Cantabile is a well known example of the centrality of food and eating in the narratives of Duras. Mme. Desbaredes, wife of the import-export director of the Fonderies de la Côte, disengages from her middle class society by drinking wine publicly in a working class cafe with Chauvin, an out-of-work laborer, and then by refusing to participate in the rituals of a formal dinner at which she is to be the hostess. Her alienation is not hers alone. The paradox of the title, meaning 'with constraint and with freedom,' is apparent in the table manners, the food served and the reaction to it. The polite, well dressed women at dinner do not just eat, they devour the chilled salmon (130). As Dina Scherzer pointed out, the dinner is the only scene which takes place in Mme. Desbaredes' home (596). It should be a moment of communion, a playing out of a series of rituals attendant upon the creation of a work of art, the slow sipping of the fine Pommard, as opposed to the swift downing in one gulp of the nameless wine in the cafe where she meets Chauvin. Such a dinner should include communal rituals like the appreciative commenting upon the delicate appearance of the duck à l'orange or the cold salmon instead of the insistence upon the violence of the killing of these "victims" (133), in order to make this meal possible or the reference to the duck "mort dans son linceul d'orange" (126). The isolation of Mme. Desbaredes and her rejection of the middle class meal is forcefully apparent when she refuses to eat and when she vomits up the meal afterwards.

Several of Marguerite Yourcenar's narratives also use food to express the opposing forces of creation and annihilation. But where denial of food is alienation for Duras, willful resistance to certain kinds of food, is empowering for Yourcenar. It is what sets apart many protagonists in her narratives. There are frequent references to mistrust of large quantities of food served at a meal, of heavily spiced sauces, stews, and of roasts of whole pieces of meat which are preferred by those with whom the protagonist associates. Nathanael, central figure of *Un Homme obscur*, is Dutch, raised among the English in Greenwich. To characterize his separateness the text focuses on the food his mother prepares. It is markedly different from the "boeuf trop cuit" (903) of their English neighbors who, for their part, wouldn't touch the Dutch vegetable stews. The mark of belonging then is the sharing of food, as Nathanael does with his girl friend, Janet (904). When Nathanael is among the North American Indians he is again isolated from society. He observes and enumerates the many methods by which the Indians kill game. While he admires the fact that they take only what is necessary for sustenance, the tonality and context show the disdain he has for eaters of meat, grease, and constructed dishes (915). He abhors the violence necessary in the killing. He prefers bayberries, strawberries, blueberries, vegetables, cheese and water to the rabbits killed with stones or the venison impaled on spikes. Curiously, when Nathanael was a cook on board an English frigate, any mention of what he cooked or the methods of preparation is absent, but later when he reads Ovid's elegies, the pleasure of the text is a gustatory one. "Il s'y plut: on recontrait parfois au détour d'une page quelques vers coulant comme du miel, un assemblage de syllabes qui laissaient dans l'âme un arrière-goût de bonheur" (927).

In *Anna Soror*, control over food is power over life. Valentine, like Nathanael, eats only fruits and vegetables (861). At her death, mourning takes place in the great hall from which all the farm products have been removed.

Hadrian, of all Yourcenar's characters, is the most interesting willful abstainer from food. His mistrust of food served in orgiastic quantity contrasts markedly with the common manners of his Roman court. Abstemiousness here becomes a clear sign of individual power. Food controlled, eaten without additives and in small quantities is an indication of Hadrian's discipline. It derives from his ability to survive on less as much as his understanding of Greek, of the non-Roman culture, of that which is other. The paradoxical nature of less is more is reminiscent of the cuisine minceur of Michel Guérard. It is another exploration of the individual alienated from food, often a vegetarian, whose simple food tastes isolate but also empower. These narratives point to the question of what is power and what is narrative. In Yourcenar's work those characters able to survive on less can define themselves apart from the society in which they exist. Their will affirms their selfhood and their self-abnegation is at once a transcendent act and a step towards self destruction and annihilation. But Hadrian knows the dangers of extremes and avoids them. He remarks that over-eating is a Roman vice (16), that the ordinary rich man would be expected to boast of gorging himself and the poor man to dream of stuffing himself, "s'empiffrer," on days of feasting. Hadrian prefers the simpler roasting preparations of army food to the fried food of the Roman marketplace for which

Yourcenar uses words like "répugnance" and "ennui." On the other hand, a positive, even religious, tonality marks the simpler foods. "Manger un fruit, c'est faire entrer en soi un bel objet vivant, étranger, nourri et favorisé comme nous par la terre; c'est consommer un sacrifice où nous nous préférons aux choses" (16). Hadrian admires the frugal soldiers and farmers smelling of garlic rather than the long official dinners of Rome. The narrative contrasts the rustic "fringale" to the Romans who "s'étouffent d'ortolans, s'inondent de sauces, et s'empoisonnent d'épices (17). A simple succession of courses, rather than the "pell-mell" presentation of a Roman dinner served in "une confusion détestable où les odeurs, les saveurs, les substances perdent leur valeur propre et leur ravissante identité" (17), is reminiscent of the complaints of Guérard, Troisgros, and Bertholle. Hadrian also prefers the fresh food of the provinces, game cooked immediately after being taken, fish freshly caught from the sea. The opposite kind of food is Roman and it becomes a metaphor of decadence. While there is appreciation for the art involved in the creation of a rare dish, the text uses words like "confectionner" and "savant dosage" to express them and such dishes made in Rome as a spiced pheasant pâté stuffed with ham contrast with dishes made "sans trop de complications" in the provinces and which are characterized as "pure" or "divinement propres" (17).

The text points to the dangers of total abstinence, which Hadrian rejects as well. He declares he would rather eat "oies grasses" his whole life than be accused by his eating companions of "une ostentation d'ascétisme" (19). He has even eaten dried fruit and has drunk his wine very slowly in order to hide from his guests his dislike for the constructed dishes which he serves at his own banquets only to please them. Finally, Yourcenar portrays Hadrian as having a clear advantage over his peers. He is more able to sustain ritual fasts then others. He flirted with what the text calls "progressive suicide" through complete abstinence, "espèce de débauche retournée où l'on va jusqu'à l'épuisement de la substance humaine" (19). However, the dangers become manifest and he avoids servitude to any system.

Aversion to certain kinds of food, disdain of excess and avoidance of the complex and the communal are empowering in Yourcenar's narratives whereas they appear alienating in Duras' texts. The abstemious Hadrian achieves an understanding of the poetic and the scientific through his discipline, by his ability to survive on less. These traits mark his superior rationality, his belief in order and his ability to impose it on his world.

The Yourcenar creation is basically an optimistic one. More typical points of view appear in films like Costa Gavras' *Tea in the Harem of Archimedes* or in Agnes Vardas' *Vagabond* which portray as a dominant motif the annihilating function of food in contemporary life, although

in very different milieux. Vardas' film, for example, traces the life of
a waif (Sandrine Bonnaire), ardently desirous of freedom to create her
own way, who abandons conventional life in order to do so. Her basic
need for food limits her freedom, however. Like the artist who refuses
creative sustenance and is left without inspiration, Sandrine's refusal
of all offers of assistance in the transformation required by society to
gain secure sources of food leads inevitably to death. A drop-out
philosophy teacher gives her a place of her own to live and tries to
teach her how to grow her own food and to cook a variety of dishes.
She rejects this because it requires an attachment to the land, a lack
of freedom. A biologist, whose care for the dying sycamores extends to
a desire to care for the vagabond, tries to give her bread, chocolate, sausage
and other food. Sandrine willingly accepts so long as it holds no strings
to crimp her freedom to act. Food is a dangerous impediment to
individuality, ultimate freedom, especially cooked food which requires
a place to transform it from its raw state. In refusing all inhibiting
relations and assistance, the vagabond also refuses individual
transformation. Alienation is inevitable and annihilation the necessary
outcome. The conflict between the simple and the complex, the individual
and the communal, the scientific and the poetic are forms of the conflict
between freedom and survival, an important theme in this film.

Food and drink are the ultimate individual and communal needs
for the poor, despondent Algerian immigrants who have given up all
ambitions in Costa Gavras' *Tea in the Harem of Archimedes*. The inability
to put food on the table is the final ultimate despair of the divorced
woman who loses her job, and hence her livelihood, as the result of
a strike. The camera focuses on the thin slice of meat, plopped on a
plate which the child refuses, ignorant of its sustaining, communal
meaning for his mother. He uses food as a toy, a gun, a non-necessity,
but unlike Vardas' vagabond, he does not consciously reject the
sustenance. Like the vagabond, the child chooses the world of fantasy
even using the last food to fulfill the fantasy. All fantasy is gone for
his mother. She can only see food at the end as sustenance and she eats,
but without joy. In *The Tea in the Harem* the teenagers who steal vast
sums from the Sporting Club use the money to fill their fantasies, the
first of which is to transform their reality by treating themselves to a
fine dinner with champagne. While the men in this movie create fantasies,
the women concentrate on providing cooked food for their families. It
is they who maintain the communal. Even those who work outside the
home serve in a cafeteria or in a bar. When their family disintegrates,
they lose their purpose and thus their power to control anything in
their lives.

As these contemporary narratives demonstrate, food is a metaphor for sustenance and membership. Its lack is a sign of alienation or death and it represents the ultimate contradiction of society and the creative process. In the narratives of 'nouvelle cuisine,' with the works of Duras, Yourcenar, and the two films cited above it appears, then, that the complex which obfuscates, the communal which alienates, and the scientific which transforms are what annihilate the simple, the individual, and the poetic. They create danger of death for the creative process.

Works Cited

Bertholle, Louisette. *French Cuisine for All*. Trans. Mary Manheim and author. Garden City: Doubleday, 1980.

Chelminski, Rudolph. *The French at Table*. New York: Morrow, 1985.

Chevalier, Patrice, associés. "Davipêche: cap sur la légèreté.' " *Elle* 2158 (18 mai 1987): 152-53.

Duras, Marguérite. *La Douleur*. Paris: P.O.L., 1985.

_____ *Moderato Cantabile*. Paris: Minuit, 1958.

_____ *Outside: Papiers d'un jour*. Paris: P.O.L., 1984.

Kramer, Samuel Noah. *The Sumerians, Their History, Culture and Character*. Chicago: Chicago U.P., 1964.

Kristeva, Julia. "The Pain of Sorrow in the Modern World: The Works of Marguérite Duras." Trans. Katharine A. Jensen. *PMLA* 102 (1987): 138-52.

Lebey, Claude. "La Nouvelle 'bouffe.' " *L'Express* 1276 (22-28 déc. 1975): 52-55.

Revel, Jean-François. *Culture and Cuisine: A Journey Through the History of Food*. Trans. Helen R. Lane. New York: Da Capo, 1984.

Scherzer, Dina. "Violence gastronomique dans 'Moderato cantabile.' " *French Review* L. 4 (1977): 596-601.

Troisgros, Jean and Pierre. *The Nouvelle Cuisine of Jean and Pierre Troisgros*. Trans. Roberta Wolfe Smoler. New York: Quill-Morrow, 1978.

Yourcenar, Marguérite. *Anna Soror*. 1981. *Oeuvres romanesques*. Paris: Pléiade-Gallimard, 1982. 851-901.

_____ *Un Homme obscur*. 1982. *Oeuvres romanesques*. Paris: Pléiade-Gallimard, 1982. 903-1000.

_____ *Mémoires d'Hadrian*. 1958. Paris: Gallimard, 1974.

Thoreau and Emerson: Vegetarianism, Bhuddism and Organic Form

Bruce R. Henderson

"The Bhuddist...is a Transcendentalist."
—Emerson, *Works* I,, p. 337.

To explore Thoreau's practice of vegetarianism is most appropriate only in the larger context of his spiritual beliefs. These were, as we know, shaped not only by his own reading and intellectual resources, but by his close friendship with Emerson, which included a period of his living under the same roof with the Emerson family and serving as a kind of handyman. There is evidence that both men were strongly affected by Eastern ideas, which in Thoreau's case especially influenced his attitude toward materialism and helped to shape his writing and his philosophy of the organic and organic form. The three philosophies of vegetarianism (which can be simultaneously both philosophy and practice), Bhuddism, and organic form are inseparably tied together in the pronouncements of these two men, so that it will be most useful to examine them accordingly. Finally, it is illuminating to trace the influence of these ideas through subsequent popular literary works, and so assess their impact on popular culture in general.

Central to understanding the appeal of vegetarianism to Thoreau is its link to spiritual pursuit, which was in turn, for both Thoreau and Emerson, the key to poetic composition. Emerson argued that "rightly, poetry is organic. We cannot know things by words and writing, but only by taking a central position in the universe and living in its forms" (v.10, 24). He describes the poet, in his essay of the same name, as speaking well "only when he speaks somewhat wildly...with the intellect released from all service and suffered to take its direction from its celestial life" (Gelpi 165). This notion of inspiration as a matter of unconscious receptivity parallels and prefigures modern psychological theory when Emerson speaks of "the projection of God in the unconscious" mind of man (Gelpi 163). Thoreau stressed the importance of the artist's preparation by saying, "Nothing goes by luck in

composition...the best you can write will be the best that you are"
(Matthiessen 50).

But this notion of inspiration also parallels Eastern thought in its
goals of living a life which leads to a purified or holy state and becoming
one with the divine inspiration. There is ample evidence, including the
titles and content of some of Emerson's poetry and direct references in
the writings of Thoreau, that both were well acquainted with Eastern
philosophy. It seems likely that each made discoveries independently.
Indeed, Thoreau's Oriental reading began as early as his college days,
before he went to live with the Emersons (Paul 69). Emerson called the
Bhagavad Gita "the first of books...the venerable oracle" (Porte 394).
He also paid dues to the Oriental Society for many years following the
visit of Philip Jogut Sangooly, who took tea with his family, much
to his daughter Ellen's delight "to have a real live Brahmin, brought
up a priest to Krishna &c, knowing Sanscrit and all the Vedas and able
to tell Father all he wanted to know, in our house here in America,
in Concord" (Rusk 397). Thoreau for his part presents several Eastern
studies in quite early writings, discussing such topics as the "Laws of
Menu," "Sayings of Confucius" and "Chinese Four Books." Another
visitor to the Emerson household, Thomas Chalmondeley, made a gift
to Thoreau of 44 Oriental books in 1854 (Harding 44).

The Eastern philosophy that the world is but a manifestation of
the universal mind, or the One with which all must strive to reunite
via their conduct in earthly life, is reflected in Emerson's poetic theory:
"But the transcendent fact is that nature is the representative of the
universal mind," he states in *Works* (v.7, 40). He goes on to say that
"so in art that aims primarily at beauty must the parts be subordinated
to ideal nature, and everything individual be abstracted, so that it shall
be the production of the universal soul" (48). A well-known passage
in his essay "Nature" further exemplifies this philosophy: "I become
a transparent eyeball; I am doing nothing; I see all; the currents of the
Universal Being circulate through me; I am part or parcel of God."
From the point of view of the artist, the Oversoul represented an "ocean
of light," a reserve of spiritual power, available to those who would
open themselves to its influence (Wagenknecht 206).

So far as practicing what he preached, on the whole it seems that
Emerson played the role of philosopher and teacher to Thoreau's more
active and practical pursuits. Concerning vegetarianism, Emerson at least
took a close interest. He owned, for example, a fifteenth-century book
by Luigi Cornaro, a Venetian noted for his diet and longevity. In his
journal he notes that, "Cornaro satisfied himself with 12 oz solid food
& 14 oz wine per day. He passed his 100th year. H. Daggett, his editor,
finds less than 12 oz vegetable food, sufficient" (Ferguson 211).

Though Emerson found Oriental doctrines congenial to his outlook, it is Thoreau who translated such principles into action in his own life. He found, for example, that work, which had in the Puritan tradition been regarded as a duty or as a penalty of man's fall, could instead become a source of joy; cultivating his beans became for Thoreau a joyous avenue to personal growth (Paul 302). This view is directly in the Bhuddist tradition of "right livelihood," in which any work, however humble, can form fertile ground for self-realization.

Thoreau also practiced vegetarianism as part of his spiritual pursuit. He felt that humanity in general would improve by forsaking the slaughter of animals for food:

Whatever my own practice may be, I have no doubt that it is a part of the destiny of the human race, in its gradual improvement, to leave off eating animals, as surely as the savage tribes have left off eating each other when they came in contact with the more civilised. (Salt 247)

And of course vegetarianism has for millennia been part of ascetic practice associated with personal spiritual improvement and clarity. At Walden Pond the staples of Thoreau's diet were rye, Indian meal (corn), potatoes and rice, of which he commented, "it was fit that I should live on rice mainly, who loved so well the philosophy of India" (Wagenknecht 22).

Besides his vegetarianism, there is good evidence that Thoreau practiced meditation as a means to access the kind of higher spiritual power about which Emerson rhapsodized. He wrote to his friend Harrison Blake that "...those who have practiced the yoga gather in Brahma the certain fruit of their works.... The Yogi, absorbed in contemplation, contributes in his degree to creation...and, united to the nature which is proper to him, he goes, he acts as animating original matter" (Paul 353). In *Walden*, in the opening passages of the "Sounds" chapter, he reports that "I sat in my sunny doorway from sunrise till noon, rapt in a revery, amidst the pines...in undisturbed solitude and stillness...I realized what the Orientals mean by contemplation and the forsaking of work." Another clue to what constituted Thoreau's reveries can be found in his pronouncement on a famous Oriental book: "In the morning I bathe my intellect in the stupendous and cosmogonal philosophy of the *Bhagavad-Gita*, in comparison with which our modern world and its literature seem puny and trivial" (Bhaktivedanta cover).

Thoreau observed that "man's art has wisely imitated those forms into which all matter is most inclined to run, as foliage and fruit," and undertook his Walden Pond experiment during which he could simply look out his front door for fresh evidence of man's links to the world of nature. Thoreau and Emerson thus laid the groundwork for others to experiment in what we now know as organic form, sometimes called 'open form' or 'composition by field' (Gelpi 163). The essential idea is that compositional manifestation of organic form is linked directly to the cultivation of the inner artist who does the composing: that is a crucial link between the literary/cultural ideas recorded by both men and the Oriental/Transcendental philosophy behind them.

Thoreau extended Emerson's idea of the artist as a medium for higher inspiration, feeling that "in the act of expression, a man's whole being, and his natural and social background as well, function organically together" (Matthiessen 62). (Echoing this notion a century later, Allen Ginsberg, when asked how he prepared to compose, answered, "I polish my mind." His interviewer misheard him and asked if he said, "polish my lines," whereupon Ginsberg insisted, "No, I polish my mind"). Believing that "great art can grow from the center of the simplest life" (Harding 8), Thoreau related the concepts of the simple life and self-reliance to respect for locality, as sufficient for both artistic and physical nourishment:

When La Mountain and Haddock dropped down in the Canadian wilderness the other day, they came near starving, or dying of cold and wet and fatigue, not knowing where to look for food nor how to shelter themselves. Thus far we have wandered from a simple and independent life. I think that a wise and independent, self-reliant man will have a complete list of the edibles to be found in a primitive country or wilderness....Here we are, deriving our breadstuffs from the West, our butter stuffs from Vermont, and our tea and coffee and sugar stuffs, and much more with which we stuff ourselves, from the other side of the globe. Why, a truly prudent man will carry such a list as the above, in his mind at least, even though he walk through Broadway or Quincy Market. He will know what are the permanent resources of the land and be prepared for the hardest of times. (Torrey 397-98)

We should now be able to trace some of the above concepts in the work of subsequent writers and so link them to cultural changes of recent times. Albert Gelpi states that Emerson's sense of the primacy of inspiration and scorn for 'rules and particulars' ushered the Dionysian ideal into American literature (165). Parallel to the embrace of open form and sensual detail is the spiritual quest of the Eastern ideal, together with the ideals of renunciation and discipline, including such practices as yoga and vegetarianism. In 1930 Carpenter, in his comprehensive study *Emerson and Asia*, credited Emerson with a cultural renaissance through which "literatures of Asia have been stimulating the leading writers of America to new explorations and new horizons of thought" (255).

Perhaps the most direct recipient of the Dionysian ideal was Walt Whitman, whom Emerson met and introduced to Orientalism. While Emerson could not approve of the "vulgarity and coarseness" of some of Whitman's verse (Gelpi 168), nevertheless the spirit and form of the later poet's work is clearly in Emerson's debt. Whitman extended the concept of individualism toward American culture as a whole, believing that "with the production of great persons, an indigenous and organic American culture would necessarily follow" and that democracy was itself "organic" in the final analysis, and in the throes of an evolutionary process (Gerster 219 & 220):

That growth and tendency of all modern theology, literature, social manners, diet, most to be dreaded, is the feebleness, inertia, the loss of power, the loss of personality being diffused—spread out over a vast democratic level...And yet the most marked peculiarity of modern philosophy is toward the special subjective, the theory of individuality. (Gerster 171)

Thoreau also met Whitman, in Brooklyn, in 1856, and received, from Emerson, a copy of *Leaves of Grass*. He did not think it vulgar, refusing to join in any public denunciation, declaring he would not "jump on that bandwagon" (Harding 13). In fact these differing reactions symbolize at least two distinct streams of influence as we examine later American literature. One leads through Melville, Dickinson, Pound, Eliot, Frost and Stevens with their celebration of the emptiness of material culture and/or existential stance and quests to come to terms with a universe from which modern men and women have become estranged. Perhaps Emerson would have felt most aligned to the cosmic, controlled and philosophical treatments of these writers. The other stream is, generally, the more sensual branch of influence—those who in their celebration of the world of the senses manage to delineate similar ideas, but in a perhaps more truly organic approach: Poe, Whitman, Gertrude Stein, Eugene O'Neill, Carl Sandburg, Henry Miller. Allen Ginsberg and the Beats, Gary Snyder.

Certainly the writers from both lists are hardly mutually exclusive in their techniques and philosophies, and in fact show extensive cross-fertilization. But we can recognize distinct approaches in their embodiments of the several strains of the original Transcendental philosophy. Although the theme of the alienation of the individual is common to most of them, to some extent it is on a more personal and celebratory level in Thoreau, Whitman and the succession of writers leading to the Beats. In addition to meeting with critical disapproval, Whitman did not have much material success with *Leaves of Grass*, which aligns him with Thoreau, whose books did not give him much worldly satisfaction either. Thoreau's name has also been linked with a tradition of dissent and even rebellion and placed with those of Dreiser, Steinbeck, Kerouac and Mailer (Meyer 155).

Yet in popular culture, the pattern of social flirtation with the Dionysian side seems to go hand in hand with the more idealistic and philosophical side. If the American intellectuals have been traditionally alienated, that very condition has given them the freedom to seek spiritual fulfillment elsewhere. During the twenties, for example, we can trace the intellectual cynicism of Pound and Eliot, perhaps reflected most clearly in the writings of F. Scott Fitzgerald, which seem to both celebrate and condemn the era. But the core or seed of the Transcendental principles inform the basic artistic aesthetic and even the form of this tradition of writing. We find it in Pound's distrust of aestheticism—that technical skill and ingenuity which can inhibit the creative process—when he asserts that Paradise is not artificial but is the 'tao,' or the divine process of nature (Gelpi 156). The notion of higher inspiration persists through more recent writers such as Kerouac, who claimed he opened his mouth and let the Holy Ghost speak, or Ginsberg, whose chanting of "Om" to open poetry readings seeks to prepare both audience and poet to share the fruits of his artistic inspiration. The idea of organic form has led to the notion of a poet writing not just collections of poems but a life-poem, reflecting the techniques of "open form" and "composition by field." Examples are the journals of Thoreau, Whitman's *Leaves*, Pound's *Cantos*, Charles Olson's *Maximus Poems* and Ginsberg's notebooks in verse and prose (Gelpi 163). Ginsberg's work is especially revealing of the several themes of Transcendental philosophy, in that while he deplores a material culture which has driven the best minds of his generation stark raving mad, he also points the way to spiritual salvation through concepts embodied in titles and poems such as "Kaddish" and "Wichita Vortex Sutra."

Ginsberg came to popularity in the 50s along with his prose counterpart Jack Kerouac. A 1957 essay by Norman Mailer heralded the arrival of the "American existentialist" whom he labeled the hipster:

...the man who knows that if our collective condition is to live with instant death by atomic war, relatively quick death by the state as "l'univers concentrationnaire," or with a slow death by conformity with every creative and rebellious instinct stifled...why then the only life-giving answer is to accept the terms of death, to live with death as immediate danger, to divorce oneself from society, to exist without roots, to set out on that uncharted journey into the rebellious imperatives of the self. (Gerster 250)

As social activism widened in the 60s and public expression of disenchantment with American material culture gained momentum, popularity of Thoreau's *Walden* grew accordingly and reintroduced Transcendental ideas to a whole new generation who found worth in the concepts of respecting and revering nature and also respecting and cultivating individual self-expression. Michael Meyer's analysis of Thoreau's political reputation at that time is revealing:

Wanting no part of the corporate adult world because it seemed diametrically opposed to a simple, meaningful, organic life style, hippies dropped out and attempted to establish communal Waldens where they could live free from the quiet desperation of a nine-to-five world....Thoreau was perceived by many...as one of the links between their values and the nonmaterialistic philosophies of the East. (184)

In fact the personal cult of Thoreau fit many 60s concerns:

He emerged as both a spokesman and an antagonist of capitalism; a food faddist; an anarchist; a sexual libertarian advocating a bodily-orgasmic response to life; . . . an ecologist. (186)

A poet such as Gary Snyder, whose writing was especially popular among college students of the 60s and 70s, continued in the Beat and Eastern traditions, undertaking monastic study in Japan for several years before returning to the United States to resume his literary activities. He also became a spokesperson for ecological concerns and for alternative social and community arrangements. We look back on the 60s as a time of widespread social experimentation with alternative family structures, back-to-the-land movements and widening concern for the preservation and protection of nature, all of which can be gathered under the spiritual umbrella of the Transcendentalist movement and its practical applications by Thoreau.

It is interesting that Thoreau admired the American Indians (as did many 60s social activists) at least for their practices of vision-quests, fasting, and relying upon local foods, even though he thought them without the higher spirit of the truly 'civilized' white culture. From this perspective the Transcendentalism of Emerson and Thoreau can be regarded as a link which brings such ancient indigenous American spirituality full-circle to the social trends which are still with us today and which gained a foothold in U.S. society during the 60s and 70s. Two such trends are vegetarianism, particularly of the macrobiotic variety (which derives from Japanese culture via George Oshawa) which stresses using foods grown seasonally in the locality of the consumer; and spiritually-related practices derived from the East such as yoga, various kinds of meditation, including Transcendental Meditation or TM, and martial arts in all their variety, including the highly ritualized Tai Chi.

Consistent with the popularized concept of 'living lightly on the earth' and the resurgence of interest in American Indian culture are the variety of alternative housing designs and ideas featured in such publications as Steward Brand's *Whole Earth Catalogue* (still being published in updated versions) which, with its subtitle "Access to Tools," also attests to the re-emergence of the practical philosophy of self-reliance. A recent pioneer in alternative architectural design was Frank Lloyd Wright, a proponent of organic form in building. He believed in using local building materials when possible and in taking into account the overall natural setting in which the structure would be located. He designed, for example, a famous house straddling a stream in Pennsylvania, built from local woods and stone (Henderson 1). Such respect for "nature's organic harmony" (Gerster 56) goes back to Emersonian philosophy such as that of his observation in "Nature:"

The charming landscape which I saw this morning is indubitably made up of some twenty or thirty farms. Miller owns this field, Locke that, and Manning the woodland beyond. There is a property on the horizon which no man has but he whose eye can integrate all the parts, that is the poet. This is the best part of these men's farms, yet to this their warranty-deeds give no title.

A minor but growing social trend is toward the macrobiotic diet, lately put forth as a possible preventative diet and/or cure for cancer (Sattilaro). Besides its obvious affiliation with organic philosophy, it is also but one of a number of holistic approaches to health which derive from Eastern medical traditions and which are rapidly gaining respectability and acceptance: acupuncture (for which one can now be licensed in the U.S.), reflexology, accupressure, herbal therapies. In the broad philosophical sense these trends dovetail with Emerson's and Thoreau's ideas of self-reliance and in particular with Thoreau's principle of finding all the inspiration and nourishment needed in one locality (such as that of Walden Pond and Concord). Thoreau offered his friend Blake the advice, "Live at home like a traveller... What a fool he must be who thinks that his El Dorado is anywhere but where he lives!" (Paul 392).

Contemporary American society continues to struggle between material desires and the yearning for personal growth and fulfillment of the spiritual order. In the past twenty years we have seen adoption of practices which have gone beyond the intellectual concepts from which they derive to an often unconscious embrace as popular trends. Witness such phenomena as tofu on sale in most U.S. supermarkets, of meditation and related physical practices becoming household words if not universal practices, of growth of hardware, auto parts and computer outlets as many more Americans attempt to rely on their own resources rather than hire the expertise of others. While influences beyond the literary ones discussed here have undoubtedly entered into these social shifts, nevertheless it seems that such changes are undeniably related to the ideas which found their origin or renaissance in the writings of Thoreau and Emerson, a tradition which subsequent generations of American writers continued and elaborated upon and have kept alive in our social consciousness.

Works Cited

Bhaktivedanta, A. C. *Bhagavad Gita As It Is*. Sydney: Dominion, 1984.
Carpenter, Frederic. *Emerson and Asia*. Cambridge: Harvard UP, 1930.

Emerson, Ralph Waldo. *The Complete Works of Ralph Waldo Emerson*. Boston: Centenary edition, 1903.

Ferguson, Alfred R., ed. *Journals and Miscellaneous Notebooks of Ralph Waldo Emerson*. Cambridge: Harvard UP, 1964.

Gelpi, Albert. "The Paradox of Organic Form." *Emerson: Prophecy, Metamorphosis and Influence*. Ed. David Levin. New York: Columbia UP, 1975. 149-170.

Gerster, Patrick G. "Aesthetic Individualism: Key to the Alienation of the American Intellectual—Studies in Ralph Waldo Emerson, Henry David Thoreau, and Walt Whitman." Diss.U of Minnesota, 1970.

Harding, Walter and Michael Meyer. *A Thoreau Handbook*. New York: NYU, 1980.

Henderson, Bruce R. *Oakland Organic*. Berkeley: Caboose Press, 1982.

Matthiessen, F.O. "The Organic Structure of Walden." *Twentieth Century Interpretations of Walden*. Ed. Richard Ruland. Englewood Cliffs: Prentice, 1968. 51-63.

Meyer, Michael. *Several More Lives to Live*. Westport, CT: Greenwood, 1977.

Moldenhauer, Joseph and Edwin Moser. *Early Essays and Miscellanies*. Princeton: Princeton UP; 1975.

Paul, Sherman. *The Shores of America*. Urbana: U of Illinois, 1958.

Porte, Joel. *Emerson in His Journals*. Cambridge: Harvard UP, 1982.

Rusk, Ralph L. *The Life of Ralph Waldo Emerson*. New York: Scribner's, 1949.

Salt, H.S. *The Life of Henry David Thoreau*. London: Bentley, 1890.

Sattilaro, Anthony. *Recalled by Life*. New York: Houghton, 1982.

Torrey, Bradford and Francis Allen, eds. *Journal of Henry David Thoreau*. New York: Dover, 1962.

Yanella, Donald. *Ralph Waldo Emerson*. Boston: Twayne, 1982.

Wagenknecht, Edward. *Ralph Waldo Emerson: Portrait of a Balanced Soul*. New York: Oxford UP, 1974.

Looking at Early American Cookbooks from an Inter-Disciplinary Perspective*

Jody Kolodzey

Old cookbooks can be approached as curiosities, or they can be appreciated as historical documents and used to reconstruct not just past lifestyles, but the tacit philosophies underlying those lifestyles. How foods were classified, for instance, indicates that they were not always seen simply as protein or carbohydrate sources, but may have been linked to a particular eschatology, such as Culpeper's ordering of herbs by astrology (Shellard 6). This paper examines traditional and popular sanctions governing the preparation of common garden vegetables such as potatoes, cabbages, etc., as represented in two centuries of American cookbooks. These gleanings are weighed against modern nutritional and agricultural data as reported in current scientific journals.

One current direction in folklore methodology is toward the study of an item of folklore—be it a performance of a folk song, the wearing of a folk costume, or a certain method of cooking asparagus—in context. In attempting to observe the cookbook in its particular milieu, we find ourselves in a situation that is not unfamiliar to anyone researching history from a perspective other than the military or political. The documentation is scanty or non-existent for most aspects of cultural history, so when attempting to reconstruct how people lived, most historians deal with contemporaneous ephemera such as letters, diaries, novels, newspapers, and cookbooks. But when what you are interested in is the role played by one of these sources—i.e., the cookbook—in its own culture, you broach circularity, for there is likely to be nothing to check your findings against. Furthermore, in dealing with popular printed sources such as cookbooks, one is confronted with a deterministic dilemma: did such encyclicals serve *to influence* eating habits, or were they themselves *influenced by* prevailing habits? Moving into a modern

*This paper was originally entitled "Into the Eye of the Potato: An Exploration of American Garden-Variety Vegetables in Folklore, Fact and Fallacy," and, as such, was presented at Folklore through Foodways, a conference of the 1985 Food and Nutrition Section of the American Home Economics Association Annual Meeting held 21-23 June 1985 at the Sheraton University City Hotel, Philadelphia, Pa.

179

parallel, we see both possibilities at work: *viz.*, Julia Child and other innovators on the one hand, purporting to steer American tastebuds in new directions, and the concurrent proliferation of "natural foods" and "cancer-preventing diet" cookbooks on the other, banking on popular trends that already exist.

The connection of extant vintage cookbooks to prominent historical personages is ubiquitous; one can currently buy facsimile editions of Martha Washington's cookbook, Gulielma (Mrs. William) Penn's cookbook, Thomas Jefferson's granddaughter's cookbook, and many others. This gives rise to several additional questions: Were these sociopolitically prominent women more inclined to keep or write cookbooks than was the average housewife? Or is it just that their manuscripts were reckoned more valuable and consequently are more likely to have bided through until the present day? And, were such women, as cookbook authors in general, leaders or followers of popular taste?

Surviving alongside the cookbooks connected with notable individuals are cookbooks that were published by various religious organizations and which ostensibly served as primers for an espoused lifestyle. One of the most interesting examples of this latter type was a vegetarian cookbook published in 1829 by the Bible Christian Church in London. Entitled *Vegetable Cookery With An Introduction Recommending Abstinence from Animal Food and Intoxicating Liquors*, it provides a fascinating glimpse into the everyday activities of this obscure sect. Of particular interest are the apparent inconsistencies, errors in logic that seem obvious to us scientifically astute denizens of the twentieth century, but were perhaps not considered so "irrational" a century and an half ago. For instance, the book contains a recipe for "Ivory Jelly," a confectionary condiment:

Ivory Jelly
    To six ounces of ivory powder put two quarts of water, cover the jar, and set it in a moderate oven till reduced nearly one half; then strain, and either let it stand to be cold and set, or, if wanted immediately, put it in a pan and set it on the fire, with nearly half a pint of sherbet, the rind of a lemon pared very thin, the juice of two or more lemons according to the size, and sugar to the taste; stir in the white of four new-laid eggs well beaten; let it boil five minutes, then run it through a flannel jelly bag dipped in hot water and wrung quite dry. The flavor may be varied by adding two table-spoonfuls of orange-flower water, or using Seville oranges instead of lemons, or a mixture of both. (137)

It strikes me as curious that the Bible Christian Church did not acknowledge the fact that ivory came from slaughtered elephants, and should therefore have fallen under their own stated taboo against food obtained at the cost of an animal's life. Perhaps they were not aware that the elephants were killed. They were not strict vegans, opposed to any food of animal origin, but ovo-lactarians who ate things such as milk and eggs that could be taken from an animal without inflicting pain. Thus, there is a chapter of the book devoted to "Omelets, Fritters, & c.", and another entitled "Creams, Flummery, & c."; the "Ivory Jelly" recipe is part of the latter.

The Bible Christian Church cookbook followed the accepted practice of including a collection of remedies for common maladies as one of its final chapters. A recommended cure for dysentery advised the sufferer to "...take a sheet of writing paper, cut it in slips, boil it in a pint and a half of milk till reduced to a pint; take it at twice" (286).

According to William Woys Weaver, this prescription was probably as efficacious as any other of the day, as it would yield a gelatinous substance that would bind the bowels (Weaver conv.). But once again, the Bible Christians were making inadvertent use of an animal product: Paper. Although compounded from wood pulp, writing paper is sized with glue, which is derived from the hooves of dead horses.

Although the sect extolled abstinence, the cookbook prescribed garlic steeped in wine as a cure for "convulsion fits" (292). Presumably, it was all right to partake of the benefits of wine—or carrion—as long as one did not directly consume the alcohol or the flesh itself. The Bible Christians proffered another medicinal use for garlic: roasting it and applying it, while still hot, directly to the corn (312). Another garlic-based remedy, from the anonymously-authored *New Family Book, or Ladies' Indispensible Companion and Housekeeper's Guide* published in 1854, also pertained to the feet; garlic rubbed on the feet at night was said to ease fever and promote circulation (59).

Although a condimentary staple in Mediterranean countries since antiquity, garlic was slow in garnering favor among Northern Europeans. In 1699, the English diarist John Evelyn inveighed against its use in salads "by reason of its intolerable Rankness" (qtd. in Quinn 162). Evelyn's writings also suggest that the taste and odor of the bulb was so abhorrent to his countrymen "that the eating of it was part of the Punishment for such as had committed the horrid'st Crimes" (162). "Garlicks, tho' used by the French, are better adapted to the uses of medicine than cookery," reproved Amelia Simmons in her *American Cookery* book of 1796 (12). Garlic was, however, liberally used in the continentally-sophisticated kitchen at Monticello; Thomas Jefferson's personal household cookbook, which was compiled by his granddaughter and is roughly contemporary with Simmons' treatise, calls for garlic in a variety of recipes, including "Boiled Leg of Mutton," wherein it is observed that the addition of "[one] small garlic... Will give it a delicately fine flavor" (68).

Even today, however, garlic suffers from a lowbrow reputation according to Abigail ("Dear Abby") van Buren and other arbiters of twentieth century Western convention; to go about with garlic on one's breath is considered offensive, a social *faux pas*. Ironically, however, one team of medical researchers concluded that, by eating garlic, a person might avoid proliferating an even more socially embarrassing odor: that of passing gas (Damrau and Ferguson 411-419). After a series of clinically controlled trials in 1949, physician Frederick Damrau and chemist Edgar A. Ferguson asserted that garlic provided "definite and consistent relief of the symptoms of heaviness after eating, flatulence, gas colic, belching and nausea" (411) by relaxing the stomach lining, but they were troubled by their inability to determine precisely why it has this effect, and so ended their report on a peculiarly vague note, an appeal to what logicians refer to as "truth by definition" (Fearnside & Holther 137):

> It is believed that these studies explain the carminative action of garlic as due to unidentified principles which we half designated as *gastroenteric allichalonae (allium,* garlic; *chalone,* to relax). [Damrau & Ferguson 419].

Thus, there is some scientific basis to the practice of cooking beans with garlic, and there are other methods of attempting to reduce the consequences of eating beans that I will address later.

Likewise, the *Ladies' Indispensible Companion's* assertion that garlic is effective in treating "indolent tumors, coughs, colds and asthma" (59) also has its modern champions. Observing that the residents of Britain are more prone to bronchitis than those residing in the vicinity of the Mediterranean, where the humidity should be equally conducive to the complaint, a Los Angeles-based otolaryngologist indicated garlic as one reason why (Ziment 193). The other reason cited was the amount of wine drunk in the Mediterranean countries. Garlic and wine were the two components of the Bible Christian Church's remedy for "convulsion fits" that I mentioned earlier, and I suspect that some attacks of bronchial asthma may have been classified as convulsions.

Another vegetable which was accepted on the table only after being established in the pharmacopeia was rhubarb.

Rhubarb debuted on the London food market in 1810; it was a dismal failure. Until then, Western Europeans brewed an astringent from the roots and admired the leaves for their ornamental beauty, but did not believe rhubarb was good for anything else (Saling 9; Rackemann 93).

Sandra Oddo's compilation of recipes from the nineteenth century— which she sees as the pivotal epoch in mainstream American cookery, attributed primarily to Benjamin Thompson's invention of the kitchen stove (4)—lists rhubarb in both the culinary (142-145) and medicinal (456) sections of the book. The medicinal value is chiefly purgative, in keeping with Culpeper *et al*: One ounce of rhubarb combined with one teaspoon saleratus [a leavening substance] and two teaspoons essence of peppermint in a pint of boiling water, taken by the tablespoonful at intervals ranging from one quarter-hour to two full hours "according to age and urgency of disease" (456), is offered as a "Simple mixture for all bowel complaints." Combined with two drachms of English saffron, two drachms of cardomom seed, a large nutmeg and "a pint of the best French brandy," then bottled and heated in a *bain marie* for twelve hours, an ounce of crushed rhubarb is recommended as a cure "for the dysentery" (456). Espoused culinary uses are of the expected confectionary variety, including recipes for pie and cake filling, a marmalade with oranges, preserves with ginger, wine and *vol au vent*. However, the last case represents something of a hybrid, with rhubarb being extolled as a spring tonic:

Sweet Vol Au Vent With Rhubarb

In the spring of the year this makes a very inviting and wholesome dish, and its qualities purify the blood, which the winter's food has rendered gross; cut about twelve sticks of rhubarb into lengths of one inch, put it in a stew pan holding about two quarts, put over it a quarter of a pound of sugar, and a tablespoon of water, set it on a sharp fire, stirring it, so to not let it get brown, or it would spoil and lose its sharp flavor; it will take but a few minutes to do; when tender, put it in a basin to cool; a few minutes before serving, fill the vol-a-vent with it, and serve cold. [Oddo 143]

Another such hybrid, "Spiced Rhubarb," appears among the "Simple Remedies" section of Elizabeth Ellicott Lea's 1853 publication, *Domestic Cookery*. Lea cites it as a treatment for "the summer disease," and recommends a dosage of two teaspoons for a one-year-old child, two tablespoons for an adult (qtd. in Weaver *Quaker* 263). "Summer disease" was a euphemism for diarrhea, so-called because during hot weather in the days before pasteurization and refrigeration, milk frequently became contaminated with diarrhea-causing bacteria (Rinzler 49).

Lea, who was a Pennsylvania Quaker, also gives a recipe for rhubarb pie, and among her contemporaneous Pennsylvania Dutch, rhubarb was called "Boigraut," meaning "pie plant" (Weaver *Sauerkraut* 127). One hundred and some-odd years later, most of the rhubarb grown in America nowadays is indeed used to make pies. Usually, the rhubarb is cooked on the stove before being poured into the pie shell and baked in the oven. Recently, Lois Burpee of the famous seed catalogue family, cautioned "never cook rhubarb in an aluminum pot because the metal spoils the flavor" (60); she also advised that, "for the best color, do not peel the stalks" (60). Nearly a century earlier, Fannie M. Farmer's *Boston Cooking School Cook Book* asserted that the best color is obtained if the stalks *are* peeled, and subsequently cooked for a very long time (476). The stalks, or stems, are the only edible part of the rhubarb plant. The leaves, though revered for their topical astringency since antiquity, contain lethal amounts of oxalic acid, a poison which crystallizes in the kidneys. Rhubarb, however, is such a garden fixture that even presumed "authorities" are prone to forget just how potentially dangerous it is. In 1961, for example, a new edition of one of the world's most revered cookbooks, the *Larouse Gastronomique*, suggested that rhubarb leaves be "eaten like spinach" (qtd. in Telephone Pioneers of America 2). About half a century earlier, in an attempt to deal with critical food shortages during World War I, the British government recommended doing the same thing (Saling 10). Sadly, it took several deaths to remind the authorities that, although rhubarb is related to spinach—and to buckwheat—it is not as wholesomely benign.

After such uncomfortably recent episodes as those, it is not so easy to disparage our colonial forebears who shunned the tomato as a "poison apple." More than half the families in America grow tomatoes each summer, and we each ate an average of more than 50 pounds of them in 1980 (Jabs 82). But the truth is that the tomato *is* poisonous, but just as in rhubarb, the poisons are confined to those parts of the plant that are not normally eaten, i.e., the foliage.

Perhaps Americans would be shunning the fruits yet had it not been for the frequently histrionic efforts of Colonel Robert Giddon Johnson, an eccentric amateur gardener. In 1830, he dramatically and defiantly ate an entire basketful of tomatoes in front of a crowd expecting him to "foam at the mouth and double over with appendicitis" on the steps of the Salem, New Jersey, courthouse (Jabs 83; Michaelson 8).

In her *Book of Household Management* serialized between 1859 and 1861, Isabella Beeton inveighed against the tomato:

...The whole plant has a disagreeable odor, and its juice, subjected to the action of the fire, emits a vapour so powerful as to cause vertigo and vomiting. (596)

However, she went on to concede:

In this country [England] it is much more cultivated than it formerly was; and the more the community becomes acquainted with the many agreeable forms in which the fruit can be prepared, the more widely will its cultivation be extended. For Ketchup, soups, and sauces, it is equally applicable, and the unripe fruit makes one of the best pickles. (597)

There are no recipes utilizing the tomato in Amelia Simmons' 1796 cookbook, which is understandable because she predates Colonel Johnson by a generation. Mrs. J. Chadwick's 1853 *Home Cookery* reflects the Colonel's influence by proffering two tomato recipes: "Tomato Sauce" and "Scalloped Tomatoes." In the latter, instructions call for the tomatoes to be "blanched" (139), which is the closest Chadwick comes to serving any vegetable raw. In both recipes, she calls for peeling the tomatoes.

Lea's *Domestic Cookery*, published the same year as Mrs. Chadwick's book, makes more liberal use of the tomato, comprising five recipes, for "Tomato Catsup," "Tomato Figs," "Tomato Jelly," "Tomato

Omelet" and "Tomato Sauce," as well as instructions on how to bake, broil, fricassee and fry the vegetable.

A nickname for the tomato that survives in parts of New England is "love apple"; there was even a *Love Apple Cookbook* published by the Vermonter Don Bevona in 1969. There is, however, no proof that the tomato functions as an aphrodisiac, as the name ostensibly implies, and it has been suggested that this misnomer derives from the French *"pommes d'amour,"* which was itself a distortion of the Italian *"pomi dei Moor,"* or "apples of the Moors," since the tomato was introduced into Italy from Morocco (Michaelson 7). When Thomas Jefferson recorded planting the first tomatoes in the New World in his garden at Monticello in 1781, he was actually *re*-introducing the vegetable into America, since it was from Mexico that Cortez brought the tomato to Morroco in 1519 (Burpee 127; Michaelson 7; Tannahil 241, 248-249). Because the sixteenth century tomato was yellow-hued, it was sometimes called the "golden apple," which was also a medieval colloquialism for the orange. One thing tomatoes and oranges have in common is a high nutrient content of ascorbic acid, vitamin C, which made them valuable contributions to a shipboard larder, in that they could protect the crew from scurvy (Weaver *SMJ* 479). Despite this benign attribute, the tomato was frequently shunned as a "poison apple."

Professor Hans Zutter at Temple University's Ambler Campus School of Horticulture believes the tomato may have been stigmatized as a result of mistaken identity (Zutter conv.). Old varieties of potato plants were wont to produce fruits that look exactly like green cherry tomatoes, and those *are* poisonous. However, he points out that such fruits have been bred out of domestic cultivars over the past 15 years (Zutter conv.). As an aside, I would like to mention that the French tendency to call the tomato after the apple pertains also to its cousin: thus, potatoes were accorded the sobriquet *"pommes de terre,"* or "apples of the soil."

Both the tomato and the potato belong to the genus Solanaceae, the deadly nightshade family, whose poison is called solanine. The eggplant is another member. The leaves and stems of all these plants are poisonous, and the edible potato tuber itself contains tiny amounts in the skin and the eyes. Solanine increases with exposure to sunlight (Crocco 625), so it is generally recommended that potatoes be stored in darkness immediately after they are harvested. "Spoilage" usually refers to potatoes that have "greened"—that is, have begun to produce chlorophyll after exposure to light—or sprouted as a result of exposure to excessive dampness. Greened or sprouted potatoes contain too much solanine and should not be eaten. Today, most commercially-grown potatoes are chemically treated with a substance to inhibit sprouting (Crocco 625). Potatoes are also less prone to sprout if they are stored in a location that is both well-ventilated and dry (Moyer 188-189), which Simmons knew as far back as 1796 (10-11).

Exactly one hundred years after Simmons, the proprietess of the Boston Cooking School was aware that sprouted potatoes were unhealthy, and advised cutting out the bad parts:

> When sprouts appear they should be removed; receiving their nourishment from starch, they deteriorate the potato. (Farmer 276)

Most modern nutritionists, however, including Seder, recommend discarding "spoiled" potatoes in their entirety (18). As potatoes sprout through the eyes, many cooks developed the habit of paring out the eyes of good potatoes as a precautionary measure before boiling; this also lent a desirable pristine whiteness to the finished dish. Such whiteness was one of the constituent qualities of the epithet "mealy."

Nowadays, the designation "mealy" is an expression of disdain for a food's texture, but to both Simmons and Chadwick, "mealiness" was considered a virtue in potatoes. Simmons revered the Irish-grown variety as "a genuine mealy rich Potato,...which takes rank of any known in any other kingdom" (Simmons 11). Of those available in the United States, she commended the smooth-skinned "How's Potato" as "the most mealy and richest flavor'd"; the "yellow rusticoat" she ranked after that, and "the red, and red rusticoat" were considered merely "tolerable" (10).

Chadwick provided the following recipe to enhance the quality of mealiness:

To Cook Potatoes, Mealy

[Pare the potatoes, then] put them into cold water, with some salt, and let them boil half an hour. Then drain the water from them, put in more cold water well salted, and let them boil till a fork runs through them. Again drain off the water and sprinkle dry salt on the potatoes, and leave the cover off but keep them in a hot place. (Chadwick 135)

Solanine is water soluble; that is the scientific basis behind Chadwick's recommending cooking the potatoes in three changes of water. Although they probably don't realize it, it is also why most people still leave the skin on their plates when they eat a potato that has been baked rather than boiled. Most solanine is bound to the underside of a potato's skin (*Lancet* 681); when consumed, the poison becomes concentrated in the digestive and nervous systems, and its effects are more severely experienced by children (Lampe 348; Henrique 3). As recently as 1979, responding to an outbreak of solanine poisoning at a London boys' school, the editors of the British medical journal *Lancet* advised "anyone who wants to eat more than a pound at a time to see that they are peeled and boiled" (681). Although she may not have been familiar with its name, these facts about solanine were not unknown to Farmer:

> Potatoes contain an acrid juice, the greater part of which lies near the skin; it passes into the water during boiling of potatoes, and escapes with the steam from a baked potato. (276)

Recognizing that the nutrients are likewise concentrated just under the skin, the evangelizing nutritionist Dr. Sylvester Graham (1794-1851), who also invented the cracker that bears his name, declared in the 1830s that "human beings may subsist from childhood to extreme old age on good potatoes and pure water alone" (20), provided that the potatoes were not peeled. Graham's influence was reflected in *The Cook's Own Cook*, written by an anonymous "Boston Housekeeper" and published in 1854:

> The vegetable kingdom affords no food more wholesome, more easily procured, easily prepared, or less expensive, than the potato. Yet although this most useful vegetable is dressed almost every day, in almost every family, for one plate that comes to the table as it should, ten are spoiled. (qtd. in Burpee 168)

The author of *The New Family Book, or Ladies' Indispensible Companion and Housekeepers' Guide*, published that same year, suggested dressing potatoes with pork fat or butter, but conceded:

> ...a plain boiled potato, when well-cooked, is the best and most wholesome; and although not a substitute for bread, is one of the most useful vegetable productions. (93)

Farmer, however, disagreed with Graham, saying of potatoes that:

> They give needed bulk to food rather than nutriment, and, lacking in proteid, should be used in combination with meat, fish, or eggs. (276)

Farmer, it should be noted, called for the potatoes to be pared—that is to say, peeled—in all of her recipes (276-287; 294), which Graham would probably have said was why she found them so lacking in nutrition. As part of his espoused vegetarian diet, Graham also extolled his whole wheat-based "Graham Bread," unleavened and sweetened only with molasses. The essential factor in all his recommendations was that the potatoes, the wheat and the sweetener will be consumed in as close to a natural state as possible. Graham was aware that the nutritional value of a food decreases the further along it is in the refinement process. Graham, whose disciples included Henry David Thoreau and Louisa May's father Bronson Alcott, was in many ways the forerunner of today's natural foods movement.

A *fin de siecle* compromise of sorts was reached between the peelers and the non-peelers, when some American housewives began following the advice in the newly-published *Twentieth Century Cookbook and Practical Housekeeping* (1900), which suggested removing a narrow belt of skin from around the potato's middle to allow the poisonous solanine to escape while it was boiled with the rest of the jacket intact. In some restaurants promoting what they perceive as *nouvelle cuisine*, I have lately observed that it is currently considered chic to serve new potatoes prepared in that fashion.

The appellation "new" potatoes refers to those which are harvested before reaching maturity, when some of the carbohydrates have not yet undergone conversion from sugar to starch. Thus, they are typically less "mealy" than mature potatoes. Farmer found them relatively undigestible and did not fully approve of them:

New potatoes may be compared to unripe fruit, the starch grains having not reached maturity; therefore, they should not be given to children or invalids. (277)

Digestibility was a major concern of the early cookbook authors. Raw foods in general were considered less digestible than foods which had been cooked, and boiling was the way almost everything was prepared. Chadwick's recipes recommend boiling most vegetables, including spinach, eggplant, cabbage and beets for a full hour (137, 141-142); three-quarters of an hour would suffice for boiling artichokes (140); one and a quarter hours was recommended for cauliflower (140); onions required between one half and three quarters of an hour (138); string beans merited two full hours (137); and potatoes could be boiled all day (135).

It is a modern fallacy that potatoes are fattening; as are most bonafide fallacies, this one is based on a mis-application of empirical logic. A plain potato has no more calories than an apple—in addition to a respectable amount of vitamin C and potassium—but the practice of eating potatoes fried in oil and laden with salt, or baked and smothered by butter and sour cream, increases the caloric and fat values considerably. The addition of a level tablespoonful of butter, for instance, will effectively double the caloric content of a baked potato from 100 to 200 calories, while it escalates the fat content from a mere trace to more than 12 grams (USDA 7, 27).

Our custom of serving potatoes with butter and/or sour cream has its antecedents in the belief, expounded in some old cookbooks, that vegetables were indigestible by themselves. In addition to their having to be cooked, a relative proportion of animal fat was considered necessary to assimilate them. The *Twentieth Century Cookbook and Practical Housekeeping*, published in Chicago in 1900, admonished that "vegetables when eaten raw are apt to ferment in the stomach," and went on to advise the practical turn-of-the-century housewife that "the lack of fat in vegetables should be supplied by using butter, or some other form of fat, with them all" (83).

Butter does, indeed, aid digestion by stimulating the stomach's production of enzymes (Weaver cov.), but the idea that vegetables are otherwise indigestible—or fat-free—is erroneous; the oleomargarine and vegetable-based cooking oils that have replaced butter and lard in most American kitchens provide a ready testament to the contrary. Even now, cans of Crisco solid vegetable shortening are manufactured with the slogan, "It's Digestible!" emblazoned on their labels.

Among the few vegetables that may actually qualify as being indigestible are various types of beans. Beans cause flatulence because they contain highly complex carbohydrates, called oligosaccharides. Human stomachs lack the specific enzymes needed to break down these oligosaccharides, which are also immune to attempted alteration by prolonged cooking. Thus, as the digestive process proceeds, the oligosaccharides reach the lower intestine and commence to ferment, releasing carbon dioxide and methane gases which in turn produce flatulence. It isn't really harmful, but flatulence is uncomfortable, and it tends to be most severe in young children and the elderly, whose digestive systems are not as efficient as those of folks in the prime of life (Hillman 128; Olson AGFD [37]; Randall 109).

Diverse methods of preparing beans have arisen in hopes of reducing the flatus factor. Vermonters sometimes add a little cider vinegar to their pots of baked beans (Jarvis 79); elsewhere in New England, the founder of the Boston Cooking School noted in her recipe for Boston Baked Beans that:

> Many feel sure that by adding with seasonings one-half tablespoon mustard, the beans are more easily digested. (Farmer 212)

Slightly off the subject, she went on to observe that:

> The fine reputation which Boston Baked Beans have gained, has been attributed to the earthen bean-pot with small top and bulging sides in which they are supposed to be cooked. (212)

Surely, a pot of such dimensions would act as a semblance of pressure cooker and ostensibly yield a more tender bean, but whether the alleged "fine reputation" implied any attenuation of flatus symptoms, she did not say.

In 1981, a woman wrote to a newspaper in Allentown, Pennsylvania, offering "a remedy that the woman in our family have used for years." She went on to recommend adding "a teaspoon of baking soda to the cooking water." The columnists' response was that while the alkali in the baking soda may soften the beans and thereby shorten the cooking time, it destroys too much of the B-vitamin thiamine and is, moreover, dubious at best as a flatus preventative (Mayer & Goldberg D5). Another method, endorsed by Dr. Joseph Rackis of the United States Department of Agriculture, is to soak the beans in water for at least three hours, change the water and cook the beans for 30 minutes, then serve if they are done or change the water again and continue cooking if they are not (Randall 109). Still, the problem with Rackis' method is that many important nutrients leach out into the soaking water and are coincidentally discarded.

Other experts call for adding castor or safflower oils, and herbs such as garlic, dill, parsley and epazote to the cooking water. Perhaps the only proven one of these is garlic, which I discussed earlier (Damrau & Ferguson 411). For those who would rather avoid the problem than fight it, Dr. Louis Rockland of the Western Regional Research Laboratory in Albany, New York, has designated a "flatulence scale" for ten common beans. In order, starting with the worst offender, they are: soybeans, pink kidney beans, black beans, pinto beans, California small white beans, Great Northern beans, baby lima beans, garbanzo beans (chick peas), large lima beans, and black-eyed peas (qtd. in Mayer & Goldberg D5).

Who is not familiar with this childhood jingle:

> Beans, beans, good for your heart,
> The more you eat, the more you fart.

Thus far, we have seen how the latter line of the couplet holds true, but there is a certain validity to the former line as well. Eating beans has been proven by independent teams of medical researchers to lower the amount of cholesterol in the blood, so they really are good for your heart (Anderson & Chen AGFD [39]; Keys 145; Randall 102, 104).

Burping is perhaps slightly more socially acceptable than flatulence, but until recently, was apparently a significant source of embarrassment to some people who ate a lot of cucumbers. The first of the "burpless hybrids" debuted in the Burpee Seed Catalogue in 1971; it was relatively seedless, with a thinner skin than the standard varieties. In breeding it, the modus operandi had been that burping was a reaction to an oil found in the seeds and under the skin of the the cucumber; diminishing these offending portions effectively eliminated the problem (Riotte 132). Similar results may be obtained by peeling the cucumbers; this is the method most advocated in vintage cookbooks, as well as the one to which most people still subscribe. Another alternative is pickling, as the oil is effectively neutralized by vinegar and brine. Occasionally, the two practices are combined, as in Penn's 1702 recipe for pickled cucumbers, which calls for cutting them open and removing the seeds, then tying them back together "with a thred" before marinating in a base of white wine vinegar spiced with mace, pepper, horse radish, shallot or garlic, mustard seed and bay leaves (qtd. in Benson 154-155).

Pickling was not, however, primarily a method of making vegetables more digestible, nor was it limited to cucumbers. In essence, pickling was one of the earliest methods of food preservation, and was used to prepare a wide variety of vegetables and fruits. Simmons provided directions for pickling barberries and melons (44); the latter, in their pickled state, she referred to as "mangoes" (44). Martha Washington's collection included, among others, recipes for pickled kidney beans (qtd. in Hess 166-167) and lettuce stalks (169-170). The latter are roughly akin to head-lettuce hearts, and were not particularly exotic. According to food writer Waverly Root, the earliest varieties of lettuce "did not form heads, but put out leaves from a tall central stalk," and were designated as "asparagus" by the ancient Greeks (224). To add to the modern readers' confusion, head lettuce, which was extremely rare before Tudor times, was referred to as "cabbage lettuce" into the nineteenth century (Hess 99).

That both cucumbers and lettuce stalks made fitting pickles may have had something to do with the fact that both were classified as "cold" vegetables in the medieval pharmacopiea. The expression "cool as a cuke" is a residual allusion to this system, wherein all vegetables were dichotomized as either hot or cold, and this distinction served, among other things, to help determine which foods should be eaten by the victim of a particular ailment. "Cold" foods were consequently given to people suffering from high fevers, and "hot" foods were prescribed to help diminish excess phlegm and other "cold" disorders (e.g., Hess 207; Tannahill 179-180). (Similarly, some modern neo-Oriental practitioners advocate the treatment of "yin" disorders such as diarrhea with "yang" foods such as brown rice (Muramoto 122).)

Another vegetable whose merits were sorely debated was cabbage. In a negative vein, Isabella Beeton observed in 1861:

> Cabbage is heavy, and a long time digesting, which has led to a belief that it is very nourishing. It is only fit for robust and active persons; the sedentary or delicate should avoid it. (Beeton 602)

The aforementioned notion that animal fats ameliorated digestibility may have been behind Gulielma Penn's advocacy of cooking a single head of cabbage with "a pound of butter or more:"

> *To Make Cabidg Poridg Without Flesh*
> Take youre Cabidge and pick them Clene
> and put them in to a pot of watter,
> and Lett it boyle so an houer,
> then putt into it a pound of butter or more,

According too youre quantaty
putt in Cloves mace peper and salt,
boyle all these together till it bee all mash,
then put slices of bred into it,
youre bred must bee put at bottom of the dish
then take 6 eggs with yelks only,
and beat them with warme Creme
pour it one the Cabidg
and sarve it up—
(qtd in Benson 152)

For numerous reasons, cabbage has endured a chronic stigma and a steady decline in popularity in America, and appears to be the first food that Celtic, Germanic and Slavic immigrants feel compelled to relinquish when they attempt to climb the social ladder. In the late nineteenth century, one cookbook author observed that its odor made cabbage reprehensible to the delicate noses of Virginia socialities (Hooker 229). Earlier, Simmons had indicted cultivation methods as the culprit, and opined that if cabbages are "grown in an old town or on old gardens, they have a rankness that may be perceived by the fresh air traveller" (14), presumably before they are even harvested, let alone cooked. Modern growers, in my experience, do not acknowledge this problem, although some concede that as cabbages cook, they may emit odors that some people find less than appetizing. Writing in *Organic Gardening*'s December 1981 issue, Marion Gorman proffered the following advice to those who "object to cabbage's cooking odor:"

It [the odor] can be reduced considerably by dropping a whole English walnut or some celery (rib, leaf or seed) into the cooking pot. (Gorman 104)

According to another modern food writer, traditional American cooking practices are to blame. She is self-righteously snide in prefacing her defence of cabbage, employing the fallacy of "forestalling disagreement" (Fearnside & Holther 101) in her insinuation that cooking cabbage only poses problems for the incompetent:

Good cooks know that the secret of cooked cabbage is to avoid boiling it to death. The longer cabbage cooks, the stronger the taste and smell—and because of this, its reputation has suffered. (Coleman n.p.)

Coleman leaves to the reader to decide whether boiling a cabbage "to death" means for five minutes or five hours; her precursors Penn and Simmons were no less vague in their respective recommendations that cabbage is done either when "it bee all mash" (Penn 152), or "when the stalk is tender" (Simmons 47). Chadwick specified an hour (142), as she did for most things, while Farmer suggested between thirty minutes and an hour (257); the latter also noted that she forestalled the odor problem by adding a quarter teaspoon of baking soda to the boiling water (Farmer 257).

Medically, it could almost be said of cabbage that what it doesn't cause, it cures. Ever since the ancient Romans prepared for their long, decadent feasts by eating cabbage leaves dipped in salt water, cabbage has been heralded as a cure for drunkenness (e.g., Quinn 174; Trachtenberg 63). Moreover, because of its extremely high vitamin C content, nutritionists currently contend that it may indeed help in that regard (Imrie 428-430). Current research sanctions cabbage as an antibiotic (Dickerman and Liberman 440); a cure for peptic ulcers (Cheney 672; *Chemical Week* 11-14-53); and a preventative for colon cancer (*Therapaeia* 39).

The problem with cabbage, however, is that it contains a goitrogenic alkaloid that blocks iodine absorption and can lead to enlargement of the thyroid. The alkaloid likewise inhabits all other members of the Brassica family, including Brussels sprouts, cauliflower, kohlrabi, broccoli, collards, kale, rutabaga, turnip, watercress, rape and mustard greens (Hartman conv.; Tampion 151; Tannahill 380). Ironically, the iodine-blocking constituents are the very same ones that give these vegetables their preferred flavors (Tampion 151).

The wanton dissemination of misconceptions about vegetables is not merely a curiosity of history. In our own self-consciously scientific age, the British popular historian Reay Tannahill erroneously wrote in his 1973 *Food in History* that:

...the pigment carotene, which puts the color in egg yolks, sweet potatoes, mangoes and carrots, can give the consumer jaundice. (Tannahill 380)

The facts are that carotene is a precursor to vitamin A and, according to pediatrician Guy Hartman, M.D., of the Kaiser-Permanente Medical Center in Fontana, California, it does not cause jaundice, which is a liver disease, but merely mimics one of the disease symptoms: effecting a yellowish cast to the skin. The condition is especially pronounced in small children—with most of the yellowish pigment collecting in their noses, palms, and the soles of their feet. It is impossible to overdose, so there is nothing to worry about, according to Hartman, "as long as mother doesn't mind an orange baby" (Hartman conv.). Indeed, a sallow complexion could be considered more a sign of health than disease, he said, as it indicates the child is receiving adequate vitamin A in a non-toxic form.

Remember your mother telling you that eating your carrots would enable you to see in the dark? She has her champions. Vitamin A supplements are frequently prescribed to treat night blindness, and carrots are among the best natural sources of vitamin A (Rodale *et al* 560, 569).

In conclusion, I would like to reiterate that my purpose here has been to show that old cookbooks may serve as repositories of what were once conscious beliefs about vegetable composition, that such beliefs have in turn affected how vegetables were prepared, and that some of those methods of preparation persist into modern times as empty rituals, sans the belief systems which fostered them. Today, we pride ourselves on our sophistication, but when we butter our peas and pare the eyes out of our potatoes, it is not necessarily because they taste better that way. We are cultivating a tradition of folklore, fact and fallacy that has been growing for as long as there have been gardens.

Works Cited

Abbott, Shirley. "The Woman With the New Stove." Introduction to facsimile edition of *Home Cookery* by Mrs. J. Chadwick, and *Ladies' Indispensible Companion.* Birmingham, Alabama: Oxmoor House, 1984.

Anderson, James W, MD, and Wen-Ju Lin Chen, PhD. "Effects of Legumes and Their Soluble Fibers on Cholesterol-Rich Lipoproteins." *American Chemical Society Abstracts of Papers*, 1982, p. AGFD (39).

Augustin, Jorge, and Johnson, S.R., and Teitzel C., and Toma, R.B., and Shaw, R.L., and True, R.H., and Hogan, J.M., and Deutsch, R.M. "Vitamin Composition of freshly Harvested and Stored Potatoes." *Journal of Food Science*, Vol. 43, No. 5 (Sept-Oct. 1978), 1566-1567.

Beeton, Mrs. Isabella. *The Book of House-Hold Management.* "Published originally by S.O. Beeton in 24 monthly parts, 1859-1861; first published in a bound edition, 1861." London: S.O. Beeton, 1861. Facsimile edition: New York: Farrar, Straus, and Giroux, 1977.

Benson, Evelyn Abraham, ed. *Penn Family Recipes.* York, PA: George Shimway, 1966.

Bevona, Don. *The Love Apple Cookbook.* New York: Funk & Wagnalls, 1969.

Bible Christian Church. *Vegetable Cookery With an Introduction Recommending Abstinence from Animal Food and Intoxication Liquors.* "By a member of the Bible Christian Church." Third edition. London: Mr. E. Wilson, & Manchester: Messrs. Clark & Others, Booksellers, 1829.

Bordia, Arun K., and Joshi, H.K., and Sanadhya, Y.K., and Bhu, N. "Effect of Essential Oil of Garlic on Serum Fibrolytic Activity in Patients With Coronary Artery Disease." *Atherosclerosis*, Vol. 28, No. 2 (October 1977), 155-159.

A Boston Housekeeper, *The Cook's Own Book.* 1854.

Bullock, Helen D. "Thomas Jefferson...Gourmet." Introduction to *Thomas Jefferson's Cookbook* by Marie Kimball. Charlottesville: University Press of Virginia, 1976, vii-xii.

Burpee, Lois. *Gardener's Companion and Cookbook.* New York: Harper and Row, 1983.

Chadwick, Mrs. J. *Home Cookery: A Collection of Tried Receipts, Both Foreign and Domestic.* Boston: Crosby, Nichols and Company, and New York: Charles S. Francis and Company, 1853. Facsimile edition. Birmingham, Ala.: Oxmoore House, Inc., 1984.

Chemical Week, 14 November 1953. "Cabbage Cure."

Cheney, Garnet, MD. "Anti-Peptic Ulcer Dietary Factor: Vitamin 'U' in the Treatment of Peptic Ulcer." *Journal of the American Dietetic Association*, Vol. 26, September 1950, 668-672.

Coleman, Mrs. Charles. "Cabbage to 'Taketh Away Freckles.'" *The Sacramento Union*, 12 March 1972, n.p.

Crocco, Stephanie, PhD. "Potato Sprouts and Greening Potatoes: Potential Toxic Reaction." *Journal of the American Medical Association*, Vol. 245, No. 6 (13 February 1981), 625.

Damrau, Frederic, MD, and Ferguson, Edgar A., Chemist. "The Modus Operandi of Carminatives: The Therapeutic Value of Garlic in Functional Gastrointestinal Disorders." *The Review of Gastroenterology*, Vol. 16, No. 5 (May 1949), 411-419.

Dickerman, J.M., and Liberman, S. "Studies on the Chemical Nature of an Antibiotic Present in Water Extracts of Cabbage." *Food Research*, September-October 1952, 438-440.

Farmer, Fannie Merrit. *The Boston Cooking-School Cook Book*. Boston, 1896. Facsimile of first edition: New York: Weathervane Books div. Crown Publishers, Inc., n.d.

Fearnside, W. Ward, and Holther, William B. *Fallacy: The Counterfeit of Argument*. Englewood Cliffs, NJ: Prentice-Hall, Inc., 1959.

Given, Meta. *Modern Encyclopedia of Cooking*. Volume Two. Chicago: J.G. Ferguson and Associates, 1948.

Gorman, Marion. "Winter Menus Starring Cabbage." *Organic Gardening and Farming*, Vol. 28, No. 12 (December 1981), 104-106.

Graham, Sylvester. *A Treatise on Bread and Bread Making*. Boston: Light & Stearns, 1 Cornhill, 1837.

Hartman, Guy. Personal conversations, 1981.

Henrique, Doris. "Plants—Know Which Ones Are Safe to Eat." University of Delaware: press release, 9 April 1980.

Hess, Karen, ed. *Martha Washington's Booke of Cookery and Booke of Sweetmeats*. New York: Columbia, 1981.

Hillman, Howard. *Kitchen Science: A Compendium of Essential Information for Every Cook*. Boston: Houghton Mifflin Company, 1981.

Hooker, Richard J. *A History of Food and Drink in America*. Indianapolis and New York: Bobbs-Merrill, 1981.

Imrie. J.A. "Emergencies in General Practice: Acute Alcohol Poisoning." *British Medical Journal*, Vol. 2, 13 August 1955, 428-430.

Jabs, Carolyn. "Heirloom Tomatoes." *1981 Old Farmer's Almanac Gardeners' Companion*, 82-84.

Jarvis, D.C., MD. *Folk Medicine*. New York: Fawcett Crest, 1958.

Keys, Ancel. "Wine, Garlic, and C[oronary] H[eart] D[isease] in Seven Countries." *The Lancet*, No. 8160, 19 January 1980, 145-145.

Lampe, Kenneth F., PhD. "Systemic Plant Poisoning in Children." *Pediatrics for the Clinician*, Vol. 54, No. 3 (September 1974), 347-351.

The Lancet, Vol. 2, No. 8144, 29 September 1979, p. 681. "Potato Poisoning."

Kimball, Marie. *Thomas Jefferson's Cook Book*. Charlottesville: University Press of Virginia, 1976.

Lea, Elizabeth Ellicott. *Domestic Cookery, Useful Receipts, and Hints to Young Housekeepers.* By Elizabeth E. Lea. "The Source of Liberal Deeds is Wise Economy." Fifth Edition. Baltimore: Cushings and Bailey, 1853. Facsimile edition: ed. William Woys Weaver. Philadelphia: University of Pennsylvania Press, 1982.

Mayer, Dr. Jean, and Goldberg, Jeanne. "Anti-Gas Remedies for Beans." *The Morning Call*, Allentown, PA, 8 April 1981, D5.

Michaelson, Mike. *The Great Tomato Cookbook.* 1975.

Moyer, Anne., ed. *The Green Thumb Cookbook.* Emmaus, PA: Rodale Press, 1977.

"Naturally Occurring Toxicants in Foods." A Report by the Institute of Food Technologists's Expert Panel on Food Safety and Nutrition and the Committee on Public Information, Chicago, March 1975.

The New Family Book, or Ladies' Indispensible Companion and Housekeepers' Guide: Addressed to Sister, Mother and Wife. Containing a variety of the most Useful Information ever published on the subject, for the price. Here Are the Very Best Directions for the Management of Children. Instructions to Ladies under Different Circumstances. Ladies' Toilette Table; Rules of Etiquette, Rules for the Formation of Good Habits; Instructions for Managing Canry Birds. And Containing a Great Variety of Recipes on Medicine, So that each person may become his or her own Physician. To which is added one of the best systems of Cookery Ever Published. The Majority of the Recipes are New and Ought to be Possessed by Every One. New York: Published at 128 Nassaue Street, 1854. Facsimile edition: Birmingham, Ala.: Oxmoor House, Inc., 1984.

Oddo, Sandra. *Home Made: An Alternative to Supermarket Living: Recipes from the Nineteenth Century, Rescued, Reinterpreted, and Commented Upon by Sandra Oddo: Including Also a Wealth of Wisdom Concerning Household Management, And a Special Section of Home Remedies.* New York: Atheneum, 1972.

Olson, Alfred C. "Flatus Causing Factors in Legumes." *ACS/CSJ Chemical Congress Proceedings*, Honolulu, Hawaii, 1-6 April 1979, p. AGFD (37).

Orcutt, Georgia, ed. *The Gardener's Adviser.* Dublin, N.H.: Yankee Books, 1983.

Penn, Gulielma Maria Springett. *Penn Family Recipes.* Ed. Evelyn Abraham Benson. York, PA: George Shimway, 1966.

Quinn, Vernon. *Vegetables in the Garden and Their Legends.* Philadelphia and New York: J.B. Lippincott Company, 1942.

Rackemann, Adelaide C. "Let's Hear It for Rhubarb!" *Flower and Garden*, February-March 1981, 93-94.

Randall, Katherine. "Full of Beans...And Good Health." *Prevention*, February 1981, 101-109.

Rinzler, Carol Ann. "Granny's Complaint." *American Health*, Vol. IV, No. 6 (July/August 1985), 48-49.

Riotte, Louise. "What Do You Mean You Can't Eat Cukes?" *Organic Gardening and Farming*. Vol. 19, No. 5 (May 1972), 132-133.

Rodale, Robert, and the Editors of *Prevention* Magazine. *The Complete Book of Vitamins.* Emmaus, PA: Rodale Press, 1984.

Root, Waverly. *Food: An Authoritative and Visual History and Dictionary of the Foods of the World.* New York: Simon and Schuster, 1980.

Saling, Ann. *Rhubarb Renaissance.* Seattle, WA: Pacific Search Press, 1978.

Shellard, E.J. "Foreword." *Culpeper's Colour Herbal.* Ed. David Potterton. London: W. Foulsham & Co. Ltd., 1983.

Simmons, Amelia. *American Cookery, or the Art of Dressing Viands, Fish, Poultry and Vegetables, and the Best Modes of Making Pates, Puffs, Pies, Tarts, Puddings, Custards and Preserves, and All Kinds of Cakes, from the Imperial Plumb to Plain Cake. Adapted to this Country and All Grades of Life.* "By Amelia Simmons, An American Orphan. Published According to Act of Congress." Hartford, CT: Hudson and Goodwin, 1796. Facsimile edition. New York: Dover Books, 1984.

"Solanine Poisoning." *British Medical Journal*, Vol. 2, No. 6203, 8 December 1975, 1438-1439.

Tampion, John. *Dangerous Plants.* New York: Universal Books, 1977.

Tannahill, Reay. *Food in History.* New York: Stein and Day, 1973.

Telephone Pioneers of America, Harry B. Thayer Chapter. "Poison in Your Back Yard." Brochure, n.d.

Therapaeia, May 1981, p. 39. "Of Cabbages and Cancer."

Time, 1 March 1976, pp. 54-55. "The Deadly Garden," and "Dr. Hartman's List of Lethal Foliage."

Toyohicko Arigo and Terumi Tamada. "Platelet Aggregation Inhibitor in Garlic." *The Lancet,* No. 8212, 17 January 1981, 150-151.

Trachtenberg, Nancy. "Produce Folklore." *Vegetarian Times* May-June 1979, p. 63.

Twentieth Century Cookbook and Practical Housekeeping. Chicago: Henneberry Co., 1900.

United States Department of Agriculture. *Nutritive Value of Foods.* Home and Garden Bulletin Number 72, rev. Sept. 1978.

Washington, Martha Dandridge Custis. *Martha Washington's Booke of Cookery and Booke of Sweetmeats.* Ed. Karen Hess. New York: Columbia university Press, 1981.

Weaver, W.L. "The Prevention of Heat Prostration by Use of Vitamin C." *Southern Medical Journal*, Vol. 41 (May 1948), 479-481.

Weaver, William Woys, ed. *A Quaker Woman's Cookbook.* Philadelphia: University of Pennsylvania Press, 1982.

_____. *Sauerkraut Yankees: Pennsylvania German Foods and Foodways.* Philadelphia: University of Pennsylvania Press, 1983.

_____. Personal conversation, 21 June 1985.

Ziment, Irwin, M.D. "What to Expect from Expectorants." *Journal of the American Medical Society.* Vol. 236, No. 2 (12 July 1976), 193-194.

Zutter, Hans. Personal conversation, 1981.

Eating Our Way Toward Wisdom:
M.F.K. Fisher's Oysters

Lee Upton

"It is impossible to enjoy without thought," M.F.K. Fisher argues (Consider 150); throughout eighteen books and for over fifty years she has portrayed thoughtful pleasure as disruptive pleasure, particularly through her subversion of cultural expectations of gender. In her culinary meditations she explores "the wilder, more insistent" appetites: "So it happens that when I write of hunger I am really writing about love and the hunger for it, and warmth and the love of it and the hunger for it" (Gastronomical 353). A prolific presence, she is our subversive food writer. Just as her work subverts expectations of genre, disrupting perimeters among the essay, the memoir, fiction, and the recipe, so too do her accounts of gender and pleasure.

Fisher has written widely on gastronomy and the sensual intelligence in evocative and passionate prose. Notably, she chose to disobey at least two childhood directives—her disobedience amounting to a lifestyle: first, to avoid the discussion of food at table (she was cautioned by her mother that it was "unseemly") and second, to "swallow" the oyster "as quickly as possible, without *thinking*" (374). *Consider the Oyster* (1941), her meditation on the eating of "that most sensitive of foods, the oyster" (Consider 180), amounts to a seduction toward consciousness. She would have us consider the oyster as a means of exploring our responses to danger, transformation, and trespass as these lead to wisdom. For Fisher, wisdom may be gained through pleasure; we may taste our way toward knowledge. Knowledge, in turn, is often disruptive of social behavior. Women who eat the oyster, a food so frequently allied to both passion and women, may consider their own passion, including their passion for one another.

Oysters provide this writer with a heuristic for reflections upon pleasure that may be acquired despite peril. A particularly suitable text, oysters connote not only possible danger to the eater who may come across a "bad one," but, as this author emphasizes, they themselves face continual hazard. From *Consider the Oyster's* opening line, "An oyster leads a dreadful but exciting life" (125) to a final account of oyster poaching and a discharged gun, Fisher engages us in the drama of transformation of both the oyster and those who eat the oyster. Finally her account rests upon actual trespass; two boys poach upon commercial oyster beds, discovering the most satisfying breakfast of their lives. Acts of trespass upon accepted behavior remain compelling rewards in her

Obliquely, *Consider the Oyster* contemplates habitual assumptions about gender. The oyster is, of course, associated with women, the female genitals, and erotic prowess. Eric Partridge notes that *oyster* is slang for "the female pudend" (843). Exploring the symbolic function of the oyster, Mircea Eliade remarks upon "the resemblance between the marine shell and the genital organs of woman, the relations between oysters, waters and the moon" (125). The oyster's very connection to women and erotic force presents Fisher with remarkable possibilities for insinuation. The qualities of passivity, patience, informality, and uncanniness—qualities frequently linked to the oyster—are also culturally assigned to women. To consider the oyster, then, is to consider cultural assignments of gender. In literature, for instance, the oyster's very inexpressivity and apparent passivity are foregrounded. Frequently the oyster is a rather comic food. Simply by subverting our expectations of the inactive oyster, Lewis Carroll gains much of his humor. His oysters are "All hopping through the frothy waves, / And scrambling to the shore." "Hold your tongue, Ma!" Carroll's young Crab cries, "you're enough to try the patience of an oyster!" Clovis in H. H. Munro's "The Match-Maker" muses: "I think oysters are more beautiful than any religion....There's nothing in Christianity or Buddhism that quite matches the sympathetic unselfishness of an oyster" (24-25).

Yet it is Jonathan Swift's remark in *Polite Conversation* that serves as Fisher's epigraph to her book: "He was a bold man that first eat an oyster." Fisher's examinations more frequently focus on courage and peril than passivity or mystification. She considers the oyster with boldness, presenting oysters as more various, more dramatic, and more appetitive than we may have supposed. Women, so frequently culturally associated with the oyster, emerge as beyond categorization and thus containment. "Men's ideas...continue to run in the old channels about oysters as well as God and war and women" (Consider 137). The oyster performs as her subversive text.

Two separate accounts of Fisher's first oyster emphasize the experience of love and death: "The First Oyster" explores an adolescent Fisher's encounter with older women's passion while the second account is framed by references to death. Such divergent thematic resonances suggest the troubling divisions which Fisher evokes.

The schoolgirl Fisher is frightened by women's appetites in "The First Oyster" and the sudden revelation of their emotions. A Christmas oyster feast is underscored with the suggestion of sexual passion between women. Fisher tastes her first oyster just as she has been asked to dance by another girl:

The oyster seemed larger. I knew that I must down it, and was equally sure that I could not. Then, as Olmsted ["the most wonderful girl in the whole school"] put her thin hand on my shoulder blades, I swallowed once, and felt light and attractive and daring, to know what I had done. (Gastronomical 373)

Fisher's sudden and distressing encounter with older women's sensuality occurs after she has danced with a second girl, a partner she finds repellent. Removing herself, she enters the school kitchen to come upon "an unknown rather than a known sensuality." Her gaze focuses upon Mrs. Cheever, the normally withdrawn housekeeper:

She stood with one hand still on the wide red shoulders of the nurse, and with the other she put the oysters left from the Christmas party on a platter. Her eyes were smeared so that they no longer looked hard and hateful, and as she watched the old woman eat steadily, voluptuously, of the fat cold molluscs, she looked so tender that I turned anxiously toward the sureness and stability of such small passions as lay in the dining room. (Gastronomical 377)

The adolescent Fisher witnesses a transformation which she cannot understand. Such "unknown" tenderness and passion repulse her. The metamorphosis of the lonely and stern housekeeper into a weeping woman who looks with tenderness upon another woman is inexplicable to the young Fisher. Her first response is to condemn the oyster she has recently swallowed, a substitute for her fear and incomprehension: "If I could still taste my first oyster, if my tongue still felt fresh and excited, it was perhaps too bad. Although things are different now, I hoped then, suddenly and violently, that I would never see one again" (377). The difference between her pleasant and lingering physical experience of the oyster and her sudden terror of the scene before her reveals the division within the young Fisher: a tongue "still...fresh and excited" and a mind stunned "violently." Fisher chooses to focus on women's passion for one another—an "unknown" because in part uncategorized behavior that overwhelms her assumptions. The oysters mediate between the women, their consumption an expression of love.

In a later account, Fisher writes of her first oyster as a "test" at table, second only to the sight, dredged out of a Louisiana bayou, of a corpse bloated with feasting shrimp. "I found it [the oyster] dangerously disgusting for several minutes, but since that memorable day I have eaten oysters whenever I could, including one very bad one in Berne which, my husband told me, would prove to have been all right if I did not die within six hours. I did not, although the last hour had me waiting with ill-concealed anxiety, my eyes on the clock and one hand lying expectantly upon the bedside bell" (Alphabet 723). Her account of the first oyster is framed by death—initially the shrimp-bloated corpse and then by a "very bad one" that might have poisoned her. She seeks to educate the reader as she herself has been; to eat the oyster is to avoid the "waste" of revulsion: "Now, having wasted too many years in shuddering at oysters, I like them. I *thoroughly* like them, so that I am willing to forego comfort and at times even safety to savor their strange cold succulence" (157). Eating the oyster is a test of honor and conscious choice. The oyster remains both strange (a repeated descriptive) and compelling.

Fisher is quick to dismiss the oyster's reputation as an aphrodisiac which allows men power over women or themselves; libido cannot be fortified and accelerated thoughtlessly:

> Women have been known to be influenced...by the schemed use of these shellfish, and there is one man named Mussolini who lives near Biloxi, in Mississippi, who swears that he has cured seven frigid virgins by the judicious feeding of long brown buck-oysters from near-by bayous.
>
> It is men, though, in astounding numbers, who will swear, in correctly modulated voices, a hundred equally strange facts. (Consider 175)

She conducts her dismissal of the oyster as "amatory food" (the phase is Lord Byron's) obliquely. In a primary anecdote a young man's hopes for erotic prowess are blunted by his very reliance upon the oyster. He consumes far too many oysters to so much as meet with the women who would test his virility. Ironically, sick from over-eating, he is taken into the care of the hotel porter who, in a parody of courtesan-like control, "tucked his arm winningly, seductively, with practiced skill, into the thin little man's, and together they wove toward a comfortable couch" (177). Fisher dismisses the oyster's unconscious influence upon women, instead focusing upon over-consumption by a man. More interesting to Fisher is consciousness of danger, trespass, and transformation as these promote wisdom. Even seduction, for Fisher, ought to be *thoughtful* if it is to be pleasurable.

Interestingly enough, gastronomy is rather dangerous for Fisher. *The Gastronomical Me* includes the story of Ora, a cook in Fisher's childhood home who killed—with her French knife—her own mother and herself. Fisher lingers a good deal on the culinary efficacy of the French knife and on the unique capacity of Ora who taught the nine-year-old Fisher both the wonder of condiments and the horror of gastronomic monotony. In another account of adolescence we learn of a "double murder and hara-kiri committed by the head-boy one good Friday" (Gastronomical 369) in the all-girl's school in which Fisher was enrolled. The first meal she prepared alone was "pure poison" (364), her own mother succumbing with an extreme allergic reaction to the berries that Fisher blithely garnished upon a pudding. Not surprisingly, this author notes of her cooking: "There was always an element of surprise, if not actual danger in my meals." Danger preoccupies her; something done well is, in fact, "dangerously perfect" (17). If eating with such consciousness is dramatic, an event that tempts us from safety and calcified patterns of thought and action, we must school ourselves in our difficult pleasures. Fisher herself found her first oyster "dangerously revolting for several minutes." Revulsion that has been overcome and transformed into pleasure may educate, she suggests, most memorably.

So simple an event as satisfying an appetite is fraught with problematics, for if food is Fisher's symbolic equivalent to love, satisfying hunger remains perilous. The oyster's own existence, from spat to full-grown bivalve, intrigues her for its very peril. An oyster, she tells us, is involved in "stress, passion and danger" (Consider 125). Yet the oyster's very sensitivity to danger protects her: "She can feel shadows as well as the urgency of milt and her delicate muscles know danger and pull shut her shells with firmness" (Consider 127). While danger is often present within Fisher's meditations, so too is transformation. She would have us acknowledge food as protean, transformed in the kitchen, within the body, and within the mind. Margaret Atwood's "Carrying Food Home in Winter" might illuminate much of Fisher: "This onion will become a motion/this grapefruit/will become a thought" (140).

Oysters themselves undergo transformation within their natural environment—an effect that Fisher dwells upon with curiosity, for this blurring of category, rather than disquieting, she finds compelling. "Almost any normal oyster never knows from one year to the next whether he is he or she, and may start at any moment, after the first year, to lay eggs where before he spent his sexual energies in being exceptionally masculine" (125). Her accounts of gender similarly disrupt categories. In the memorable "Feminine Ending" we learn that Juanito is actually Juanita; through her passion for a man she reveals the sexuality she disguised as a child for her own survival. Yet when the man she loves marries another woman, Juanita once again assumes the identity of a child—a boy. "Juanita would be free again, as much as anyone can be who has once known hunger and gone unfed...." (572).

For Fisher, appetite may educate beyond constraints. The transformation of categories emerges as trespass. A display of appetite in women is a challenge to gender conceptions, exemplified by one male character who cries out of the author, "She likes it, she likes good food...She cannot be a real woman" (Serve 119). To take delight in good food, to write with precision of the fleeting sensation of taste, is to be mistaken for a man. By advocating appetite this author advocates women's ability to assume pleasure and the power of discrimination. In "I Was Really Very Hungry"—an account in part of Fisher's own considerable capacity to consume—she describes "a young servant in

Northern Burgundy who was almost frighteningly fanatical about food, like a medieval woman possessed by a devil" (As 37). In another story the landlady Madam Biarnet "ate like a mad woman, crumbs falling from her mouth, her cheeks bulging, her eyes glistening and darting about the plates..." (Gastronomical 402). These are outrageous cameos of appetite. Elsewhere Fisher refers to an anecdote by Jean-Louis Vaudoyer in which a woman's capacity for pleasure trespasses upon male sensibility. Fisher quotes the woman: "Ah...what a pity that I do not have little taste-buds clear to the bottom of my stomach!" Fisher adds that "such a remark could not seem anything but gross to an ascetic man, partly because a woman said it and partly because all such frank gastronomic pleasures are inexplicable to him." She adds that to anyone who has "eaten, digested, and then *thought*...such a blatantly sensual remark...is not only comprehensible but highly intelligent" (Consider 181). To increase the ability to taste and judge—and thus, as a woman, to trespass upon conventional assumptions of women's capacity—is Fisher's higher good.

Trespass, finally, leads to pleasure as artificial boundaries are crossed. The closing anecdote within *Consider the Oyster* highlights trespass as a means of discovering pleasure. Two boys in a boat take refuge from a storm in a Chesapeake Bay cove. The next morning they discover directly below them "oyster beds as perfect as something in a dream":

> They pulled off their clothes and swam down through the stilled water, and brought up oysters bigger than their hands, and sat there in the cool fresh grayness of the dawn, cracking open the shells and sucking down the firm fish within. When each little boy had emptied his shells, he dove down for more, and all the hidden fears of the hard night vanished as they ate, and dove, and ate, naked as they were born in the growing light.
>
> The end of the story was that a bullet plunked into their little cabin wall, because they were stealing oysters from one of the most famous privately owned beds of the most delicious strain of the whole Atlantic Coast. The guard frightened them, and then, pitied them and let them go, and they headed into the bay full of the best breakfast they were ever to eat in their lives, wiser but not sadder little boys.(Consider 184)

By trespassing, however unknowingly, beyond boundaries, by following their hungers and repeatedly diving, they are rendered "wiser but not sadder."

Rabelais tells us "appetite grows by eating." One story in particular may illustrate Fisher's awareness of the importance of assuming the habit of eating with full consciousness. In "To Feed Such Hunger" she creates her negative example, a parable of nourishment denied; significantly, a woman's hunger remains unsatisfied. We are introduced to a young Czech student, Maritza, who is in love with a German student, Klorr. Maritza is repeatedly referred to as a food; she is a "lump," a "pudding," a "potato"; she lives with the passivity we commonly associate with the oyster. In Maritza's room Fisher discovers what amounts to a tableau of ungratified desire.

> It [the table] was set up by the fireplace, with a linen tablecloth, and placed precisely on it were a plate of beautiful grapes with dark pink skins, an empty champagne bottle and a fine glass, and a little round cake with a piece out of it. It looked like the kind of table a butler arranges in the second act of an old-fashioned bedroom comedy, except that there was only one glass, one plate, one fork.
>
> I knew Klorr had been supping there, while Maritza lay naked on the bed and moaned for him. And I knew that he had put the empty grapeskins on her unprotesting flesh without ever touching her. (Gastronomical 415-416)

The arrangement excludes the woman; there is "only one glass, one plate, one fork." The woman herself is made into a form of table ("Maritza was lying there in that light, naked except for a few crumbs and grapeskins on her belly"). She is in a nearly unconscious state when Fisher enters the room. Pointedly, Fisher's narrative alludes to shame: "It was as if Maritza had been shamed in some way that only women could know about." To shame in Fisher's work is to refuse to affirm life, to refuse to eat and in turn to be refused. In another essay shame is linked with the oyster. (Fisher writes "Once I knowingly ate a 'bad one'in the Pompeiian Room at the Bern-Palace rather than cry them shame." Consider 158). Yet in "To Feed Such Hunger" Maritza suffers shame— and excitement without fulfillment. Ironically, by massaging Maritza back to sensibility and thus aiding another woman in "coming to consciousness," Fisher herself assumes greater power. Her reprimand executed to Klorr strengthens her French accent; anger improves her tongue.

A fuller pleasure requires our engagement beyond cultural strictures: "It is as if our bodies, wiser than we who wear them, call out for encouragement and strength and, *in spite of us and of the patterns of proper behavior we have learned*, compel us to answer and to eat" (Alphabet, 683, emphasis mine). Fisher's is a meditation in favor of knowledge, "to answer and to eat"—unlike Maritza unable either to answer or eat, or Klorr who ritualizes his contempt of her.

Significantly, Fisher writes of her daughter's first introduction to dining in terms that suggest eating as a journey in consciousness: "she is us; she is whatever tender creature can thus begin the long nibbling through the invisible tunnel of the world" (As 88). Fisher's gastronomical writing interrogates desire as much as it displays desire. In turn she incites desire within the reader. For Fisher there are hardly any innocent pleasures; with luck and with the conscious testing of our powers we may eat our way toward wisdom that subverts our categorizations of gender and, in turn, our categorizations of pleasure.

Works Cited

Atwood, Margaret. "Carrying Food Home in Winter." *Selected Poems 1965-1975*. Boston: Houghton, 1976: 139-140.

Carroll, Lewis. *Alice in Wonderland: The Annotated Alice*. New York: Macmillan, 1984.

Eliade, Mircea. *Images and Symbols: Studies in Religious Symbolism*. Trans. Philip Mairet. New York: Sheed and Ward, 1961.

Fisher, M.F.K. *An Alphabet for Gourmets*. In *The Art of Eating*. New York: Vintage, 1976.

―――― *As They Were*. New York: Vintage, 1983.

―――― *Consider the Oyster*. In *The Art of Eating*.

―――― *The Gastronomical Me*. In *The Art of Eating*.

―――― *Serve It Forth*. In *The Art of Eating*.

Munro, H.H. "The Matchmaker." *The Chronicles of Clovis*. New York: Lane, 1919.

Partridge, Eric. *A Dictionary of Slang and Unconventional English*. Eighth Edition. New York: Macmillan, 1984.

Dessert

Cultural Meaning and Use of Food:
A Selective Bibliography (1973-1987)

Karen Madeira

It is hoped that the categorization and specific references in this bibliography will be useful in directing those who are interested in pursuing particular areas in the study of cultural aspects of the human approach to food. It should be noted that although the references in each topic category are limited in number, those that are listed should provide an informative departure point for the interested student of culture and food.

Simply enough, a selective bibliography should be structured in such a way as to be useful to those who are inclined to further exploration of a topic of particular interest. This bibliography was compiled with thoughtful attention given to that point. Therefore, it contains a limited selection of bibliographic material from a specific period of time. The time period of 1973 to 1986 was chosen as a limiting factor for inclusion of the bibliographic citations in order to include particular articles pertinent to the topic, as well as to reflect the scope of the social science literature of the past fourteen years. During that time a proliferation of written descriptions, explanations, and various theoretical analyses of cultural aspects of food may be found. This is not to say that academic interest in this topic is exclusively characteristic of that period in time. It is to say that in the past fourteen years the humanities and social science research literature has reflected the increasing legitimacy of cultural aspects of food as a field of study that developed as a result of scholarly efforts in such disciplines as anthropology, archeology, sociology, psychology, history, linguistics, literature, nutrition, food science, and consumer studies.

The mutual interest and contemporary intellectual curiosity shared by many in seemingly diverse disciplines is evidenced in research articles and books about food and culture. The recent emergence of a research journal entitled "Food and Foodways," illustrates this contemporary academic focus. Publications of this nature demonstrate the continued emphasis that is being placed on the study of food as a significant and complex cultural phenomena worthy of serious academic consideration.

The categories of references on cultural aspects of food presented here were selected from the vast realm of possible topic categories that have been addressed by researchers between 1973 and 1987. The division of information into six topic areas in this bibliography was achieved by using principles of categorization involving: definition/classification of food for selection; meaning, use and symbolism of food; patterns of food-related behavior; and beliefs.

In choosing the bibliographic material to be included, it seemed appropriate to begin with *General References* on culture and food. The next category in the bibliography is *Cultural Meaning of Food* and includes references about the concept of food and what meaning food holds for people. The third category is divided into four components and addresses *The Human Pattern of Eating. Food Symbolism* is the fourth category, which is focussed on selected examples in the study of non-nutritive uses of food. Although many of the references in the fifth category involve symbolic identity and are appropriate for inclusion in the previous category of references, a separate category, *Ethnicity and Assimilation*, was created for them. *Food Ideology* is the sixth and last category in the bibliography and contains citations pertaining to the use of food in relation to belief systems.

General References and Review Articles

The following list of citations include: comprehensive overviews on the topic of culture and food; basic introductory information about the relationship between culture and food; reviews of literature and annotated bibliographies and references for further in-depth study of specific topics.

Arnott, M.L. (Ed.) 1976. *Gastronomy: the anthropology of food and food habits.* Mouton Pubs., The Hague.

Axelson, M.L. 1986. *The impact of culture on food-related behavior.* Annual Review of Nutrition 6: 345.

Bryant, C., Courtney, A., Markesbery, B., and DeWalt, K. 1985. *The Cultural Feast*, West Publishing Co., St. Paul, MN.

Farb, P. and Armelagos, G. 1980. *Consuming Passions*, Houghton Mifflin Co., Boston (or 1983 Pocket Books).

Foster, G. and Anderson, B. 1981. "Food in a cultural context." In *Food and People*, D. Kirk and E. Eliason, p. 12, Boyd and Fraser Publ. Co., San Francisco.

Freedman, R.L. (Ed.) 1981. *Human Food Uses. A Cross-Cultural, Comprehensive Annotated Bibliography*, Greenwood Press, Westport, CT.

Freedman, R.L. (Ed.) 1983. *Human Food Uses. A Cross-Cultural, Comprehensive Annotated Bibliography: Supplement*, Greenwood Press, Westport, CT.

Fenton, A. and Kisban, E. (Eds.) 1986. *Food in Change. Eating Habits from the Middle Ages to the Present Day*, John Donald Publishers, Edinburgh.

Gordon, B. 1983. "Why we choose the foods we do." *Nutrition Today*. March/April: 17.

Khare, R.S. and Roa, M.S.A. (Eds.) 1986. *Food, Society, and Culture. Aspects in South Asian Food Systems*, Carolina Academic Press, Durham, NC.

Lowenberg, M. 1974. *The development of food patterns.* J. Amer. Dietet. Assoc. 65: 263.

Lowenberg, M.E., Todhunter, E.N., Wilson, E.D., Savage, J.R. and Lubawaski, J.L. 1979. *Food and People*, John Wiley and Sons, NY.

Sanjur, D. 1982. "Factors influencing the patterning of food habits." Ch. 2. In *Social and Cultural Perspectives in Nutrition*, p. 21. Prentice-Hall, Inc., Englewood Cliffs, NJ.

Visser, M. 1986. *Much Depends on Dinner*, McClelland and Stewart, Ltd., Toronto.

Wilson, C. 1979. *Food—Custom and Nurture*, (An Annotated Bibliography on Sociological Aspects of Nutrition) J. Nutr. Educ. Supp. 1, 11 (4).

Cultural Meaning of Food

Inclusive in this category of references are articles that may be used in a selective study of the broad topic of cultural definition and meaning of food. Food takes on meaning in every culture and conversely, cultural meaning is transmitted via the use of food in various contexts. The connotative meaning of food and classification of meanings as they are culturally defined are addressed in these references in terms of theory, observation, and empirical research.

Bass, M.A., Owsley, D.W. and McNutt, V.D. 1985. "Food preferences and food prestige ratings by black women in East Tennessee." *Ecology of Food and Nutrition* 16: 75.

Fewster, W.J., Bostian, L.R. and Powers, R.D. 1973. "Measuring the connotative meanings of foods." *Home Economics Research* 2(1): 44.

Hertzler, A.A., Wenkam, N. and Standal, B. 1982. "Classifying cultural food habits and meanings." *J. Amer. Dietet. Assoc.* 80: 421.

Hodgson, P.A. 1977. "The many faces of food—as seen through the eyes of the artist." *J. Amer. Dietet. Assoc.* 71: 248.

Jellinek, N.W. 1973. "The meanings of flavors and textures." *Food Tech.* 27(1): 46.

Levy, S.J. 1981. "Interpreting consumer mythology: a structural approach to consumer behavior." *J. of Marketing* 45: 49.

*McCracken, G. 1985. "Culture and consumption: A theoretical account of the structure and movement of cultural meaning of consumer goods." *J. Con. Research.* 13: 71.

McCracken, R.D. 1982. "Cultural differences in food preferences and meanings." *Human Organization* 41(2): 161.

Pollock, N.J. 1985. "The concept of food in a Pacific society: a Fijian example." *Ecology of Food and Nutrition* 17(3): 195.

Shutz, H.G., Rucker, M.H., Russell, G.F. 1975. "Food and food-use classification systems." *Food Technology* 29(3): 50.

*(Although food is not the primary focus of this article, this reference is an appropriate resource for a clear definition and explanation of cultural meaning and its transmission, which is applicable to food as a consumer good.)

Worsley, A. 1980. "Thought for food: investigation of cognitive aspects of food."
    Ecol. Food and Nutr. 9: 65.

Patterns of Eating

Four components of the human pattern of eating were identified
and discussed by Farb and Armelagos (1983): selection of a limited number
of foods from the environment; manner of preparation of food; traditional
principle of flavoring staple foods; and food rules. This conceptual
framework presented by these authors provides a useful structure for
categorization of pertinent references. Patterns of eating of any group
or individual are shaped by culture and have been investigated
quantitatively as well as qualitatively by researchers in the hopes of
explaining, understanding and predicting food-related behavior.
References highlighting each of these four components of the human
pattern of eating were selected for this section.

Selection of a Limited Number of Substances for Use as "Food"

References in this subcategory address the concept of classification
of substances according to edibility criteria and various other principles
that may be used within a culture to define what is and is not considered
to be "food" appropriate for inclusion in cuisine. They help to illustrate
and explain patterns of acceptance and rejection which may not be shared
by every culture or every group in the selection of a limited number
of substances used for human consumption.

Aaronson, S. 1986. "A role for algae as human food in antiquity." *Food and Foodways*
    1(3): 311.
Fallon, A. and Rozin, P. 1983. "The psychological bases of food rejections by humans."
    Ecol. Food and Nutri. 13: 15.
Gade, D. 1976. "Horsemeat as human food in France." *Ecol. of Food and Nutr.*
    5: 1.
Harris, M. 1985. *Good To Eat*, Simon and Schuster, Inc., NY.
Lackey, C.J. 1978. "Pica—A nutritional anthropology concern." In *The Anthropology
    of Health*, E.E. Bauwens (Ed.), p. 121. C.V. Mosby Co., St. Louis
Kok, R. 1983. "The production of insects for human food." *Can. Inst. Food Sci.
    Technol. J.* 16(1): 5.
Rozin, P., Fallon, A. and Augustoni-Ziskind, M. 1986. "The child's conception of
    food: the development of acceptable and rejection substances." *J. Nutr. Educ.*
    18: 75.
Schwabe, C. 1979. *Unmentionable Cuisine*, Univ. Press of Virginia, Charlottesville.
Simoons, F.J., Schonfeld-Leber and H.L. Issel. 1979. "Cultural deterrents to use of
    fish as human food." *Oceanus* 22: 67.

Manner of Preparation and the Use of Flavor Principles

All human groups manipulate and prepare food prior to eating it.
Study of manipulation and preparation of food encompasses the concepts
of cultural adaptation to the environment, cultural determination of

cooking taxonomies and appropriate preparation techniques, the use of characteristic flavors, as well as development of preferences in these matters. The following citations are focussed on preparation of food in cultural terms.

Bennion, M. 1976. "Food preparation in colonial America." *J. Am. Dietet. Assoc.* 69: 16.

Jerome, N.W. 1981. "The U.S. dietary pattern from an anthropological perspective." *Food Technol.* 35(2): 37.

Kuper, J. (Ed.) 1977. *The Anthropologists' Cookbook*, Universe Books, NY.

Pangborn, R.M. 1975. "Cross-cultural aspects of flavor preferences." *Food Technol.* 29(6): 34.

Phillips, D.E. and Bass, M.A. 1976. "Food preservation practices of selected homemakers in East Tennessee." *Ecol. Food Nutr.* 5: 29.

Rozin, P. 1978. "The use of characteristic flavorings in human culinary practice." In *Flavor: Its Chemical, Behavioral, and Commercial Aspects*, C.M. Apt (Ed.), p. 101. Westview Press, Boulder, CO.

Rozin, E. 1973. *The Flavor-Principle Cookbook*, Hawthorn, NY.

Sihler, A.L. 1973. *Baking and roasting*. Am. Anthrop. 75: 1721.

Wilson, C.S. 1975. "Rice, fish and coconuts—the bases of Southeast Asian flavors." *Food Tech.* 29(6): 42.

Culturally Defined Rules of Eating

Rules of eating are diverse and as a topic of study may refer to any aspect of eating in which culturally defined prescriptions of acceptability are an underlying factor. These rules may range from those of contemporary standards of etiquette to long-standing guidelines as part of traditional religious dietary law. Appropriate food combinations, the definition of a meal, and who eats what, when, are also cases in which culturally defined and transmitted rules of eating prevail. The references presented here highlight only a minute portion of research, observations, and discussion concerning some of these rules of eating.

Charles N. and Kerr, M. 1986. "Eating properly, the family and state benefit." *Sociology* 20(3): 412.

Douglas, M. 1975. "Deciphering a meal." In *Implicit Meanings*, Chpt. 16, Routledge and Kegan Paul ltd., London.

Douglas, M. and Gross, J. 1981. "Food and culture: measuring the intricacy of rule systems." *Social Science Information* 20: 1.

Goode, J.G., Curtis, K. and Theophano, J. 1984. "Meal format, meal cycles, and menu negotiation in the maintenance of an Italian-American community." In *Food in the Social Order*, M. Douglas (Ed.), p. 143. Russell Sage Foundation, NY.

Jelliffe, D.B. and Jelliffe, E.F.P. 1978. "Food habits and taboos: how have they protected man in his environment?" *Prog. Hum. Nutr.* 2: 67.

Koestlin, K. 1981. "Taboo and preference: culture construct and reality." In *Food in Perspective: Proceedings of the Third International Conference in*

Ethnological Food Research, A. Fenton and T. Owen (Eds.), p. 165. John Donald
Publishers, Ltd., Edinburgh.

Lévi-Strauss, C. 1978. *The Origin of Table Manners*," Jonathan Cape, London.

Niewind, A.C., Krondl, M. and Van't Foort, T. 1986. "Combinations of foods and
their compatability." *Ecology of Food and Nutrition* 19: 131.

Pangborn, R.M. 1975. "Cross-cultural aspects of flavor preferences." *Food Technol.*
29(6): 34.

Tolksdorf, U. 1981. "Development and decline of preferences and taboos in matters
of food and drink." In *Food in Perspective: Proceedings of the Third
International Conference on Ethnological Food Research*, A. Fenton and T.
Owen (Eds.), p. 325. John Donald Publishers, Ltd., Edinburgh.

Wilson, C. 1973. "Food taboos of childbirth: the Malay example." *Ecology of Food
and Nutrition* 2(4): 267.

Food Symbolism: Selective Examples of Non-Nutritive Uses of Food

Non-nutritive uses of food (Farb and Armelagos, 1983) refer to those
uses that are not primarily associated with satisfying physical hunger
and nourishment of the human body. There have been numerous
examples of such uses that hale been cited in the literature and that
may be observed personally in everyday life in any culture. Non-nutritive
uses of food have not been extensively researched, but it can be said
that most non-nutritive uses of food are symbolic uses. A classic example
is the use of food as an integral part of social interaction. Food is used
as a vehicle to initiate, maintain and end relationships. Food is often
used symbolically within the social organization of a culture or group
to denote status, prestige, or identity of some kind. The following
references represent selective examples of how food is used in these ways.

Anderson, G. and Alleyne, J.M. 1983. "Ethnicity, food preferences and habits of
consumption as factors in social interaction." *Canadian Ethnic Studies*, 11
(1):83.

Counihan, C.M., 1985. "What does it mean to be fat, thin, and female in the United
States: a review essay." *Food and Foodways* 1(1): 77.

de Garine, I.L. 1976. "Food, tradition and prestige." In *Food, Man, and Society*,
D. Walcher, N. Kretchmer and H.L. Barnett (Eds.), p. 150. Plenum Press, NY.

Ek-Nilsson, K. 1981. "The social functions of festival food: a few thoughts on an
investigation in Northern Sweden." In *Food in Perspective: Proceedings of
the Third International Conference on Ethnological Food Research*, A Fenton
and T. Owen (Eds.), p. 77. John Donald Publishers, Ltd., Edinburgh.

Gofton, L.R. 1986. "Social change, market change: drinking men in North East
England." *Food and Foodways* 1(3): 253.

Goody, J. 1982. *Cooking, Cuisine and Class*, Cambridge University Press, Cambridge,
England.

Kerr, M. and Charles, N. 1986. "Servers and providers: the distribution of food within
the family." *The Sociological Review* 34(1): 115.

March, K.S. 1987. "Hospitality, women, and the efficacy of beer." *Food and Foodways*
1(4): 351.

Mead, M. 1976. "Comments on the division of labor in occupations concerned with food." *J. Amer. Diet. Assn.* 68: 321.

Pollock, D.K., 1985. "Food and sexual identity among the Culina." *Food and Foodways* 1(1): 25.

Sadalla, E. and Burroughs, J. 1982. "Profiles in eating." *Psychology Today.* 15(10): 51.

Taylor, L. 1976. "Coffee: the bottomless cup." In *The American Dimension*, W. Arens and S.P. Montague (Eds.), p. 144. Alfred Publishing, Port Washington, NY.

Widdowson, J. "Food and traditional verbal modes in the social control of children." In *Food in Perspective: Proceedings of the Third International Conference on Ethnological Food Research*, A. Fenton and T. Owen (Eds.), p. 377. John Donald Publishers, Ltd., Edinburgh.

Ethnicity and Food-Related Changes Associated with Acculturation and Assimilation

Patterns of food consumption are influenced by cultural change. Acculturation is the process of change experienced when two or more cultures come in prolonged contact with each other. Assimilation of different food habits, attitudes and beliefs by individuals may result during that process. The study of ethnicity and associated food habits has been of interest to those in academic communities who study acculturation and assimilation in various cultural settings. The following references touch on food-related aspects of ethnicity, acculturation, assimilation and change in food habits.

Barer-Stein, T. 1979. *You Eat What You Are*, McClelland and Stewart Ltd., Toronto.

Belasco, W.J. 1987. "Ethnic fast food: the corporate melting pot." *Food and Foodways* 2(1): 1.

Brown, L.K. and Mussell, K. 1984. *Ethnic and Regional Foodways in the United States*, The Univ. of Tenn. Press, Knoxville, TN.

Carlson, E., Kipps, M. and Thomson, J. 1984. "Influences on the food habits of some ethnic minorities in the United Kingdom." *Human Nutr.: Applied Nutr.* 38A: 85.

Dewey, K.G., strode, M.A. and Fitch, Y.R. 1984. "Dietary change among migrant and non-migrant Mexican-American families in Northern California." *Ecol. Food and Nutr.* 14: 11.

Freedman, M.R. and Gravetti, L.E. 1984. "Diet patterns of first, second and third generation Greek-American women." *Ecol. Food and Nutr.* 14: 185.

Grivetti, L.E. and Paquette, M.B. 1978. "Nontraditional ethnic food choices among first generation Chinese in California." *J. Nutr. Educ.* 10(3): 109.

Hrboticky, N. and Krondl, M. 1984. "Acculturation to Canadian foods by Chinese immigrant boys: changes in perceived flavour, health value and prestige of foods." *Appetite* 5: 117.

Jabbra, N. 1983. "Assimilation and acculturation of Lebanese extended families in Nova Scotia." *Canadian Ethnic Studies* 15(1): 54.

Levenstein, H. 1985. "The American response to Italian food, 1880-1930." *Food and Foodways* 1(1): 1.

Lippe-Stokes, S. 1973. "Eskimo story-knife tales: reflections of change in food habits." *Ecol. of Food and Nutri.* 2: 27.

Pasquali, E.A. 1985. "The impact of acculturation on the eating habits of elderly immigrants: a Cuban example." *J. Nutr. for the Elder.* 5(1): 27.

Rasanen, M. 1981. "The diffusion channels of urban food habits." In *Food in Perspective: Proceedings of the Third International Conference on Ethnological Food Research*, A. Fenton and T. Owen (Eds.), p. 209. John Donald Publishers, Ltd., Edinburgh.

Theodoratus, R.J. "Greek Immigrant cuisine in America: continuity and change." In *Food in Perspective: Proceedings of the Third International Conference on Ethnological Food Research*, A. Fenton and T. Owen (Eds.), p. 313. John Donald Publishers, Ltd., Edinburgh.

Wallendorf, M. and Reilly, M. 1983. "Ethnic migration, assimilation, and consumption." *J. Consumer Research* 10(3): 292.

Food Ideology

Three belief systems that are relevant to the study of cultural aspects of food are: world view, religion, and health beliefs. Food ideology encompasses aspects of beliefs and shared concepts associated with these belief systems. How one views the physical world, the supernatural world, and how the body functions will have an impact on food-related attitudes, beliefs and habits. Classification of foods, dietary rules, and prescribed uses of food for health reasons are influenced by these systems within a cultural context. Selected aspects of food ideology are explored in the following references.

Religion and Food

Apte, M.L. and Katona-Apte, J. "The significance of food in religious ideology and ritual behavior in Marathi myths." In *Food in Perspective: Proceedings of the Third International Conference on Ethnological Food Research*, A. Fenton and T. Owen (Eds.), p. 9. John Donald Publishers, Ltd., Edinburgh.

Grivetti, L.E. and Pangborn, R.M. 1974. "Origin of selected old testament dietary prohibitions." *J. Amer. Dietet. Assoc.* 65:634.

Land-Bogues, J. 1976. "Rastafarian food habits." *Cajanus* 9: 228.

Lowenberg, M.E., Todhunter, E., Wilson, E., Savage, J. and Lubawski, J. 1979. "Food, people and religion." Ch. 6 in *Food and People*, p. 166. John Wiley and Sons, NY.

Sakr, A.H. 1975. "Fasting in Islam." *J. Am. Dietet. Assoc.* 67: 17.

Simoons, F. 1973. "The sacred cow and the Constitution of India." *Ecol. Food Nutri.* 2: 281.

Simoons, F. 1974. "The purificatory role of the five product of the cow in Hinduism." *Ecol. Food Nutri.* 3: 21.

Simoons, F.J. 1978. "Traditional use and avoidance of foods of animal origin: a culture-historical view." *BioScience* 28: 178.

Springer, K. and Thomas, J. 1983. "Rastafarians in Britain: a preliminary study of their food habits and beliefs." *Human Nutrition: Applied Nutrition* 37A(2): 120.

Van Esterik, P. 1986. "Feeding their faith: recipe knowledge among Thai Buddhist women." *Food and Foodways* 1(2): 197.

World View and Health Beliefs: "Hot-Cold" and "Yin-Yang" Foods Chang, B. 1974. "Some dietary beliefs in Chinese folk culture." *J. Amer. Dietet. Assoc.* 65: 436.

Foster, G.M. 1979. "Humoral traces in United States folk medicine." *Med. Anthrop. Newsletter* 10(2): 17.

Logan, M.H. 1977. "Anthropological research on the hot-cold theory of disease: some methodological suggestions." *Med. Anthrop.* 1: 87.

Ludman, E. and Newman, J. 1984. "Yin and Yang in the health-related food practices of three Chinese groups." *J. of Nutr. Educ.* 16(1): 3.

Molony, C. 1975. "Systematic valence coding of Mexican "Hot-Cold" food." *Ecol. of Food and Nutr.* 4: 67.

Wilson, C.S., 1981. "Food in a medical system: prescriptions and proscriptions in health and illness among Malays." In *Food in Perspective: Proceedings of the Third International Conference on Ethnological Food Research*, A. Fenton and T. Owen (Eds.), p. 391. John Donald Publishers, Ltd., Edinburg.

Yeung, D.L., Cheung, L.W.Y. Sabry, J.H. 1973. "The hot-cold food concept in Chinese culture and its application in a Canadian-Chinese community." *J. Can. Diet. Assn.* 34: 1974.

Other Food Beliefs and Associated Values

Freeland-Graves, J.H., Greneinger, S.A. and Young, R.K. 1986. "Health practices, attitudes, and beliefs of vegetarians and non-vegetarians." *J. Amer. Dietet. Assoc.* 86(7): 913.

Harrison, K.R., Campbell, M.L. and Bond Jr., J.B. 1982. "Food-related value-orientations, socio-economic status, and diet patterns of senior citizens." *Canadian Home Economics J.* 32(3): 137.

Schafer, R. and Yetley, E.A. 1975. "Social psychology of food faddism." *Journal of The Amer. Dietet. Assoc.* 66: 129.

Sims, L. 1978. "Food-related value orientations, attitudes and beliefs of vegetarians and non-vegetarians." *Ecol. of Food and Nutrition* 7: 23.

Steelman, V.P. 1976. "Attitudes toward food as indicators of subcultural value systems." *Home Ec. Research J.* 5(1): 21.

Wolff, R.J. 1973. "Who eats for health." *Am. J. Clin. Nutr.* 26: 438.

Contributors

Delmer Davis received his B.A. and M.A. in English from Pacific Union College in California. His Ph.D. in American Literature is from the University of Colorado. He has taught English at Walla Walla College, Loma Linda University, and Andrews University, serving also as chair of the English Department in the latter two universities. He is presently Dean of the School of Graduate Studies at Andrews University. He has made presentations and published articles on such writers as Samuel Sewall, Willa Cather, and Betty MacDonald.

Michael P. Dean is Director of Undergraduate English at the University of Mississippi. A native Floridian, he has had a long-standing interest in the work of Marjorie Kinnan Rawlings. Among his publications are essays on the work of W.J. Cash, William Faulkner, and Ellen Douglas.

Lynne L. Gelber is Professor of French at Skidmore College where she chaired the Department of Foreign Languages and Literatures. She also created and coordinated Skidmore's Junior Year Programs Abroad in France and Spain. She is currently working on a book-length manuscript on *Food as a Metaphor in Contemporary French Narrative*. The chapter included in *Cooking by the Book* was supported in part by R. Green and grants from Skidmore College while on sabbatical leave and New York University where she was Scholar-in-Residence and Research Fellow in the Faculty Resources Network program funded by the Ford Foundation.

Sue Hart was educated in Michigan, New York and Montana, and has been teaching English in the Montana University System for a number of years. She is a professor at Eastern Montana College, Billings, where she has directed the Women's Studies Program for over twenty years in addition to her teaching duties. Courses like Women in Literature, Montana Writers, and Women and the Frontier Experience allow her to combine her love for Montana and her admiration for the pioneers with her academic concerns in Women's Studies and English.

Bruce Henderson is Assistant Professor of English at Fairleigh Dickinson Univ. in N.J. In addition to scholarship in the field of American literature, he has been a nutrition activist, publishing two editions of the vegetarian guide, *Oakland Organic* (Caboose Press 1985). The essay included in *Cooking by the Book* combines these interests. He also writes fiction and is currently at work on his second novel.

Kate Kane is a doctoral candidate in radio/television/film at Northwestern University. Her research interests are questions of power and popular culture.

Jody Kolodzey is a doctoral candidate in the Department of Folklore and Folklife at the University of Pennsylvania.

Anne LeCroy collects cookbooks, is a week-end cook, and enjoys experimenting with recipes that use ingredients mentioned in various literary works ranging from ancient comedy to modern amateur detective. "I'm still hunting the perfect tomato aspic recipe." Anne is professor of English and Humanities at East Tennessee State University. She has also worked with the Episcopal Church USA in various capacities— translator, editor, inclusive language consultant, and writer. Academic background includes Bryn Mawr B.A. and M.A., Ph.D from University of Cincinnati, postdoctral work at Johns Hopkins, Duke, and Sewanee.

Susan J. Leonardi is assistant professor of English at the University of Maryland, College Park and author of *Dangerous by Degrees: Women at Oxford and the Somerville College Novelists* (Rutgers University Press, 1989). She has also published in *PMLA, Novel, Women's Studies*, and *Perspectives*. She is currently at work, with her collaborator Rebecca A. Pope, on a book about the figure of the diva in literature by women, tentatively titled *To Have a Voice: The Politics of the Diva*. In addition to her academic pursuits, she writes fiction, cooks, parents, and engages in an endless search for the perfect pen and the tasty tomato.

Tobe Levin is a lecturer in English and Women's Studies with the University of Maryland European Division and adjunct lecturer, the University of Frankfurt, where she offers courses in Jewish and Afro-American women's fiction. She earned the Ph.D. in Comparative Literature from Cornell University after having received an M.A. in French from N.Y.U. in Paris and a maitrise from I'Universite de Paris III (la Sorbonne nouvelle). A contributing editor to the Women's Studies Quarterly, her essays have appeared in *Ngambika. Studies of Women in African Literature* (ed. Davies and Graves. Africa World P. 1985), the *Women's Studies International Forum, The Women's Review of Books*, the West German feminist magazine *Emma*, and elsewhere. She has edited an anthology on female circumcision (Frauenoffensive: Munich, 1979) and is currently translating Verena Stefan's Wortgetreu ich traume to be published jointly by Seal Press/The Women's Press.

Cecilia Macheski is Associate Professor of English at LaGuardia Community College of the City University of New York. She received her doctorate in 1984 from the Graduate School of the City University, where she wrote her dissertation on Elizabeth Inchbald. With Mary Anne Schofield she is co-editor of *Fetter'd or Free? British Women Novelists, 1660-1815* (Ohio University Press), and the forthcoming *Curtain Calls: British and American Women in the Theater*. She is the recipient of a Fulbright grant to pursue lecture and research in women's studies at Victoria University in Wellington, New Zealand.

Karen Madeira is assistant professor in the Department of Consumer Studies at the University of Guelph, Ontario, Canada. She teaches courses in cultural aspects of food, consumer acceptance of food, and sensory evaluation of food. She holds a B.A. degree in Psychology, an M.S. in Consumer Studies and a Ph.D. in Food Science. Her background and interests have included study and work experience in the area of consumer foods and cultural anthropology. Her current research interests include study of acceptance of ethnic food, social context of eating in food acceptance, and patterns of food consumption and habits.

Lynn Veach Sadler has a B.A. from Duke University and an M.A. and a Ph.D. from the University of Illinois at Champaign-Urbana. A Miltonist, she has published four books (on Milton, Bunyan, Carew, and Drabble), as well as over fifty articles, and is currently at work on a book on Anita Brookner. She won an Extraordinary Undergraduate Teaching Award at Drake University, was a panelist at the First International Milton Symposium in England, and has directed a National Endowment for the Humanities summer Seminar for College Teachers on "The Novel of Slave Unrest." She began working with computers in 1977, is a pioneer in and gives workshops in CAC (Computer-Assisted Composition; her coinage) and in educational computing applications around the country, has co-authored software, founded and edits the *Computer-Assisted Composition Journal*, and runs the "Computers and the Humanities" Strand of the Popular Culture Association. She is the Vice-President for Academic Affairs at Methodist College.

Mary Anne Schofield, Professor of English, St. Bonaventure University, is the editor of *Cooking by the Book*. She is a scholar of eighteenth-century feminine fiction, the author of several books on Eliza Haywood, the most popular of eighteenth-century women writers, the co-editor of *Fetter'd or Free?* and *Curtain Calls*, books about eighteenth-century women novelists and dramatists, and the author of *Masking and Unmasking the Feminine Mind*. She is the founder and co-editor of *The Barbara Pym Newsletter*. She has published articles in *Eighteenth-century Studies, Ariel, Tulsa Studies in Women's Literature, and other journals*. Currently, she is at work on a study of the feminine fiction of World War II.

Andrew Stubbs is Assistant Professor of English at Wilfrid Laurier University in Waterloo, Canada. His published work includes studies of Canadian writing and writers. He is currently working on a reading of the novels of William Styron.

Lee Upton's essays have appeared in *Soundings: An Interdisciplinary Journal, Field: Contemporary Poetry and Poetics, Poesis, The Denver Quarterly, Critique: Studies in Modern Fiction* and *Studies in Short*

Fiction. A book of her poetry, *The Invention of Kindness*, was published by the University of Alabama Press, and she is a 1987-1988 winner of the Pushcart Prize. Her second book of poems is forthcoming from Atlantic Monthly Press. She is an Assistant Professor of English at Lafayette College.

Sharon Wilson is Professor of English and Women's Studies and Director of the Writing Minor at the University of Northern Colorado. Founding Co-President of the Margaret Atwood Society, she has written about modern literature, romance, and film and has published extensively on Atwood, including "Sexual Politics in Margaret Atwood's Art" in Van Spanckeren and Castro's *Margaret Atwood: Vision and Forms.*

Index